6AA

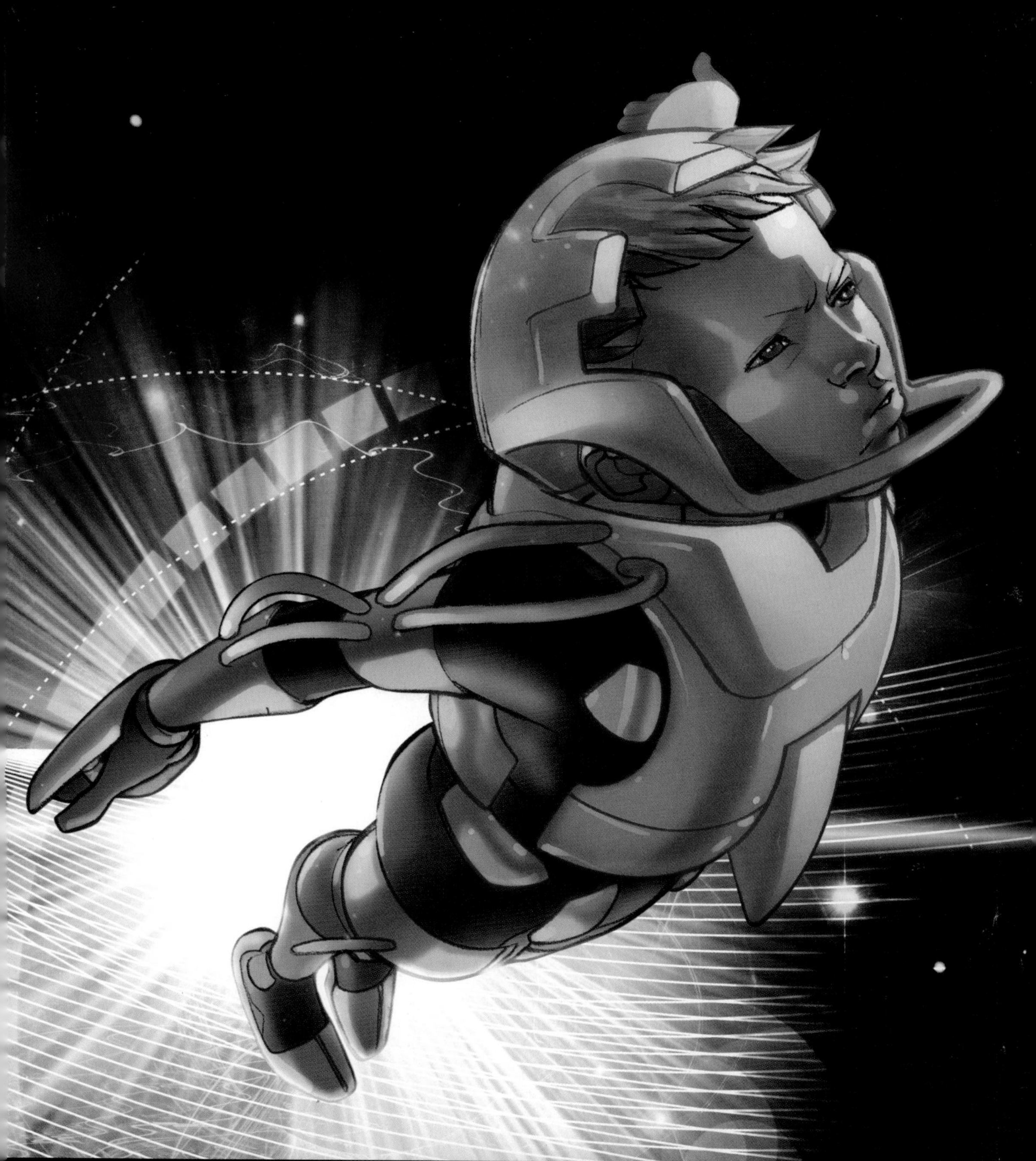

ORSON SCOTT CARD

ENDER'S GAME

BATTLE SCHOOL

ORSON SCOTT CARD

ENDER'S GAME

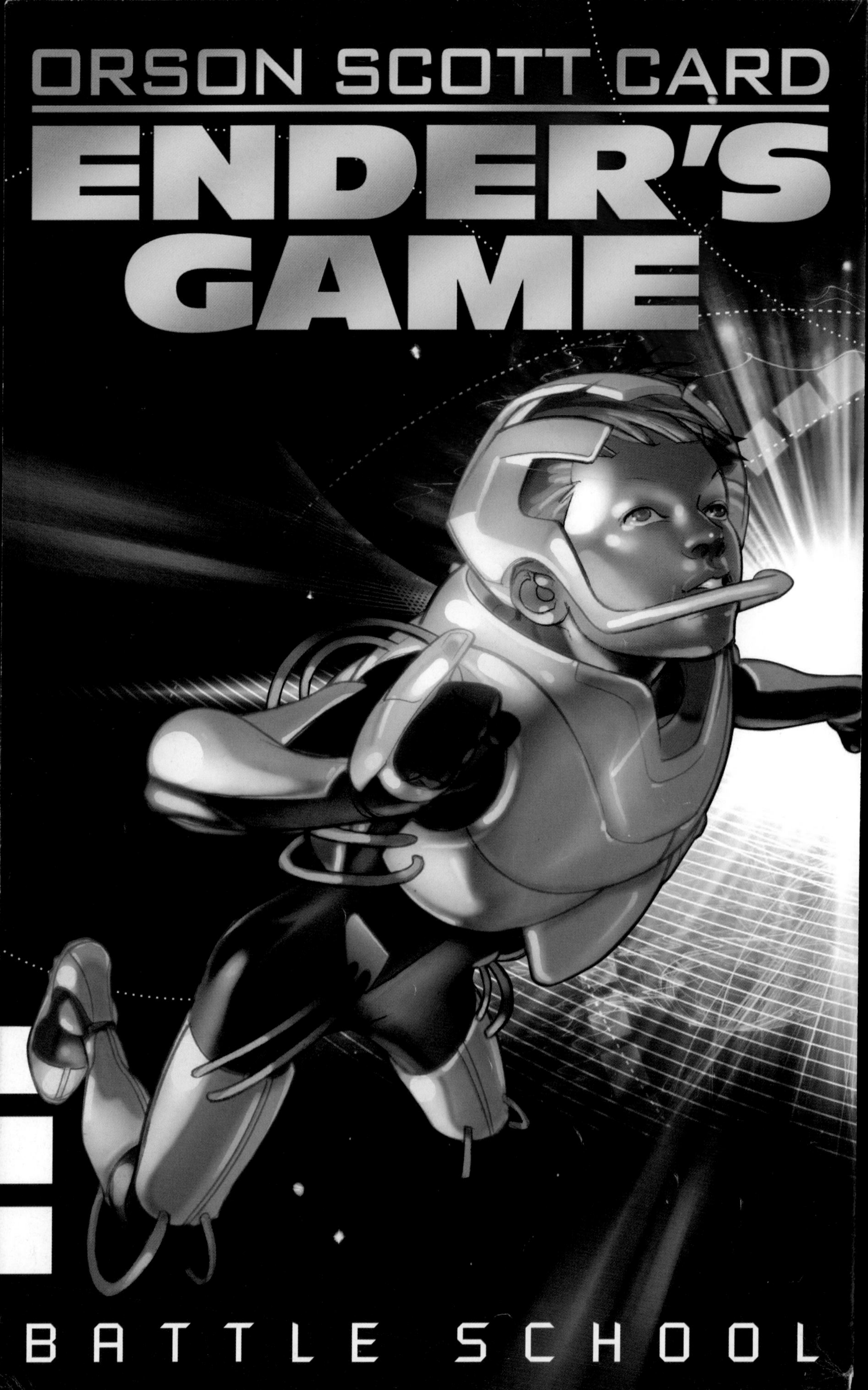

BATTLE SCHOOL

Creative Director & Executive Director:
ORSON SCOTT CARD
Script: **CHRISTOPHER YOST**
Art: **PASQUAL FERRY**
Color Art: **FRANK D'ARMATA**
Lettering: **VC'S CORY PETIT**
Story Consultant: **JAKE BLACK**
Cover Art: **PASQUAL FERRY
& FRANK D'ARMATA**
Editor: **JORDAN D. WHITE**
Consulting Editor: **NICK LOWE**
Senior Editor: **MARK PANICCIA**

Special thanks to
**KRISTINE CARD,
KATHLEEN BELLAMY,
DARIEN ROBBINS,
ANDREW BAUGHAN,
RALPH MACCHIO,
LAUREN SANKOVITCH,
JIM NAUSEDAS,
JIM MCCANN,
ARUNE SINGH,
CHRIS ALLO
& JEFF SUTER**

Collection Editor: **JENNIFER GRÜNWALD**
Editorial Assistant: **ALEX STARBUCK**
Assistant Editors: **CORY LEVINE
& JOHN DENNING**
Editor, Special Projects:
MARK D. BEAZLEY
Senior Editor, Special Projects:
JEFF YOUNGQUIST
Senior Vice President of Sales:
DAVID GABRIEL
Senior Vice President of Strategic
Development: **RUWAN JAYATILLEKE**
Book designer: **RODOLFO MURAGUCHI**

Editor in Chief: **JOE QUESADA**
Publisher: **DAN BUCKLEY**
Executive Producer: **ALAN FINE**

ENDER'S GAME: BATTLE SCHOOL. Contains material originally published in magazine form as ENDER'S GAME: BATTLE SCHOOL #1-5. First printing 2009. ISBN# 978-0-7851-3580-7. Published by MARVEL PUBLISHING, INC., a subsidiary of MARVEL ENTERTAINMENT, INC. OFFICE OF PUBLICATION: 417 5th Avenue, New York, NY 10016. Copyright © 2008 and 2009 Orson Scott Card. All rights reserved. $24.99 per copy in the U.S. (GST #R127032852); Canadian Agreement #40668537. All characters featured in this issue and the distinctive names and likenesses thereof, and all related indicia are trademarks of Orson Scott Card. No similarity between any of the names, characters, persons, and/or institutions in this magazine with those of any living or dead person or institution is intended, and any such similarity which may exist is purely coincidental. **Printed in the U.S.A.** ALAN FINE, CEO Marvel Publishing Division and EVP & CMO Marvel Characters B.V.; DAN BUCKLEY, President of Publishing - Print & Digital Media; JIM SOKOLOWSKI, Chief Operating Officer; DAVID GABRIEL, SVP of Publishing Sales & Circulation; DAVID BOGART, SVP of Business Affairs & Talent Management; MICHAEL PASCIULLO, VP Merchandising & Communications; JIM O'KEEFE, VP of Operations & Logistics; DAN CARR, Executive Director of Publishing Technology; JUSTIN F. GABRIE, Director of Publishing & Editorial Operations; SUSAN CRESPI, Editorial Operations Manager; ALEX MORALES, Publishing Operations Manager; STAN LEE, Chairman Emeritus. For information regarding advertising in Marvel Comics or on Marvel.com, please contact Mitch Dane, Advertising Director at mdane@marvel.com. For Marvel subscription inquiries, please call 800-217-9158.

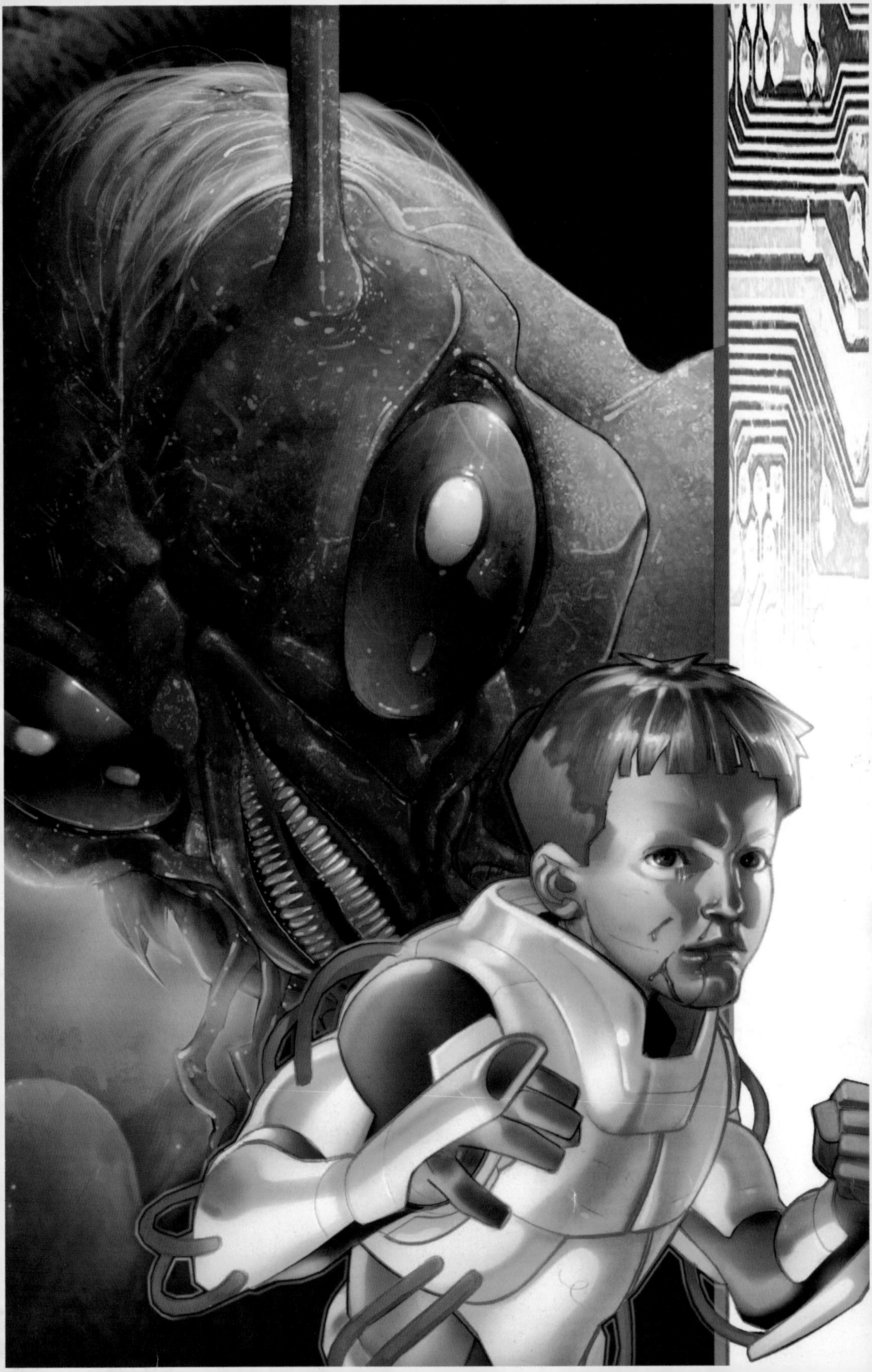

"I've watched through his eyes, I've
listened through his ears, and I tell you
he's the one. Or at least as close
as we're going to get."

"That's what you said about the brother."

"The brother tested out impossible. For
other reasons. Nothing to do with his
ability."

"Same with the sister. And there are
doubts about him. He's too malleable.
Too willing to submerge himself in
someone else's will."

"Not if the other person is his enemy."

"So what do we do? Surround him with
enemies all the time?"

"If we have to."

"I thought you said you liked this kid."

"If the Formics get him, they'll make me
look like his favorite uncle."

"All right. We're saving the world, after
all. Take him."

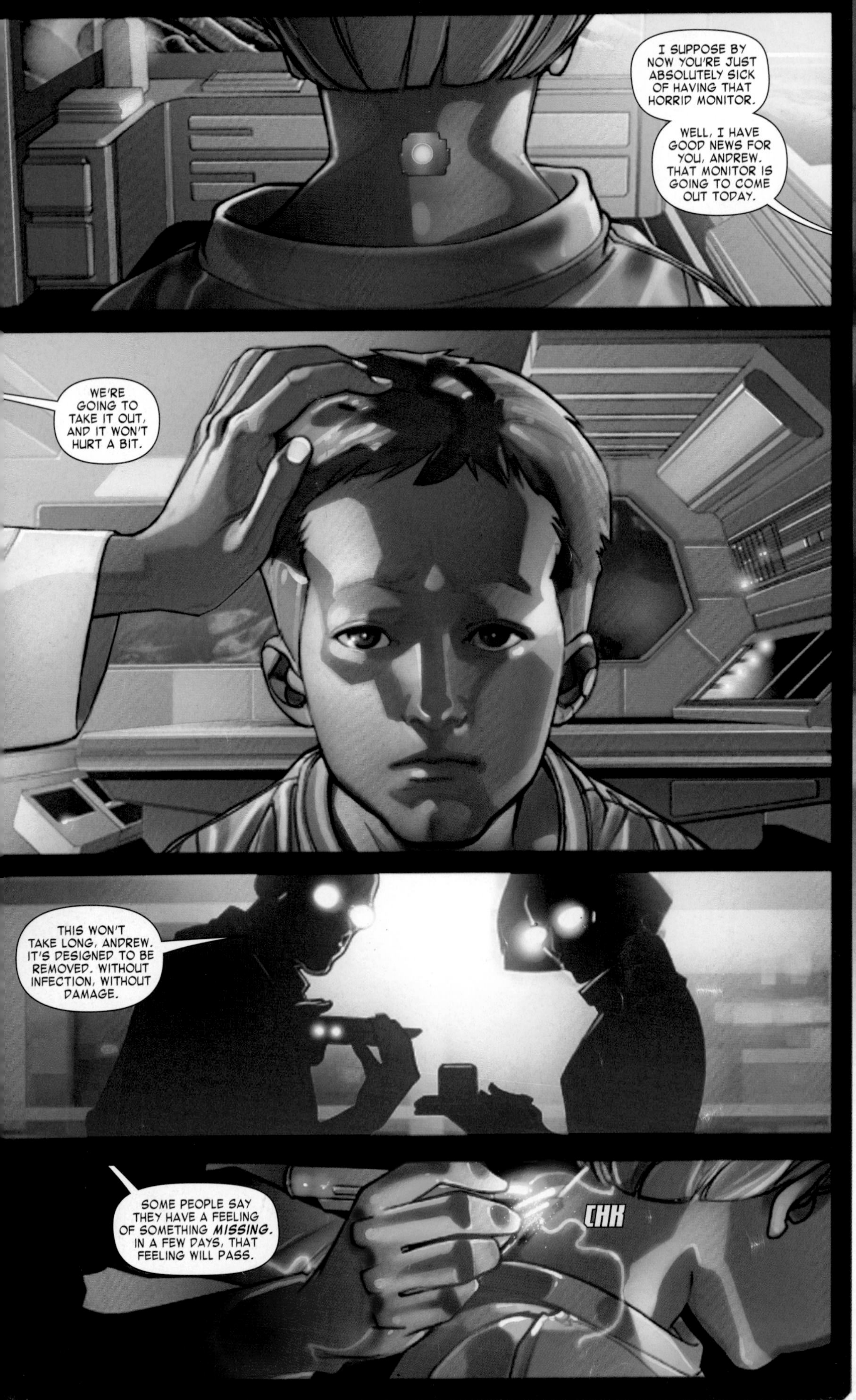
I SUPPOSE BY NOW YOU'RE JUST ABSOLUTELY SICK OF HAVING THAT HORRID MONITOR.
WELL, I HAVE GOOD NEWS FOR YOU, ANDREW. THAT MONITOR IS GOING TO COME OUT TODAY.
WE'RE GOING TO TAKE IT OUT, AND IT WON'T HURT A BIT.
THIS WON'T TAKE LONG, ANDREW. IT'S DESIGNED TO BE REMOVED. WITHOUT INFECTION, WITHOUT DAMAGE.
SOME PEOPLE SAY THEY HAVE A FEELING OF SOMETHING *MISSING.* IN A FEW DAYS, THAT FEELING WILL PASS.
CHK

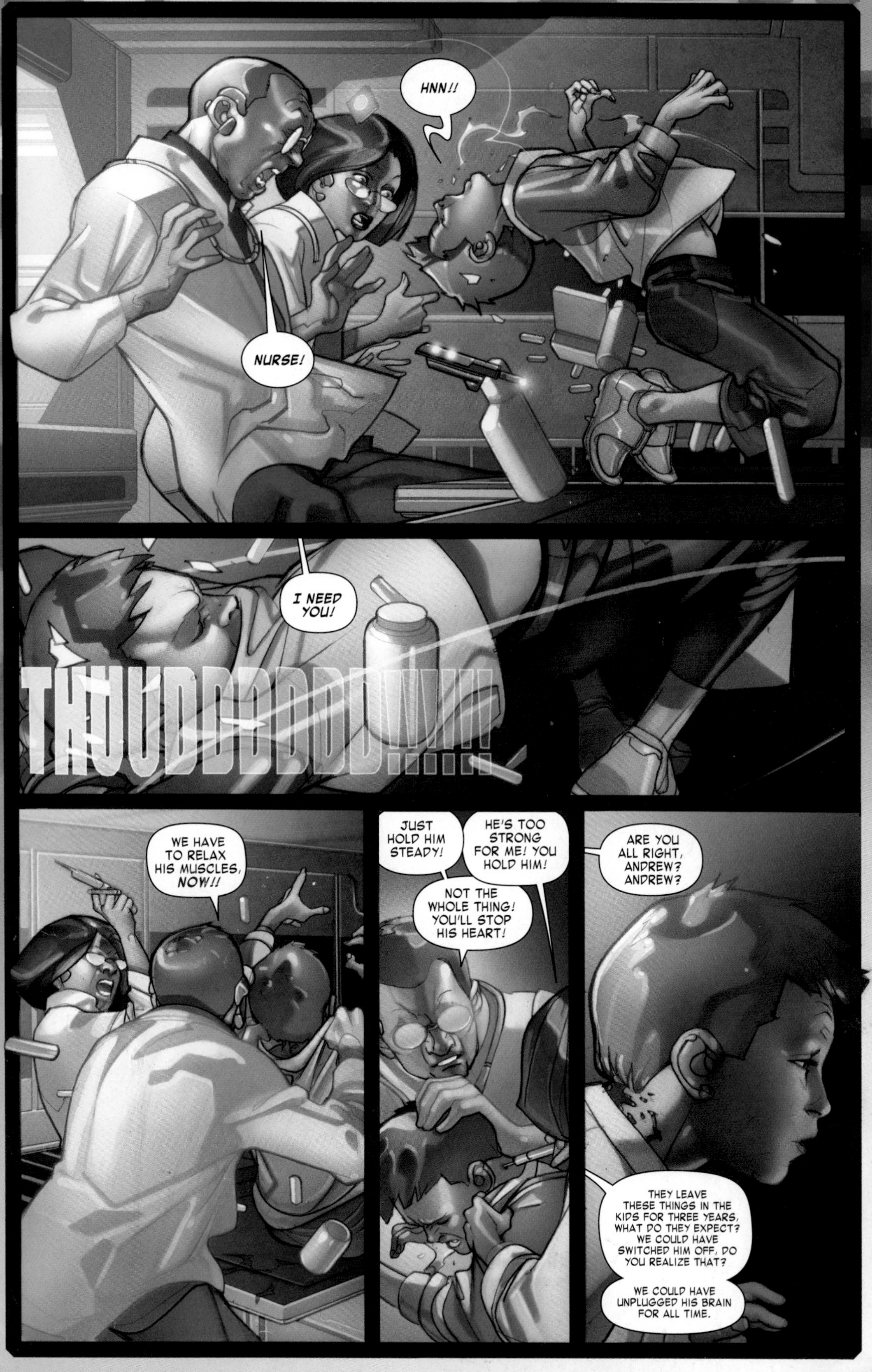
HNN!!
NURSE!
I NEED YOU!
THUDDDDDDD!!!!!!!
WE HAVE TO RELAX HIS MUSCLES, NOW!!
JUST HOLD HIM STEADY!
HE'S TOO STRONG FOR ME! YOU HOLD HIM!
NOT THE WHOLE THING! YOU'LL STOP HIS HEART!
ARE YOU ALL RIGHT, ANDREW? ANDREW?
THEY LEAVE THESE THINGS IN THE KIDS FOR THREE YEARS, WHAT DO THEY EXPECT? WE COULD HAVE SWITCHED HIM OFF, DO YOU REALIZE THAT?
WE COULD HAVE UNPLUGGED HIS BRAIN FOR ALL TIME.

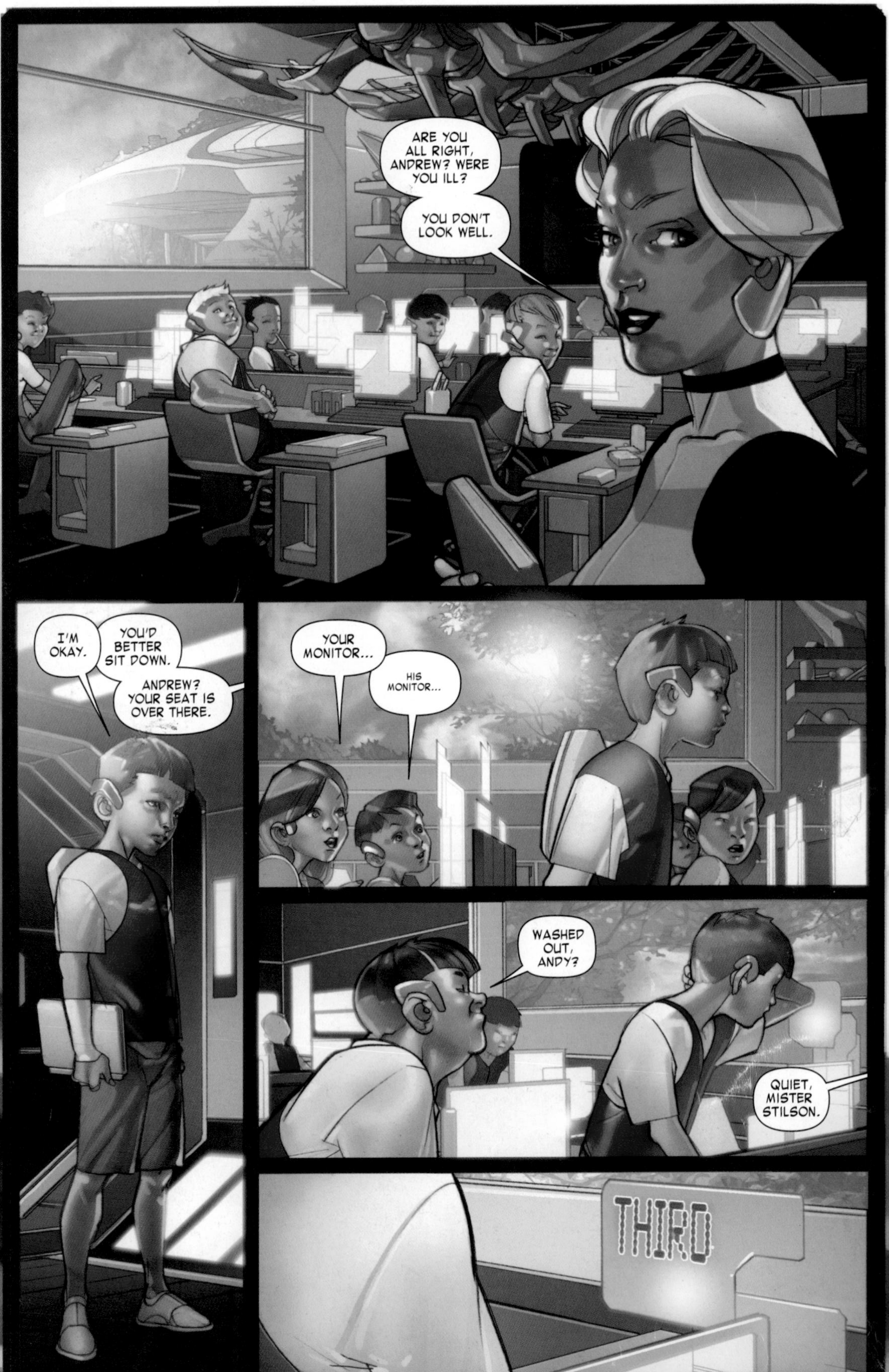
ARE YOU ALL RIGHT, ANDREW? WERE YOU ILL?
YOU DON'T LOOK WELL.
I'M OKAY.
YOU'D BETTER SIT DOWN.
ANDREW? YOUR SEAT IS OVER THERE.
YOUR MONITOR...
HIS MONITOR...
WASHED OUT, ANDY?
QUIET, MISTER STILSON.
THIRD

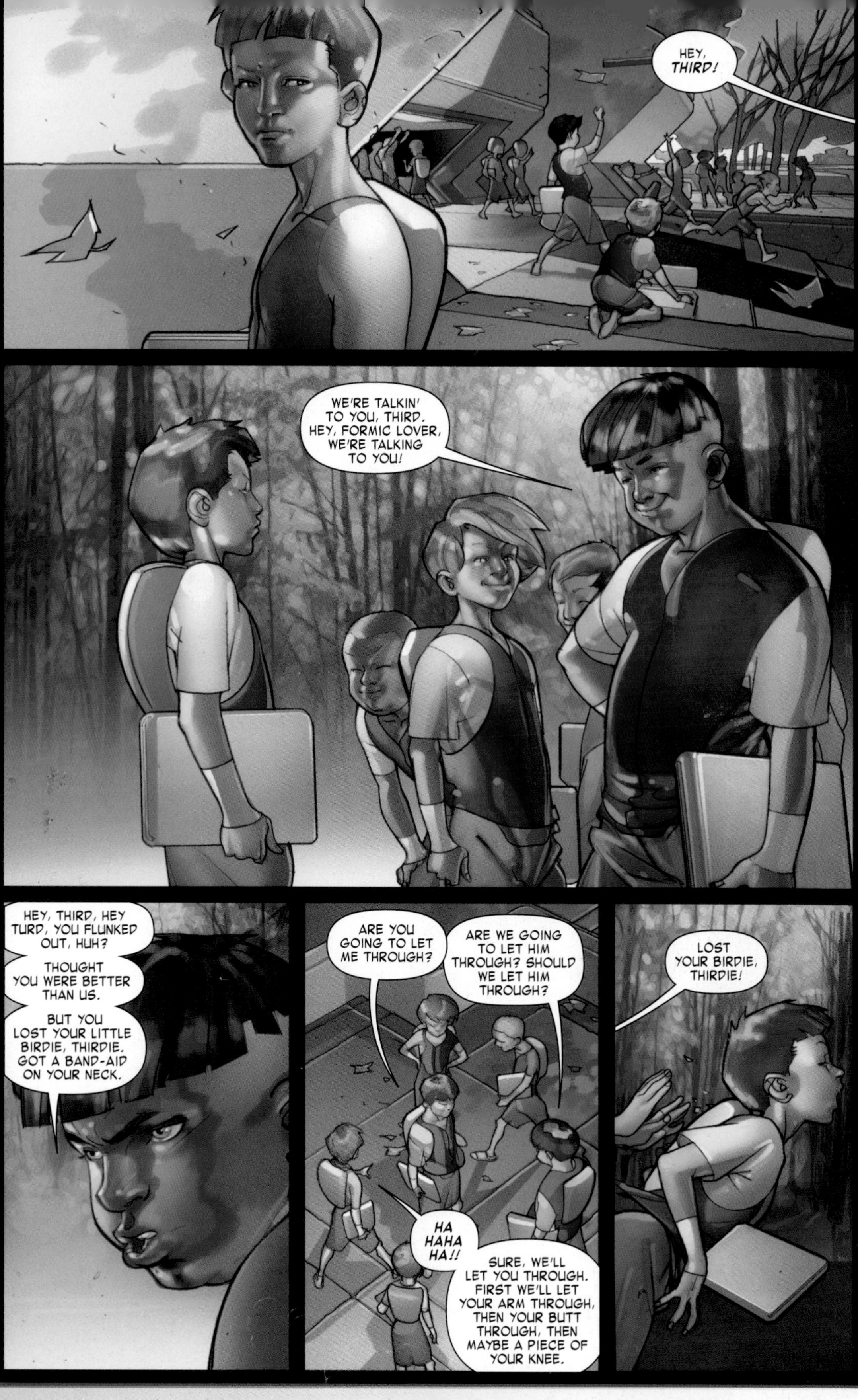
HEY, THIRD!
WE'RE TALKIN' TO YOU, THIRD. HEY, FORMIC LOVER, WE'RE TALKING TO YOU!
HEY, THIRD, HEY TURD, YOU FLUNKED OUT, HUH?
THOUGHT YOU WERE BETTER THAN US.
BUT YOU LOST YOUR LITTLE BIRDIE, THIRDIE. GOT A BAND-AID ON YOUR NECK.
ARE YOU GOING TO LET ME THROUGH?
ARE WE GOING TO LET HIM THROUGH? SHOULD WE LET HIM THROUGH?
HA HAHA HA!!
SURE, WE'LL LET YOU THROUGH. FIRST WE'LL LET YOUR ARM THROUGH, THEN YOUR BUTT THROUGH, THEN MAYBE A PIECE OF YOUR KNEE.
LOST YOUR BIRDIE, THIRDIE!

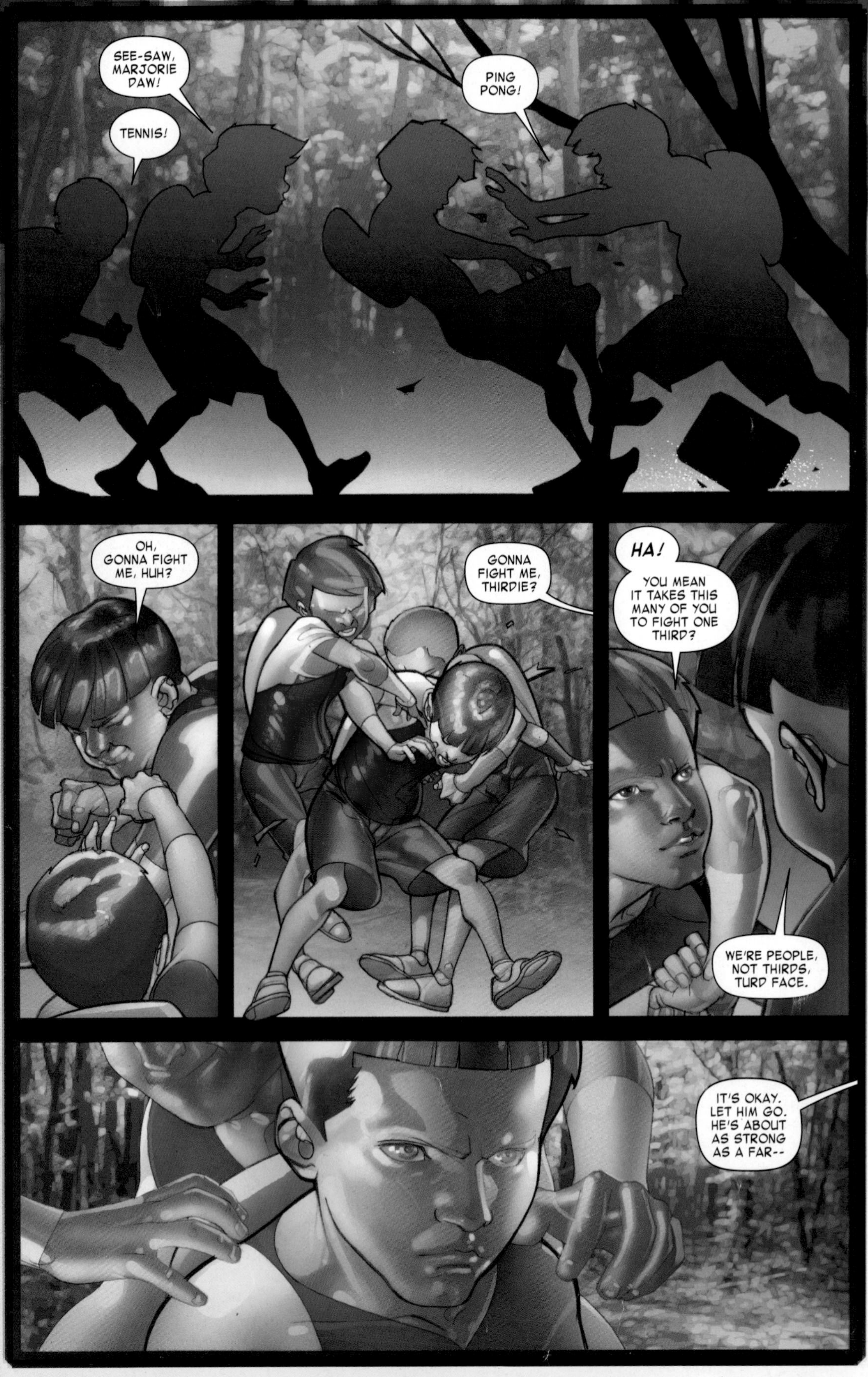
SEE-SAW, MARJORIE DAW!
TENNIS!
PING PONG!
OH, GONNA FIGHT ME, HUH?
GONNA FIGHT ME, THIRDIE?
HA!
YOU MEAN IT TAKES THIS MANY OF YOU TO FIGHT ONE THIRD?
WE'RE PEOPLE, NOT THIRDS, TURD FACE.
IT'S OKAY. LET HIM GO. HE'S ABOUT AS STRONG AS A FAR--

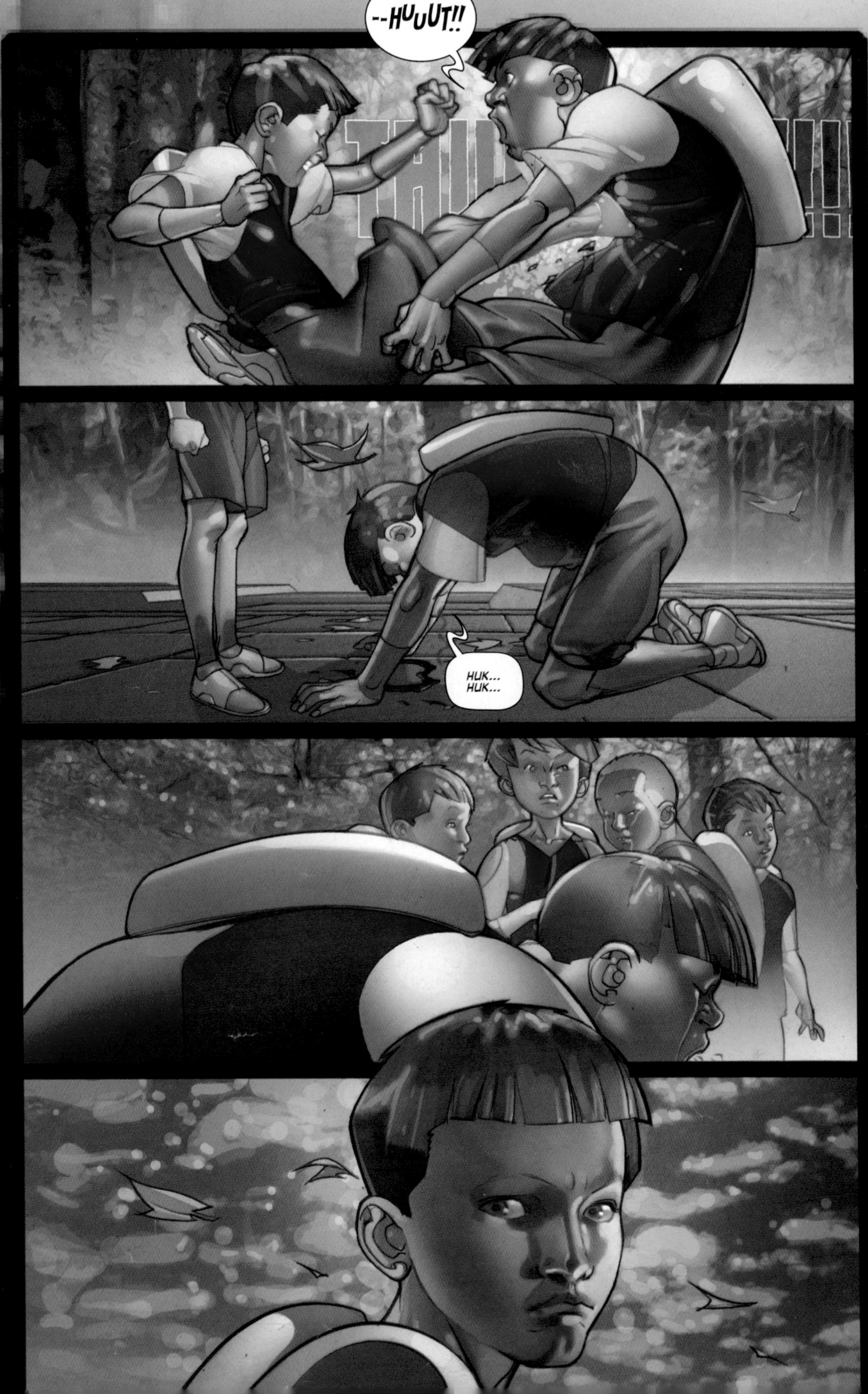
--HUUUT!!
HUK...
HUK...

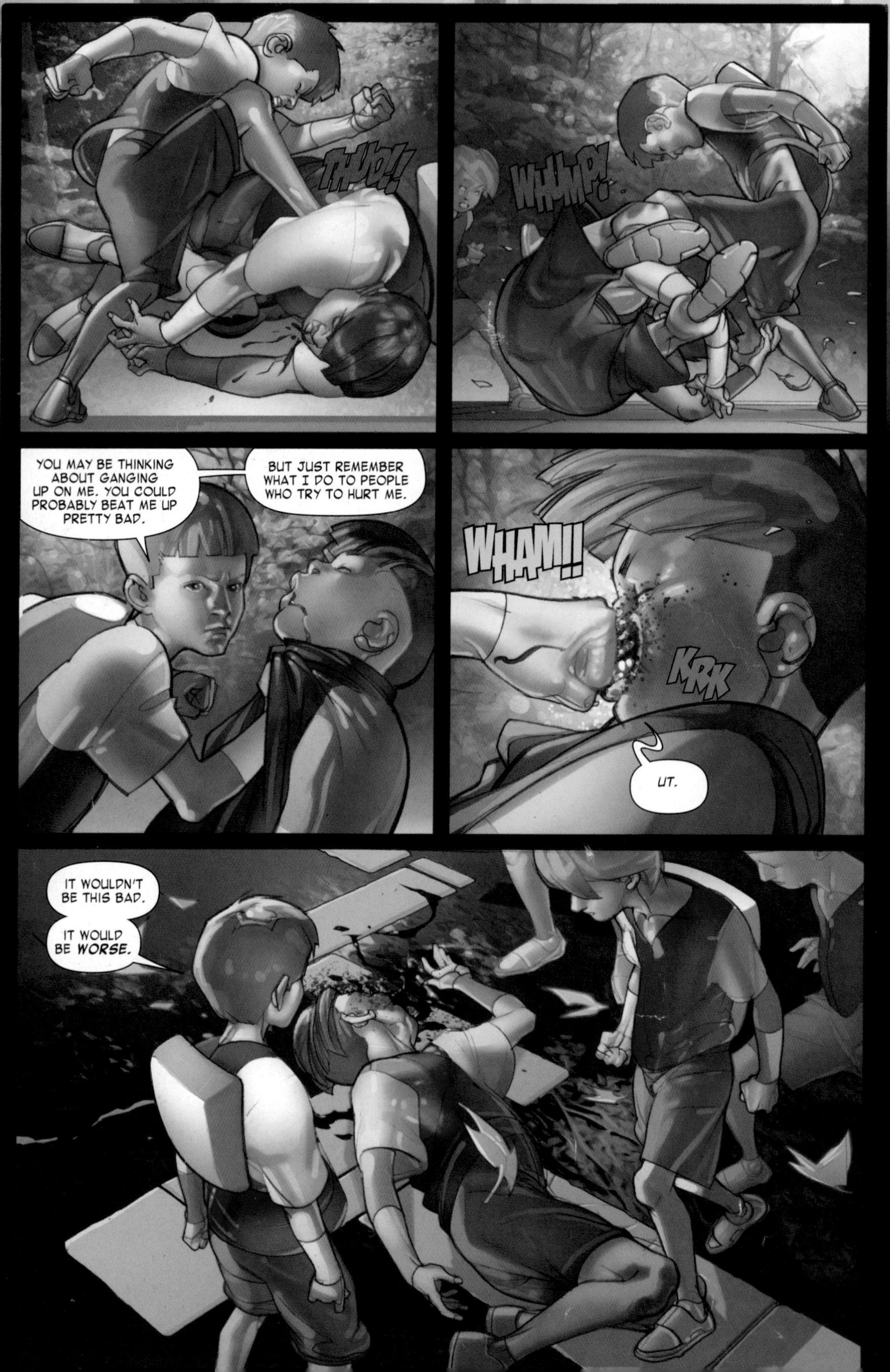
THUD!!
WHUMP!!
YOU MAY BE THINKING ABOUT GANGING UP ON ME. YOU COULD PROBABLY BEAT ME UP PRETTY BAD.
BUT JUST REMEMBER WHAT I DO TO PEOPLE WHO TRY TO HURT ME.
WHAM!!
KRK
UT.
IT WOULDN'T BE THIS BAD.
IT WOULD BE *WORSE.*

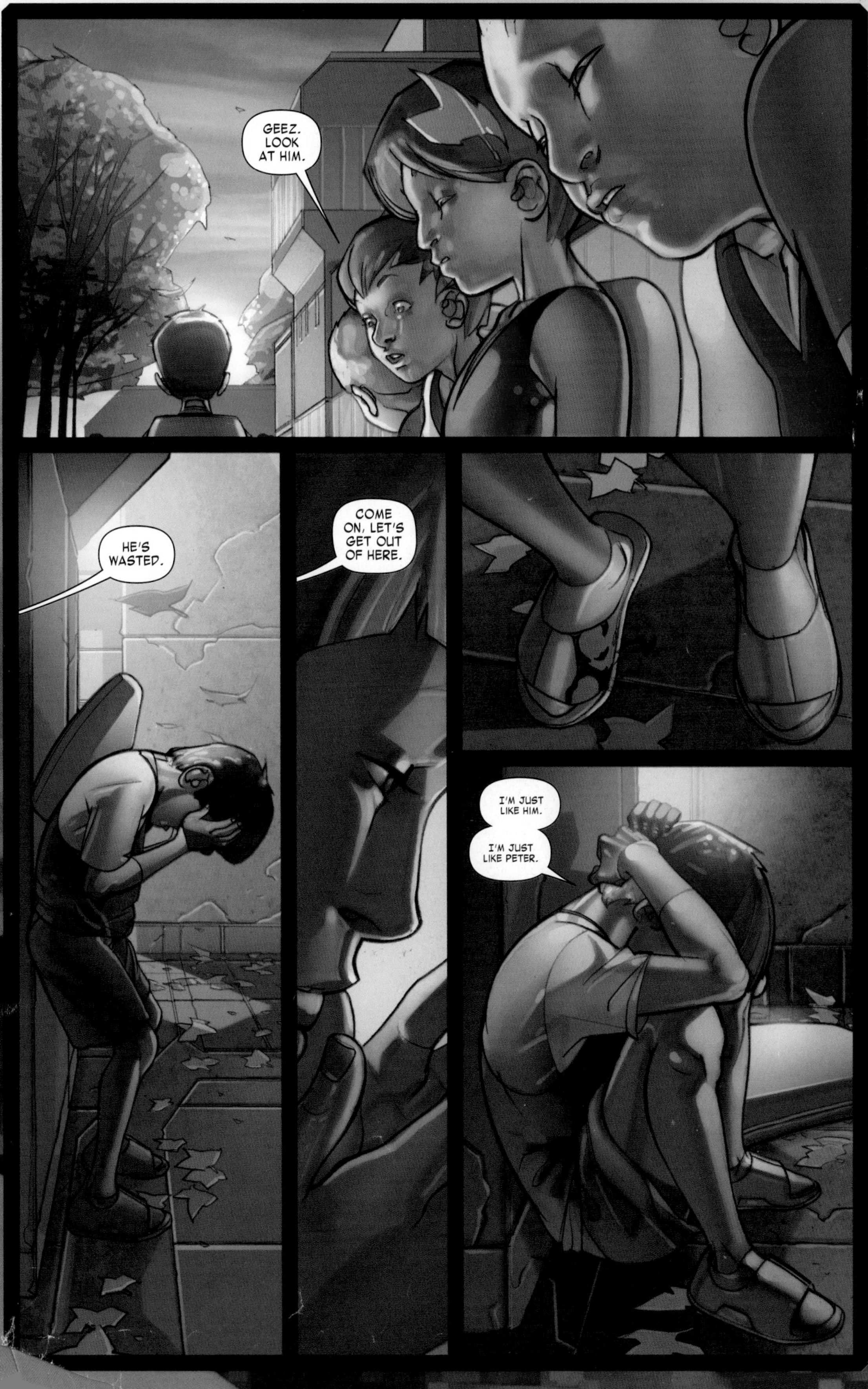
GEEZ. LOOK AT HIM.
HE'S WASTED.
COME ON, LET'S GET OUT OF HERE.
I'M JUST LIKE HIM.
I'M JUST LIKE PETER.

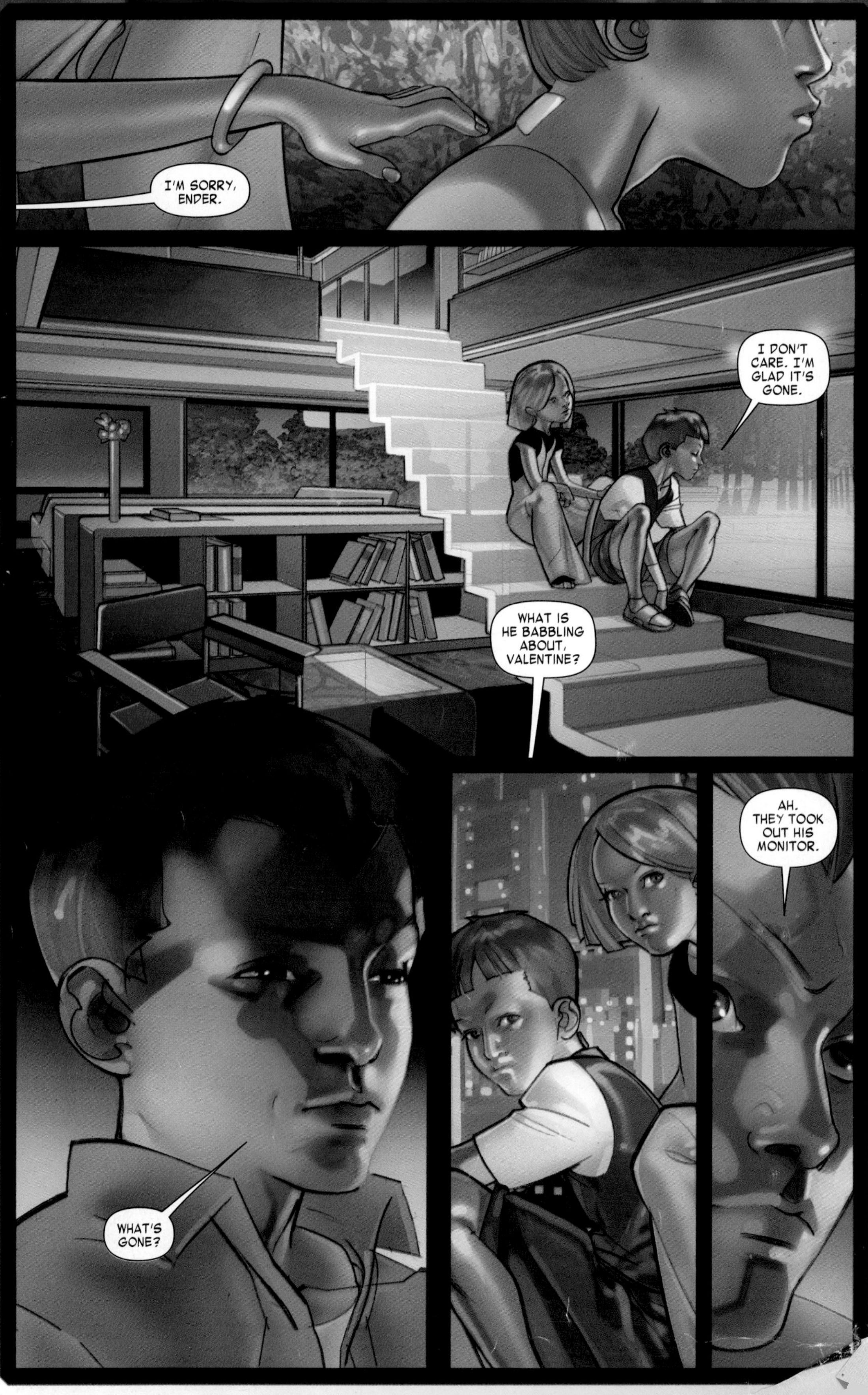
I'M SORRY, ENDER.
I DON'T CARE. I'M GLAD IT'S GONE.
WHAT IS HE BABBLING ABOUT, VALENTINE?
WHAT'S GONE?
AH. THEY TOOK OUT HIS MONITOR.

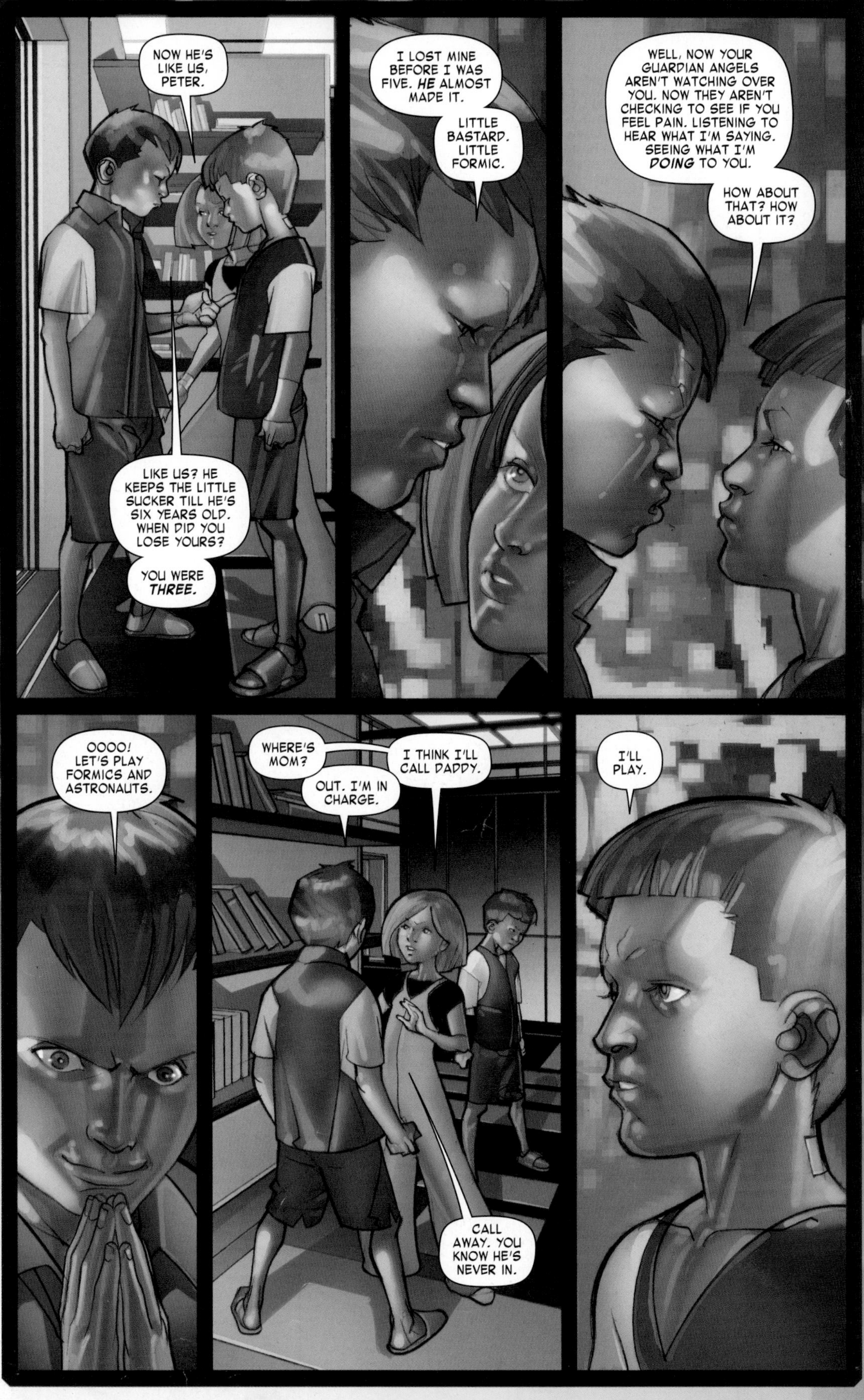
NOW HE'S LIKE US, PETER.
LIKE US? HE KEEPS THE LITTLE SUCKER TILL HE'S SIX YEARS OLD. WHEN DID YOU LOSE YOURS?
YOU WERE *THREE.*
I LOST MINE BEFORE I WAS FIVE. *HE* ALMOST MADE IT.
LITTLE BASTARD. LITTLE FORMIC.
WELL, NOW YOUR GUARDIAN ANGELS AREN'T WATCHING OVER YOU. NOW THEY AREN'T CHECKING TO SEE IF YOU FEEL PAIN. LISTENING TO HEAR WHAT I'M SAYING. SEEING WHAT I'M *DOING* TO YOU.
HOW ABOUT THAT? HOW ABOUT IT?
OOOO! LET'S PLAY FORMICS AND ASTRONAUTS.
WHERE'S MOM?
OUT. I'M IN CHARGE.
I THINK I'LL CALL DADDY.
CALL AWAY. YOU KNOW HE'S NEVER IN.
I'LL PLAY.

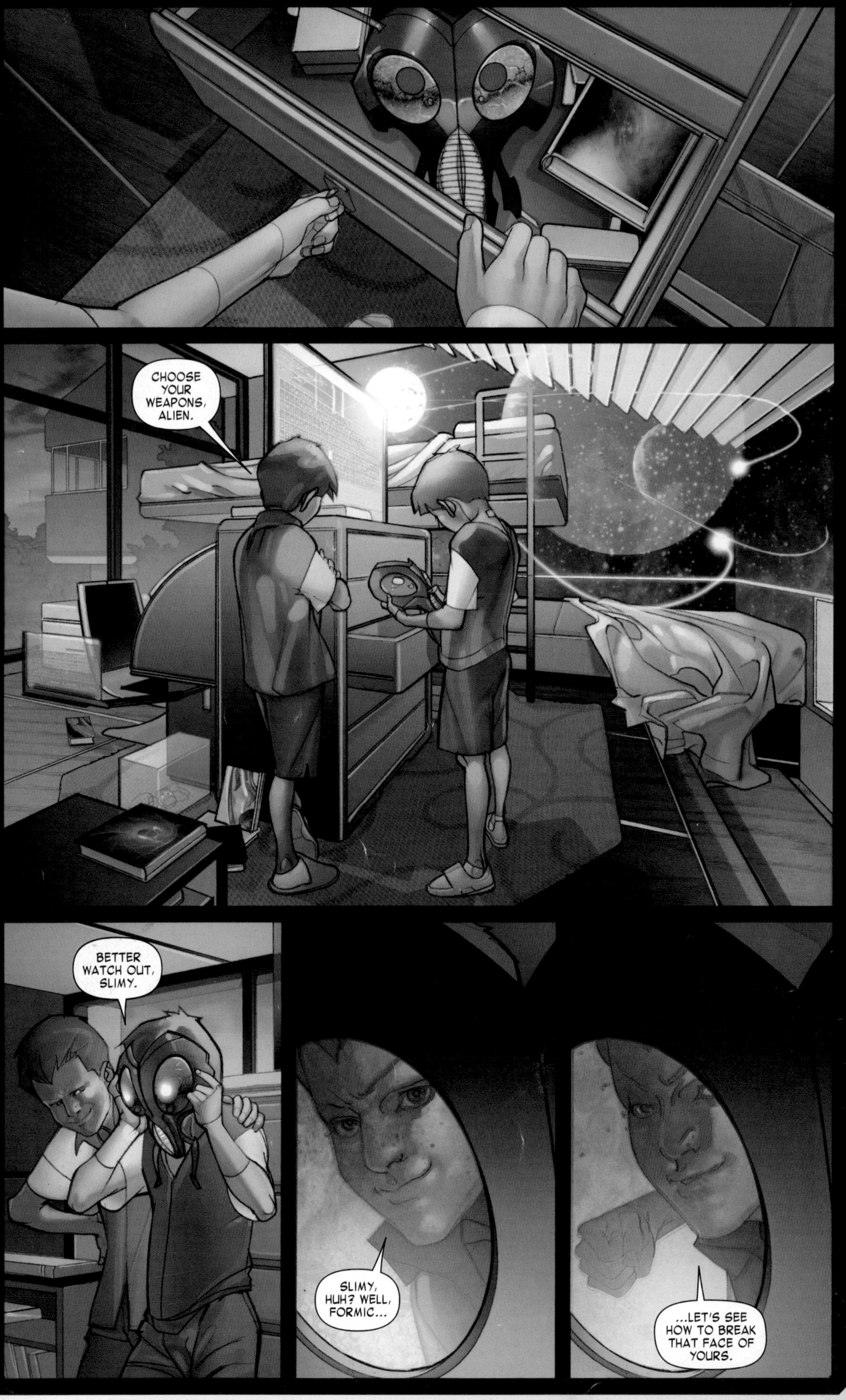
CHOOSE YOUR WEAPONS, ALIEN.
BETTER WATCH OUT, SLIMY.
SLIMY, HUH? WELL, FORMIC...
...LET'S SEE HOW TO BREAK THAT FACE OF YOURS.

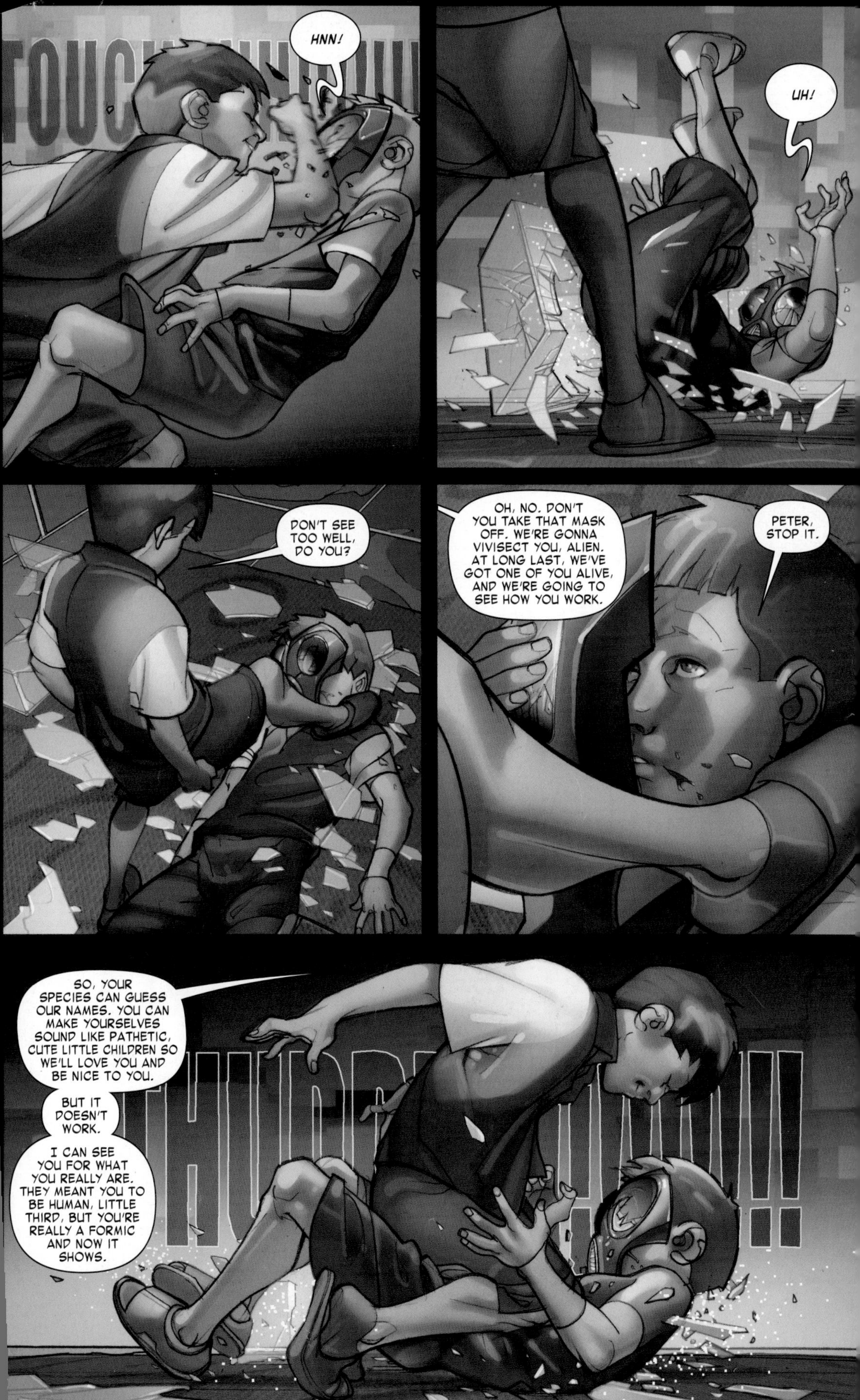
TOUCH
HNN!
UH!
DON'T SEE TOO WELL, DO YOU?
OH, NO. DON'T YOU TAKE THAT MASK OFF. WE'RE GONNA VIVISECT YOU, ALIEN. AT LONG LAST, WE'VE GOT ONE OF YOU ALIVE, AND WE'RE GOING TO SEE HOW YOU WORK.
PETER, STOP IT.
SO, YOUR SPECIES CAN GUESS OUR NAMES. YOU CAN MAKE YOURSELVES SOUND LIKE PATHETIC, CUTE LITTLE CHILDREN SO WE'LL LOVE YOU AND BE NICE TO YOU.
BUT IT DOESN'T WORK.
I CAN SEE YOU FOR WHAT YOU REALLY ARE. THEY MEANT YOU TO BE HUMAN, LITTLE THIRD, BUT YOU'RE REALLY A FORMIC AND NOW IT SHOWS.

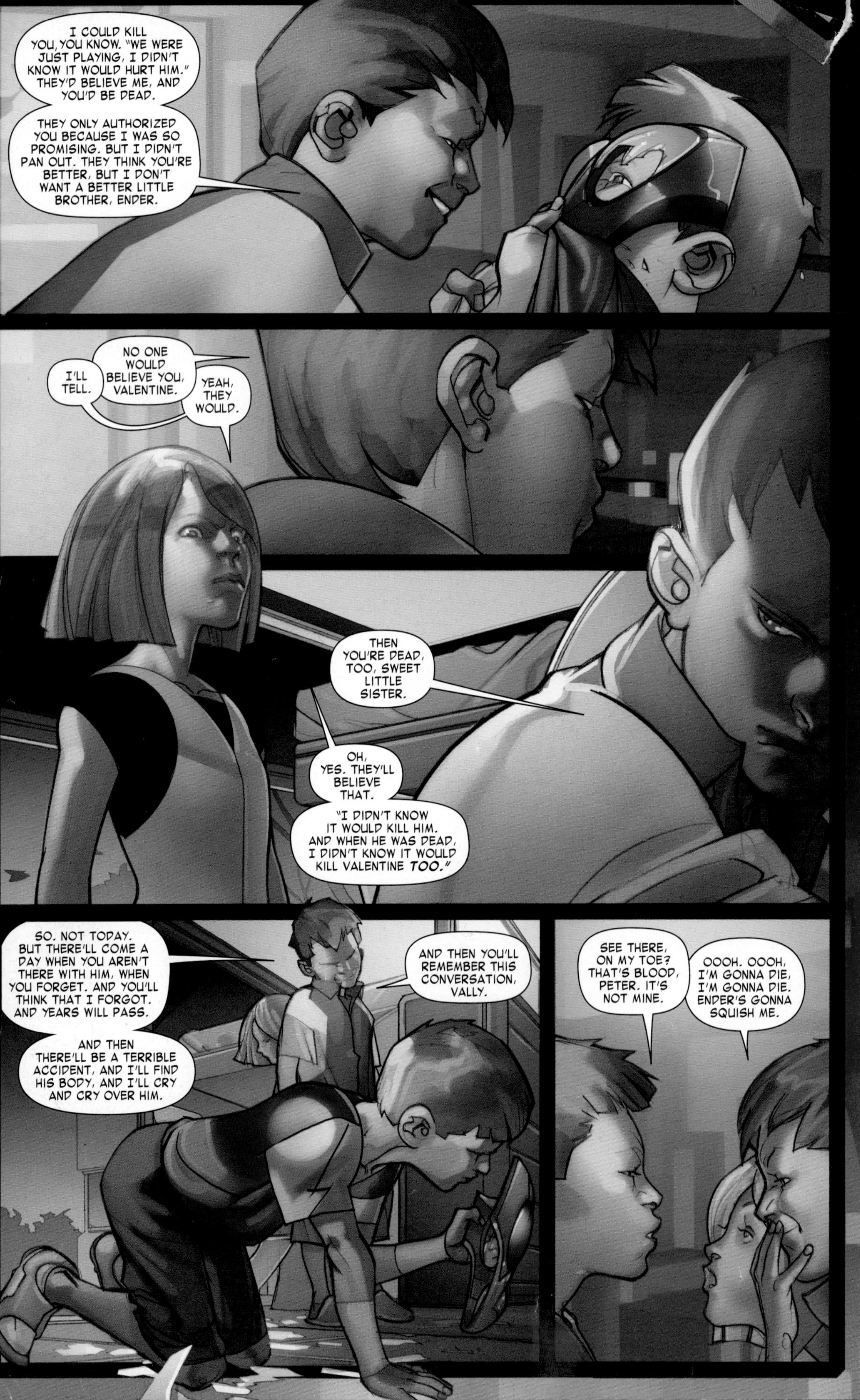
I COULD KILL YOU, YOU KNOW. "WE WERE JUST PLAYING, I DIDN'T KNOW IT WOULD HURT HIM." THEY'D BELIEVE ME, AND YOU'D BE DEAD.
THEY ONLY AUTHORIZED YOU BECAUSE I WAS SO PROMISING. BUT I DIDN'T PAN OUT. THEY THINK YOU'RE BETTER, BUT I DON'T WANT A BETTER LITTLE BROTHER, ENDER.
I'LL TELL.
NO ONE WOULD BELIEVE YOU, VALENTINE.
YEAH, THEY WOULD.
THEN YOU'RE DEAD, TOO, SWEET LITTLE SISTER.
OH, YES. THEY'LL BELIEVE THAT.
"I DIDN'T KNOW IT WOULD KILL HIM. AND WHEN HE WAS DEAD, I DIDN'T KNOW IT WOULD KILL VALENTINE *TOO.*"
SO. NOT TODAY. BUT THERE'LL COME A DAY WHEN YOU AREN'T THERE WITH HIM, WHEN YOU FORGET. AND YOU'LL THINK THAT I FORGOT. AND YEARS WILL PASS.
AND THEN THERE'LL BE A TERRIBLE ACCIDENT, AND I'LL FIND HIS BODY, AND I'LL CRY AND CRY OVER HIM.
AND THEN YOU'LL REMEMBER THIS CONVERSATION, VALLY.
SEE THERE, ON MY TOE? THAT'S BLOOD, PETER. IT'S NOT MINE.
OOOH. OOOH, I'M GONNA DIE, I'M GONNA DIE. ENDER'S GONNA SQUISH ME.

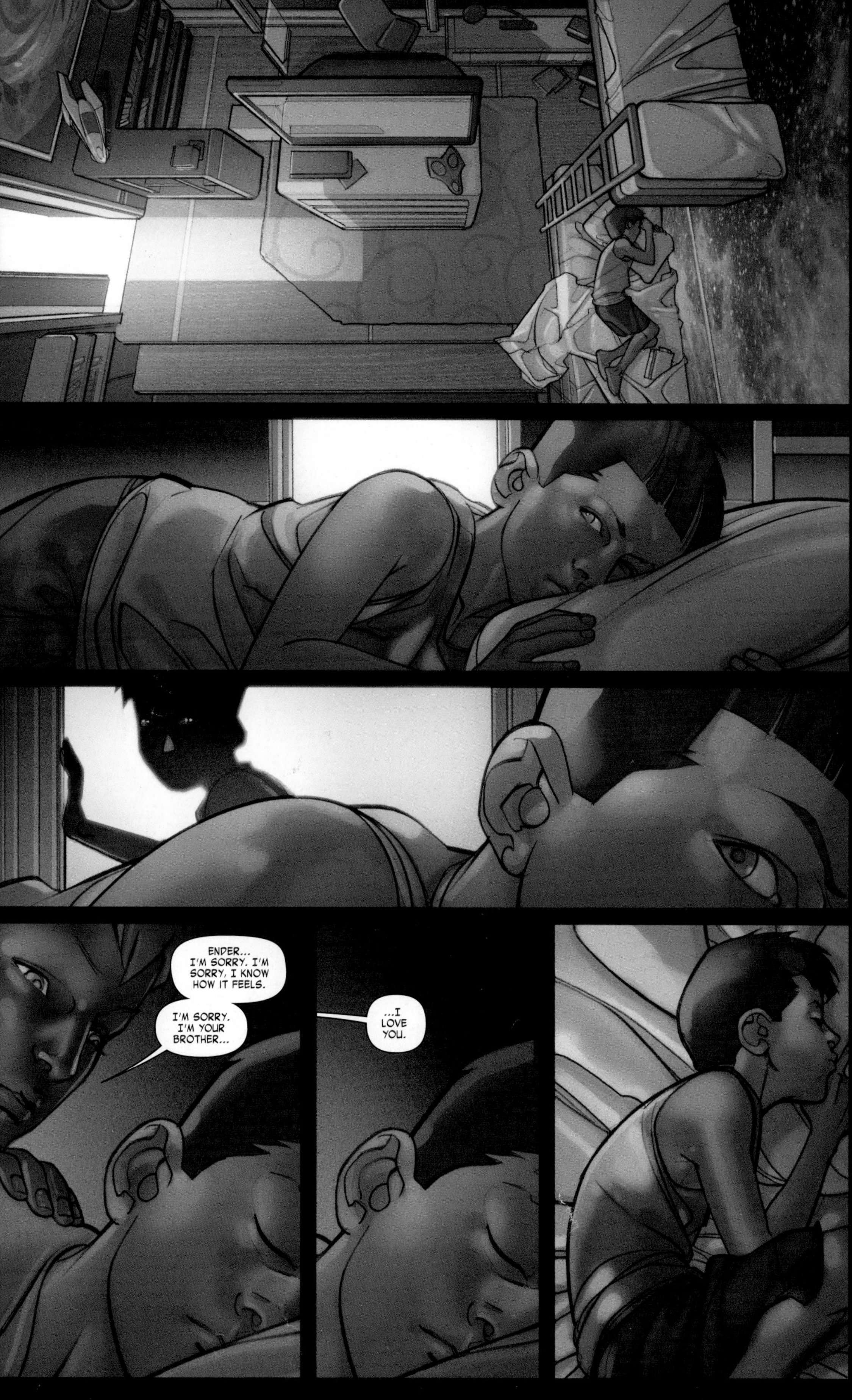
ENDER... I'M SORRY. I'M SORRY, I KNOW HOW IT FEELS.
I'M SORRY. I'M YOUR BROTHER...
...I LOVE YOU.

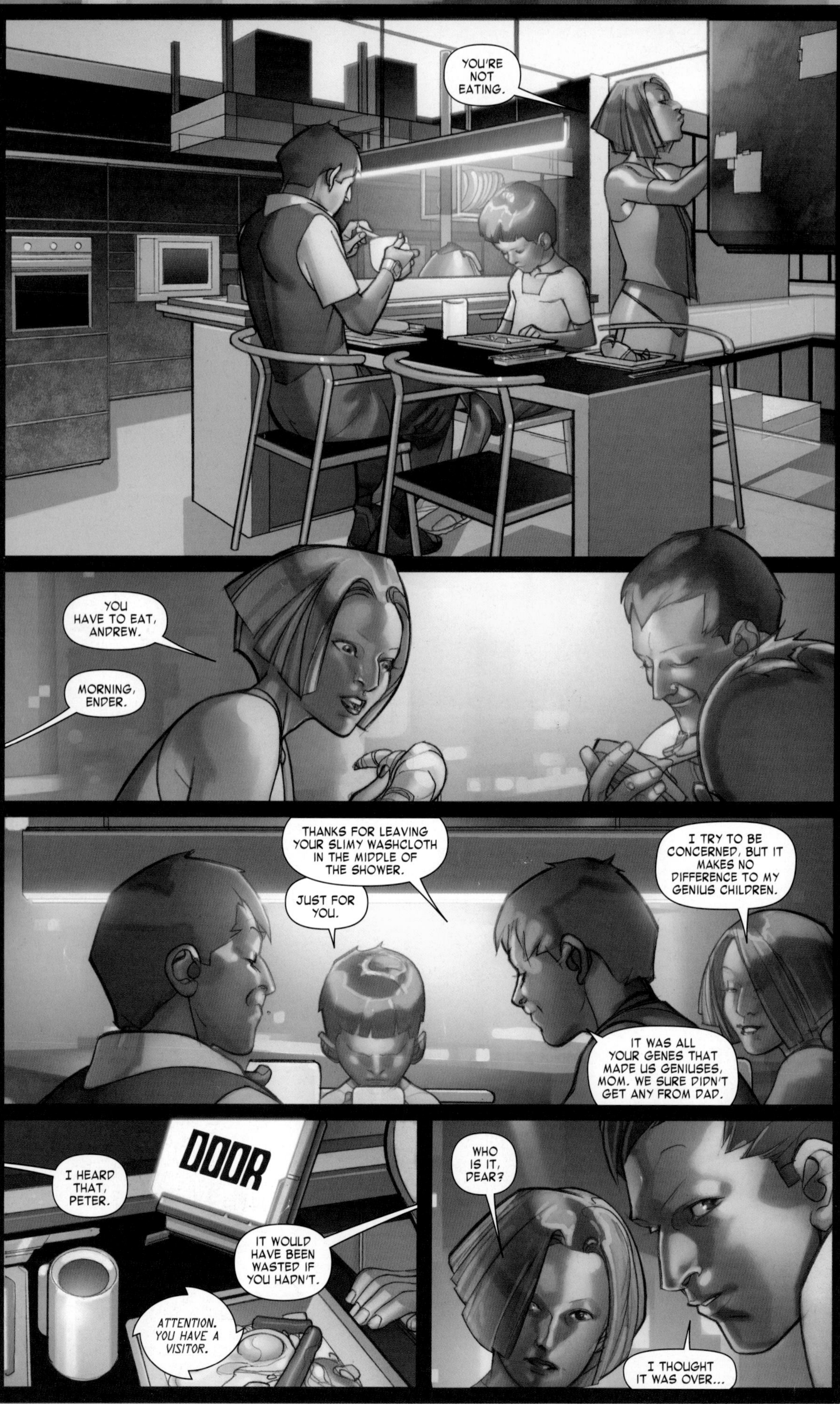
YOU'RE NOT EATING.
YOU HAVE TO EAT, ANDREW.
MORNING, ENDER.
THANKS FOR LEAVING YOUR SLIMY WASHCLOTH IN THE MIDDLE OF THE SHOWER.
JUST FOR YOU.
I TRY TO BE CONCERNED, BUT IT MAKES NO DIFFERENCE TO MY GENIUS CHILDREN.
IT WAS ALL YOUR GENES THAT MADE US GENIUSES, MOM. WE SURE DIDN'T GET ANY FROM DAD.
I HEARD THAT, PETER.
DOOR
IT WOULD HAVE BEEN WASTED IF YOU HADN'T.
ATTENTION. YOU HAVE A VISITOR.
WHO IS IT, DEAR?
I THOUGHT IT WAS OVER...

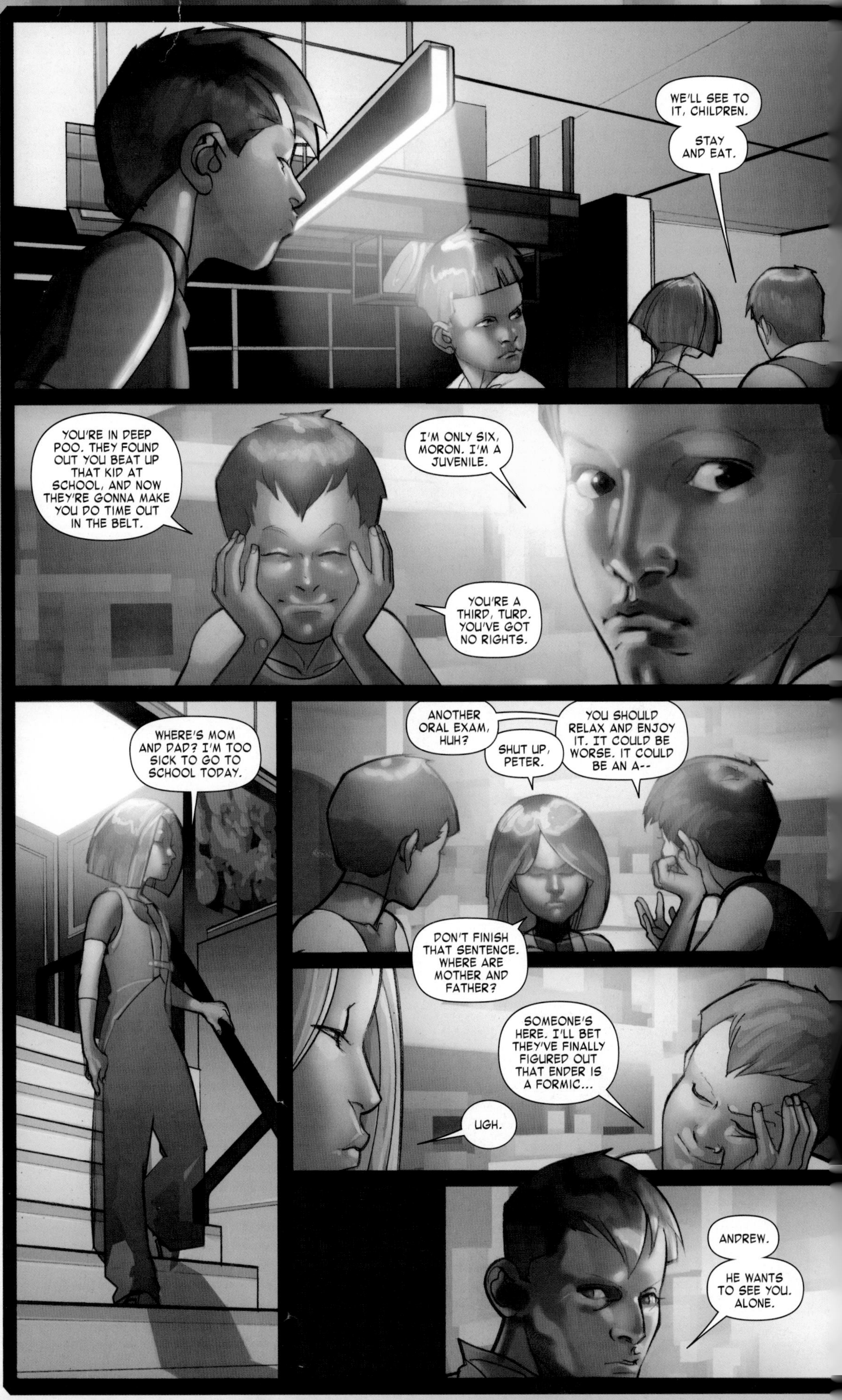
WE'LL SEE TO IT, CHILDREN.
STAY AND EAT.
YOU'RE IN DEEP POO. THEY FOUND OUT YOU BEAT UP THAT KID AT SCHOOL, AND NOW THEY'RE GONNA MAKE YOU DO TIME OUT IN THE BELT.
I'M ONLY SIX, MORON. I'M A JUVENILE.
YOU'RE A THIRD, TURD. YOU'VE GOT NO RIGHTS.
WHERE'S MOM AND DAD? I'M TOO SICK TO GO TO SCHOOL TODAY.
ANOTHER ORAL EXAM, HUH?
SHUT UP, PETER.
YOU SHOULD RELAX AND ENJOY IT. IT COULD BE WORSE. IT COULD BE AN A--
DON'T FINISH THAT SENTENCE. WHERE ARE MOTHER AND FATHER?
SOMEONE'S HERE. I'LL BET THEY'VE FINALLY FIGURED OUT THAT ENDER IS A FORMIC...
UGH.
ANDREW.
HE WANTS TO SEE YOU. ALONE.

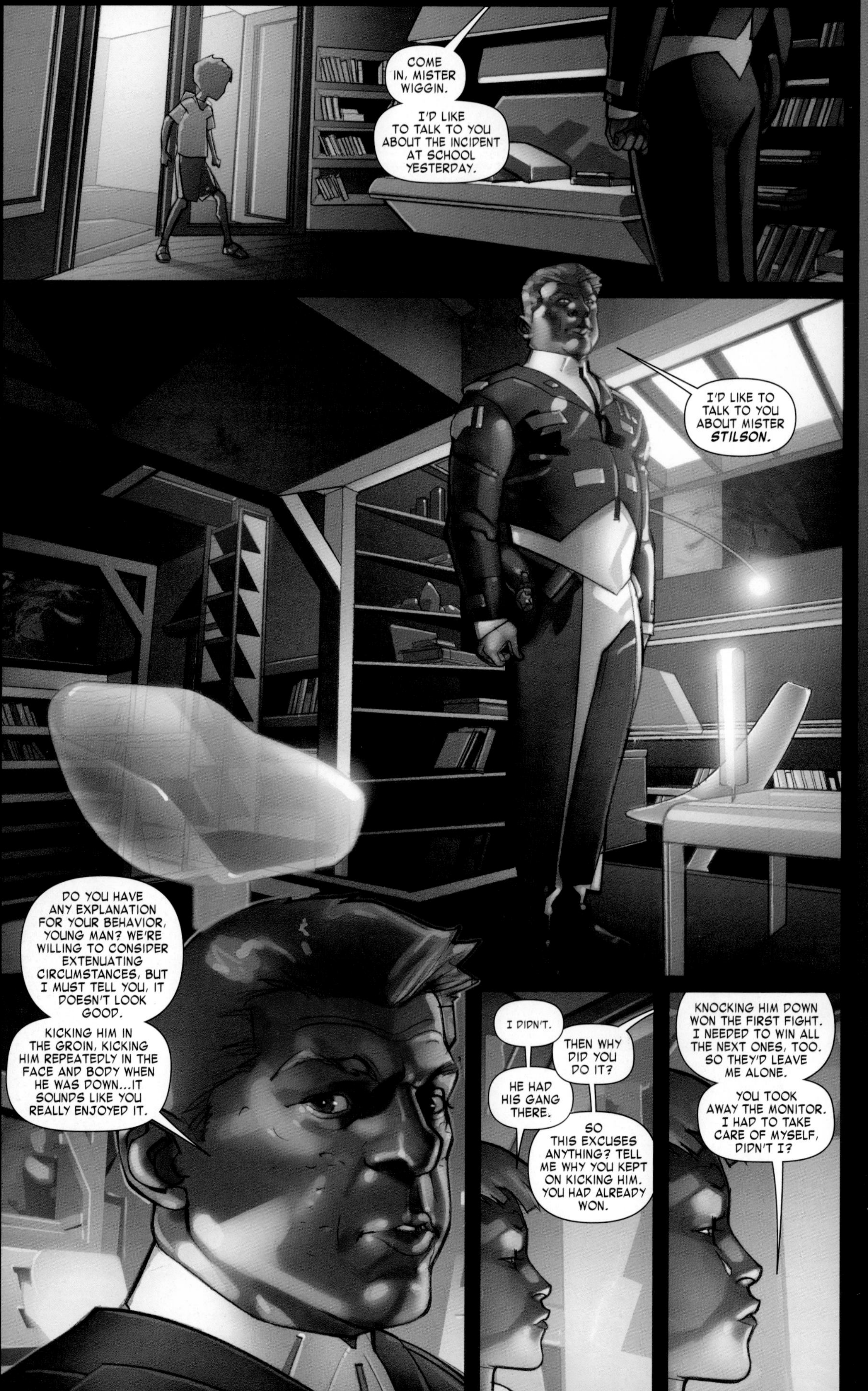
COME IN, MISTER WIGGIN.
I'D LIKE TO TALK TO YOU ABOUT THE INCIDENT AT SCHOOL YESTERDAY.
I'D LIKE TO TALK TO YOU ABOUT MISTER STILSON.
DO YOU HAVE ANY EXPLANATION FOR YOUR BEHAVIOR, YOUNG MAN? WE'RE WILLING TO CONSIDER EXTENUATING CIRCUMSTANCES, BUT I MUST TELL YOU, IT DOESN'T LOOK GOOD.
KICKING HIM IN THE GROIN, KICKING HIM REPEATEDLY IN THE FACE AND BODY WHEN HE WAS DOWN...IT SOUNDS LIKE YOU REALLY ENJOYED IT.
I DIDN'T.
THEN WHY DID YOU DO IT?
HE HAD HIS GANG THERE.
SO THIS EXCUSES ANYTHING? TELL ME WHY YOU KEPT ON KICKING HIM. YOU HAD ALREADY WON.
KNOCKING HIM DOWN WON THE FIRST FIGHT. I NEEDED TO WIN ALL THE NEXT ONES, TOO. SO THEY'D LEAVE ME ALONE.
YOU TOOK AWAY THE MONITOR. I HAD TO TAKE CARE OF MYSELF, DIDN'T I?

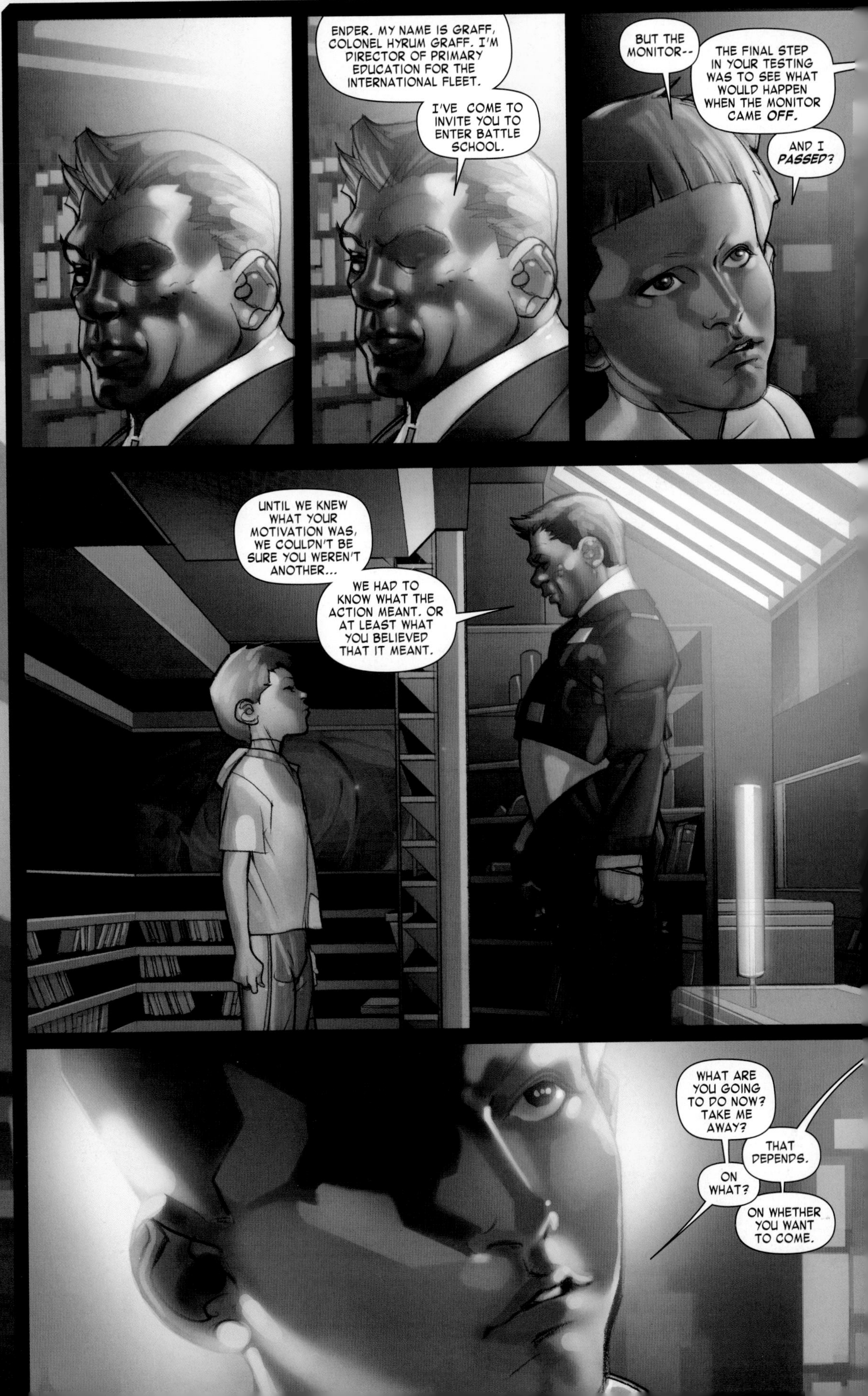

ENDER. MY NAME IS GRAFF, COLONEL HYRUM GRAFF. I'M DIRECTOR OF PRIMARY EDUCATION FOR THE INTERNATIONAL FLEET.
I'VE COME TO INVITE YOU TO ENTER BATTLE SCHOOL.
BUT THE MONITOR--
THE FINAL STEP IN YOUR TESTING WAS TO SEE WHAT WOULD HAPPEN WHEN THE MONITOR CAME *OFF.*
AND I *PASSED?*
UNTIL WE KNEW WHAT YOUR MOTIVATION WAS, WE COULDN'T BE SURE YOU WEREN'T ANOTHER...
WE HAD TO KNOW WHAT THE ACTION MEANT. OR AT LEAST WHAT YOU BELIEVED THAT IT MEANT.
WHAT ARE YOU GOING TO DO NOW? TAKE ME AWAY?
THAT DEPENDS.
ON WHAT?
ON WHETHER YOU WANT TO COME.

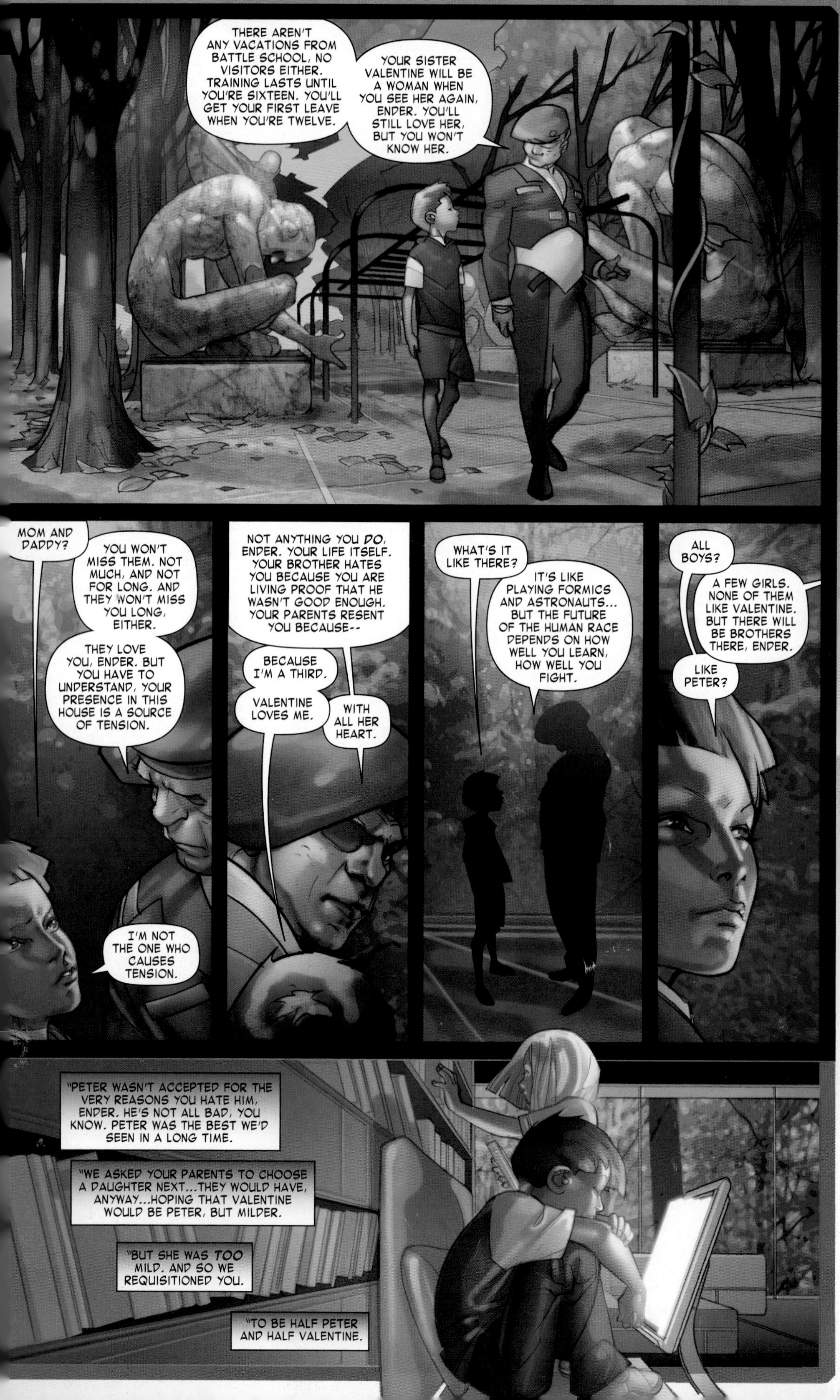

THERE AREN'T ANY VACATIONS FROM BATTLE SCHOOL, NO VISITORS EITHER. TRAINING LASTS UNTIL YOU'RE SIXTEEN. YOU'LL GET YOUR FIRST LEAVE WHEN YOU'RE TWELVE.
YOUR SISTER VALENTINE WILL BE A WOMAN WHEN YOU SEE HER AGAIN, ENDER. YOU'LL STILL LOVE HER, BUT YOU WON'T KNOW HER.
MOM AND DADDY?
YOU WON'T MISS THEM. NOT MUCH, AND NOT FOR LONG. AND THEY WON'T MISS YOU LONG, EITHER.
THEY LOVE YOU, ENDER. BUT YOU HAVE TO UNDERSTAND, YOUR PRESENCE IN THIS HOUSE IS A SOURCE OF TENSION.
I'M NOT THE ONE WHO CAUSES TENSION.
NOT ANYTHING YOU *DO*, ENDER. YOUR LIFE ITSELF. YOUR BROTHER HATES YOU BECAUSE YOU ARE LIVING PROOF THAT HE WASN'T GOOD ENOUGH. YOUR PARENTS RESENT YOU BECAUSE--
BECAUSE I'M A THIRD.
VALENTINE LOVES ME.
WITH ALL HER HEART.
WHAT'S IT LIKE THERE?
IT'S LIKE PLAYING FORMICS AND ASTRONAUTS... BUT THE FUTURE OF THE HUMAN RACE DEPENDS ON HOW WELL YOU LEARN, HOW WELL YOU FIGHT.
ALL BOYS?
A FEW GIRLS. NONE OF THEM LIKE VALENTINE. BUT THERE WILL BE BROTHERS THERE, ENDER.
LIKE PETER?
"PETER WASN'T ACCEPTED FOR THE VERY REASONS YOU HATE HIM, ENDER. HE'S NOT ALL BAD, YOU KNOW. PETER WAS THE BEST WE'D SEEN IN A LONG TIME.
"WE ASKED YOUR PARENTS TO CHOOSE A DAUGHTER NEXT...THEY WOULD HAVE, ANYWAY...HOPING THAT VALENTINE WOULD BE PETER, BUT MILDER.
"BUT SHE WAS *TOO* MILD. AND SO WE REQUISITIONED YOU.
"TO BE HALF PETER AND HALF VALENTINE.

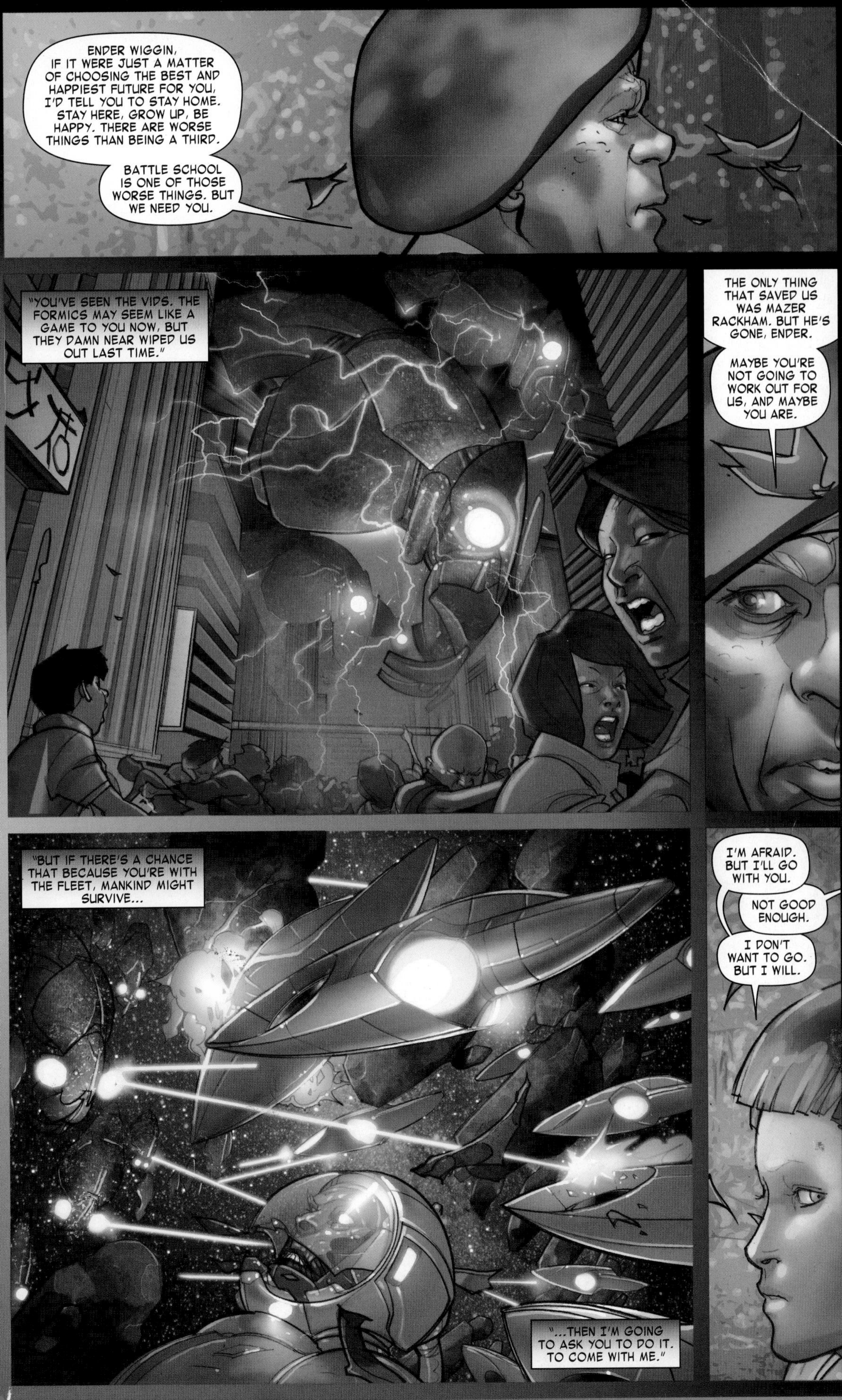

ENDER WIGGIN, IF IT WERE JUST A MATTER OF CHOOSING THE BEST AND HAPPIEST FUTURE FOR YOU, I'D TELL YOU TO STAY HOME. STAY HERE, GROW UP, BE HAPPY. THERE ARE WORSE THINGS THAN BEING A THIRD.
BATTLE SCHOOL IS ONE OF THOSE WORSE THINGS. BUT WE NEED YOU.
"YOU'VE SEEN THE VIDS. THE FORMICS MAY SEEM LIKE A GAME TO YOU NOW, BUT THEY DAMN NEAR WIPED US OUT LAST TIME."
THE ONLY THING THAT SAVED US WAS MAZER RACKHAM. BUT HE'S GONE, ENDER.
MAYBE YOU'RE NOT GOING TO WORK OUT FOR US, AND MAYBE YOU ARE.
"BUT IF THERE'S A CHANCE THAT BECAUSE YOU'RE WITH THE FLEET, MANKIND MIGHT SURVIVE...
"...THEN I'M GOING TO ASK YOU TO DO IT. TO COME WITH ME."
I'M AFRAID. BUT I'LL GO WITH YOU.
NOT GOOD ENOUGH.
I DON'T WANT TO GO. BUT I WILL.

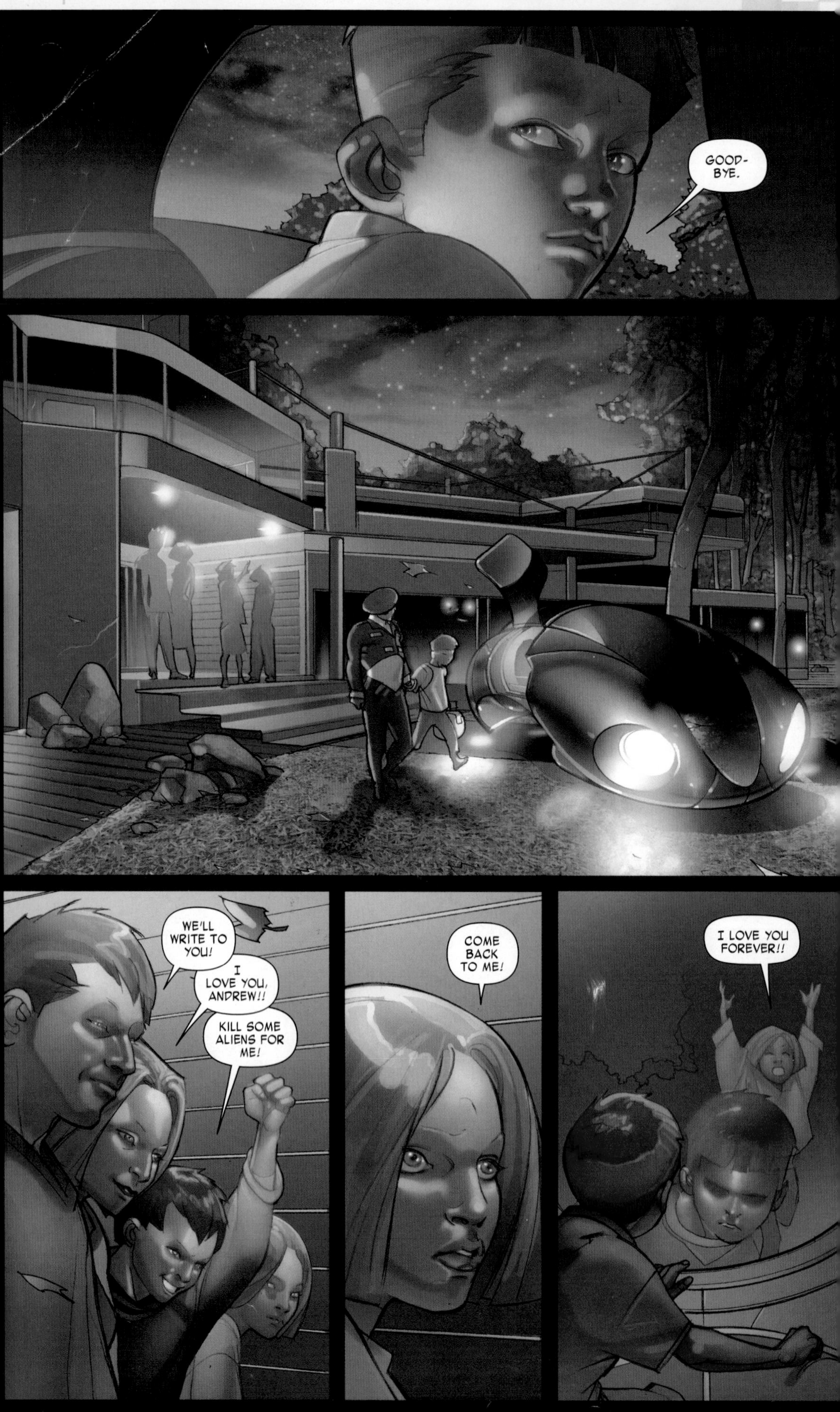
GOOD-BYE.
WE'LL WRITE TO YOU!
I LOVE YOU, ANDREW!!
KILL SOME ALIENS FOR ME!
COME BACK TO ME!
I LOVE YOU FOREVER!!

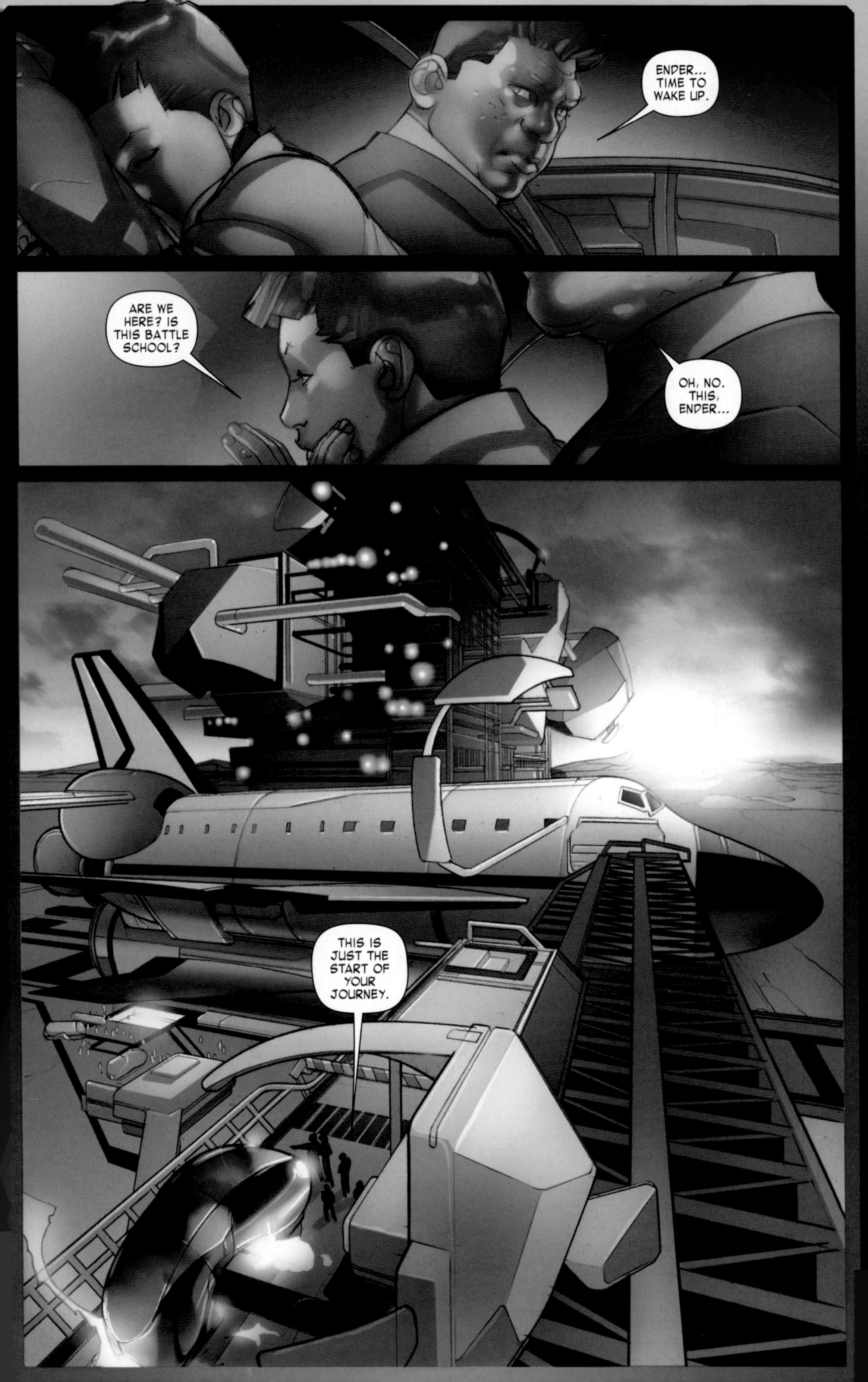
ENDER... TIME TO WAKE UP.
ARE WE HERE? IS THIS BATTLE SCHOOL?
OH, NO. THIS, ENDER...
THIS IS JUST THE START OF YOUR JOURNEY.

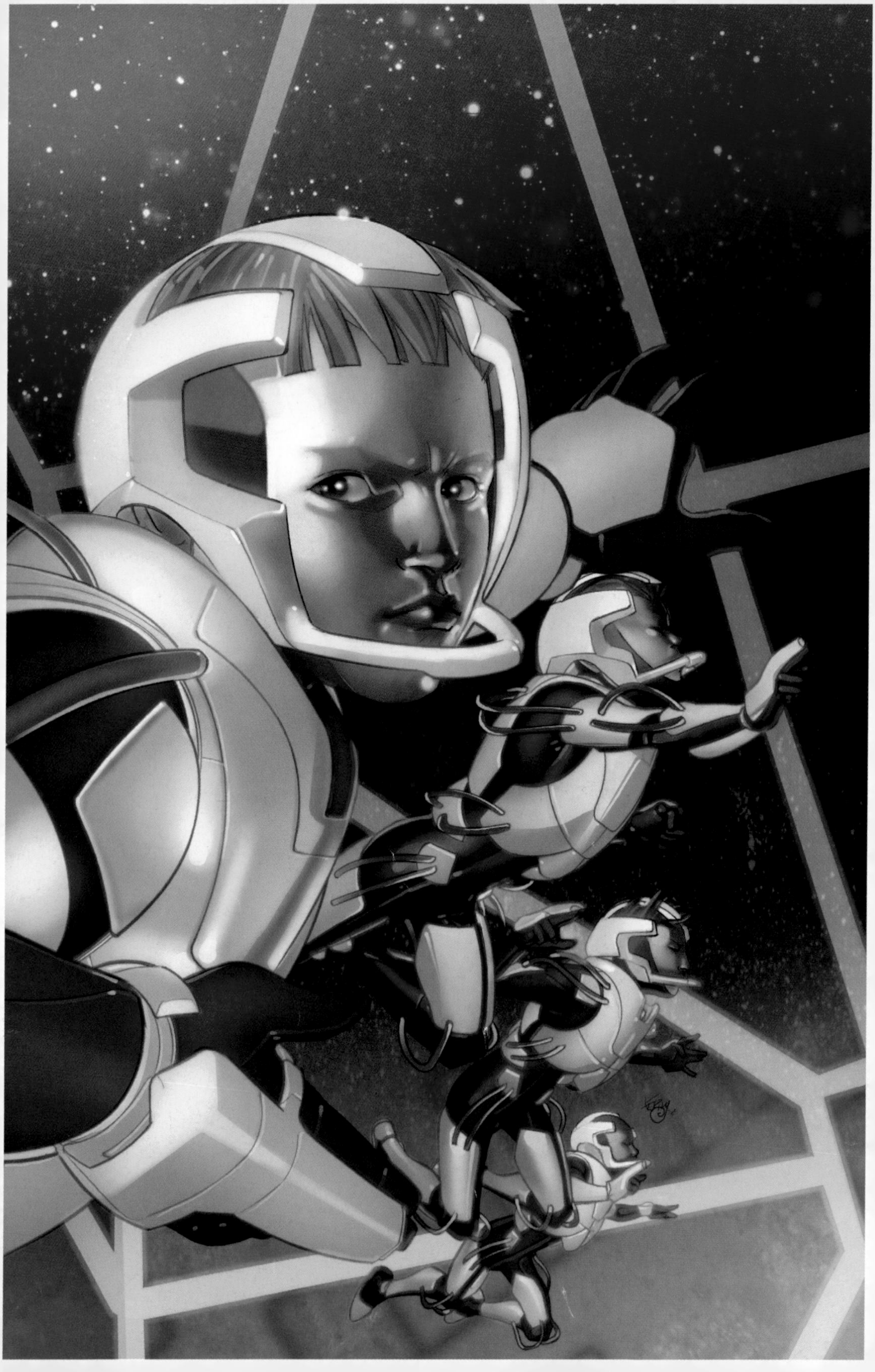

INTERNATIONAL FLEET PSYCHOLOGICAL REPORT #0026584
SUBJECT: WIGGIN, ANDREW "ENDER"
FILED BY: COLONEL HYRUM GRAFF
CROSS REFERENCE: WIGGIN, PETER and WIGGIN, VALENTINE

After the second invasion by the alien FORMICS, International Fleet
began the BATTLE SCHOOL initiative to find and train the greatest
minds humanity had to offer, preparing them to lead the International
Fleet in a potential THIRD INVASION.

Training begins at SIX YEARS OLD.

I.F. had chosen PETER WIGGIN for monitoring some years ago,
implanting a MONITOR CHIP in him. Peter was too aggressive, but
showed considerable promise. We requisitioned a second child
from the Wiggins, a girl, hoping to weed out excessive aggression.
VALENTINE was equally promising, but was too noncompetitive. And
while population laws forbade a another child, I.F. exempted the
Wiggins for a THIRD... Ender.

We monitored Ender the longest of the three children, and saw how he
was influenced equally by Peter AND Valentine. Peter tormented Ender
viciously throughout his life, and Valentine was Ender's only support.
Concerns arose that Ender subjugated his will to BOTH of them, that he
was too malleable.

I disagreed. So we gave Ender a final test... and took out his monitor.
He was immediately attacked by a school bully, and Ender dealt with
the student with... finality. Upon direct questioning, Ender revealed
that his brutality against the student was a tactical decision, and not
cruelty for the sake of cruelty.

I invited Ender to Battle School. And now I pray that he's strong
enough to survive it. For all our sakes.

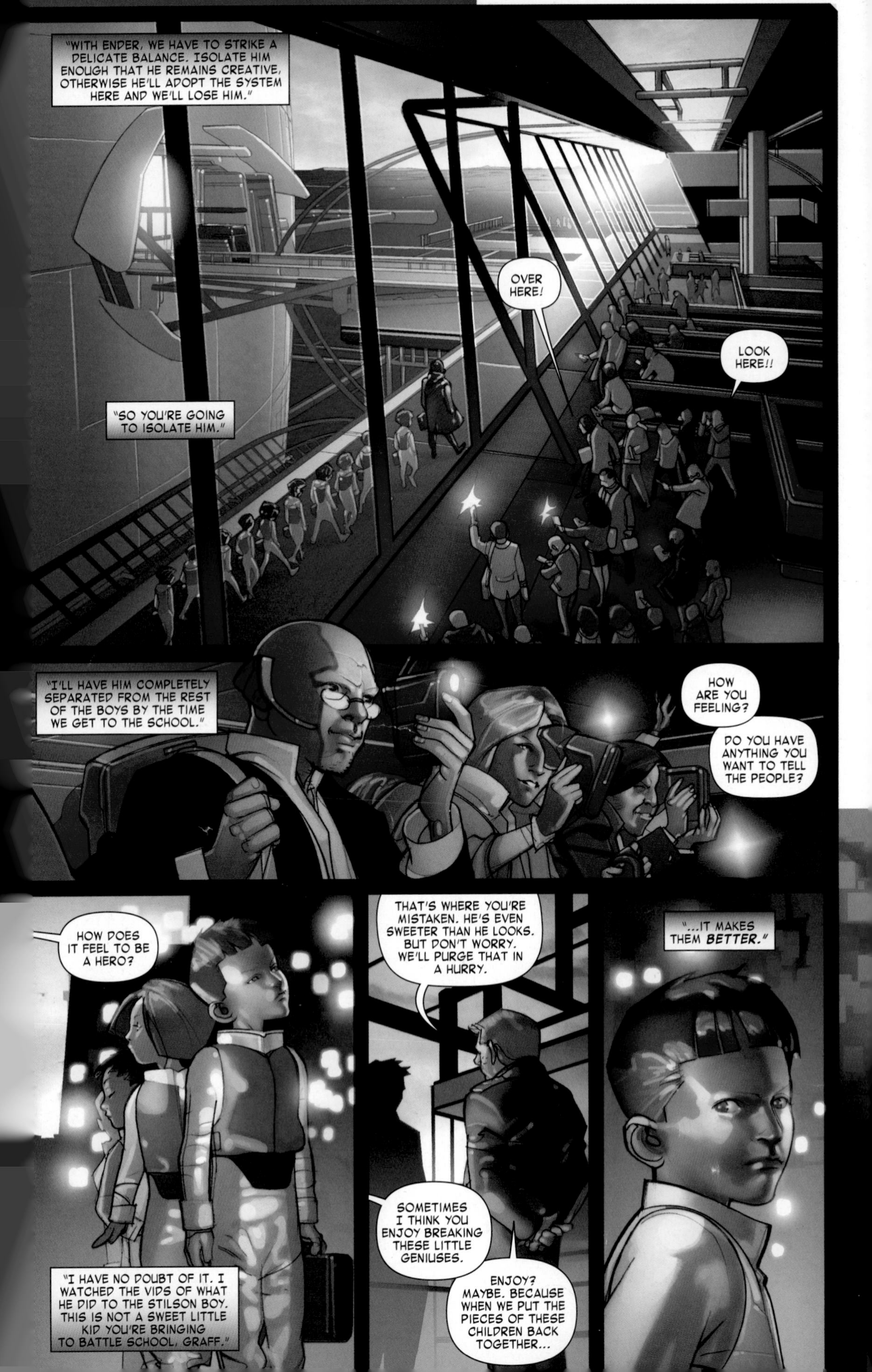
"WITH ENDER, WE HAVE TO STRIKE A DELICATE BALANCE. ISOLATE HIM ENOUGH THAT HE REMAINS CREATIVE, OTHERWISE HE'LL ADOPT THE SYSTEM HERE AND WE'LL LOSE HIM."
OVER HERE!
LOOK HERE!!
"SO YOU'RE GOING TO ISOLATE HIM."
"I'LL HAVE HIM COMPLETELY SEPARATED FROM THE REST OF THE BOYS BY THE TIME WE GET TO THE SCHOOL."
HOW ARE YOU FEELING?
DO YOU HAVE ANYTHING YOU WANT TO TELL THE PEOPLE?
HOW DOES IT FEEL TO BE A HERO?
"I HAVE NO DOUBT OF IT. I WATCHED THE VIDS OF WHAT HE DID TO THE STILSON BOY. THIS IS NOT A SWEET LITTLE KID YOU'RE BRINGING TO BATTLE SCHOOL, GRAFF."
THAT'S WHERE YOU'RE MISTAKEN. HE'S EVEN SWEETER THAN HE LOOKS. BUT DON'T WORRY. WE'LL PURGE THAT IN A HURRY.
SOMETIMES I THINK YOU ENJOY BREAKING THESE LITTLE GENIUSES.
ENJOY? MAYBE. BECAUSE WHEN WE PUT THE PIECES OF THESE CHILDREN BACK TOGETHER...
"...IT MAKES THEM BETTER."

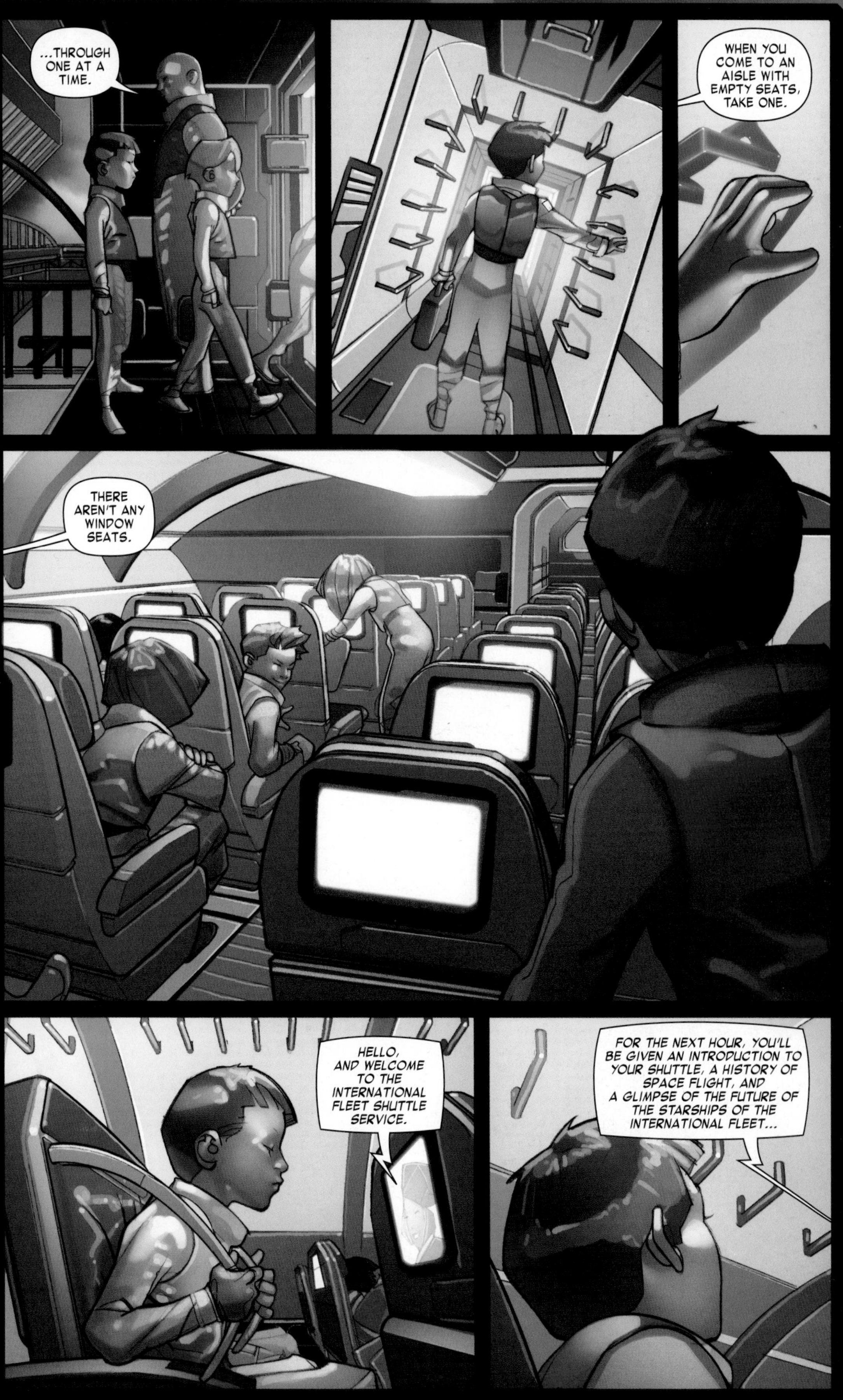
...THROUGH ONE AT A TIME.
WHEN YOU COME TO AN AISLE WITH EMPTY SEATS, TAKE ONE.
THERE AREN'T ANY WINDOW SEATS.
HELLO, AND WELCOME TO THE INTERNATIONAL FLEET SHUTTLE SERVICE.
FOR THE NEXT HOUR, YOU'LL BE GIVEN AN INTRODUCTION TO YOUR SHUTTLE, A HISTORY OF SPACE FLIGHT, AND A GLIMPSE OF THE FUTURE OF THE STARSHIPS OF THE INTERNATIONAL FLEET...

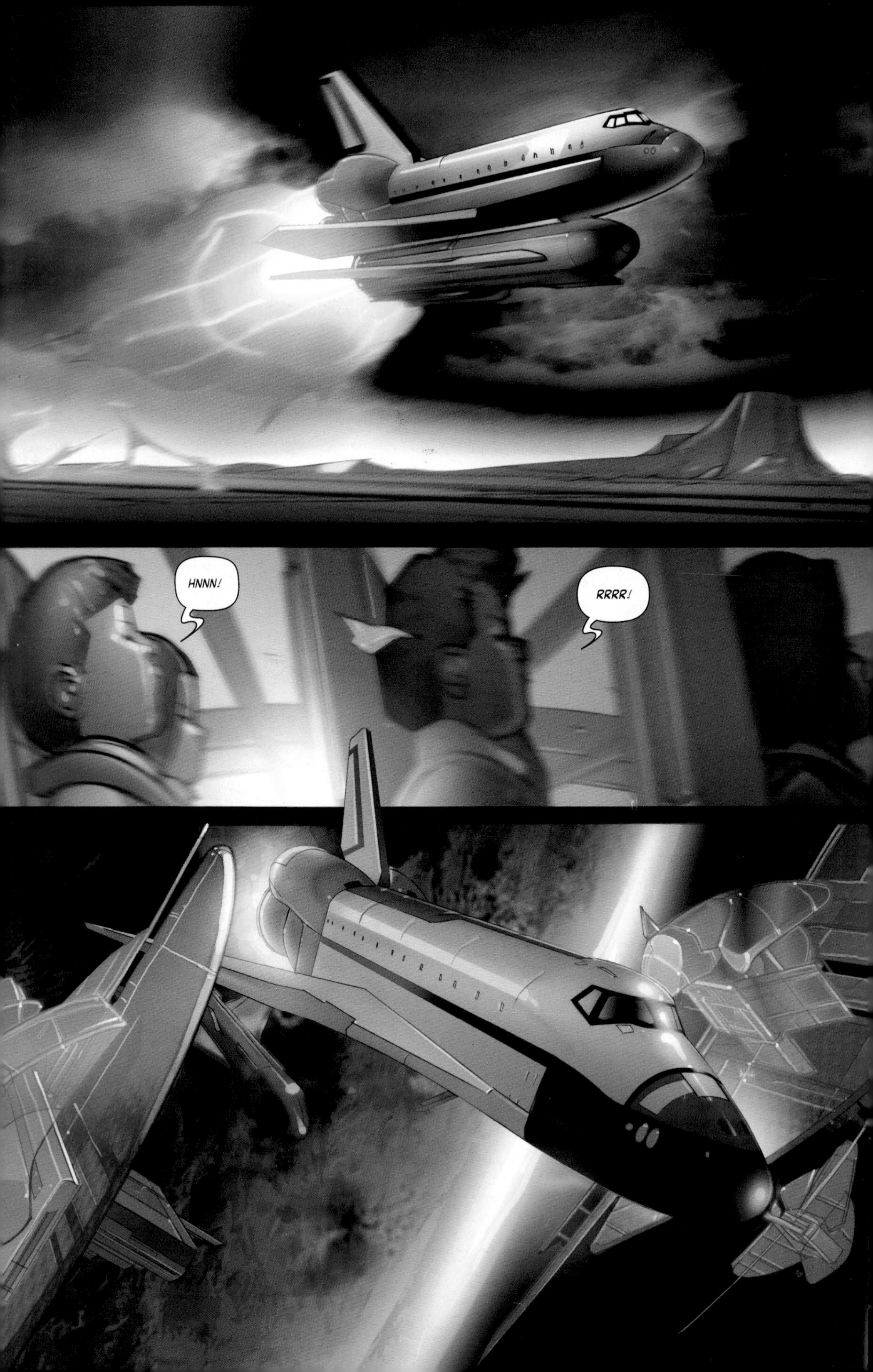
HNNN!
RRRR!

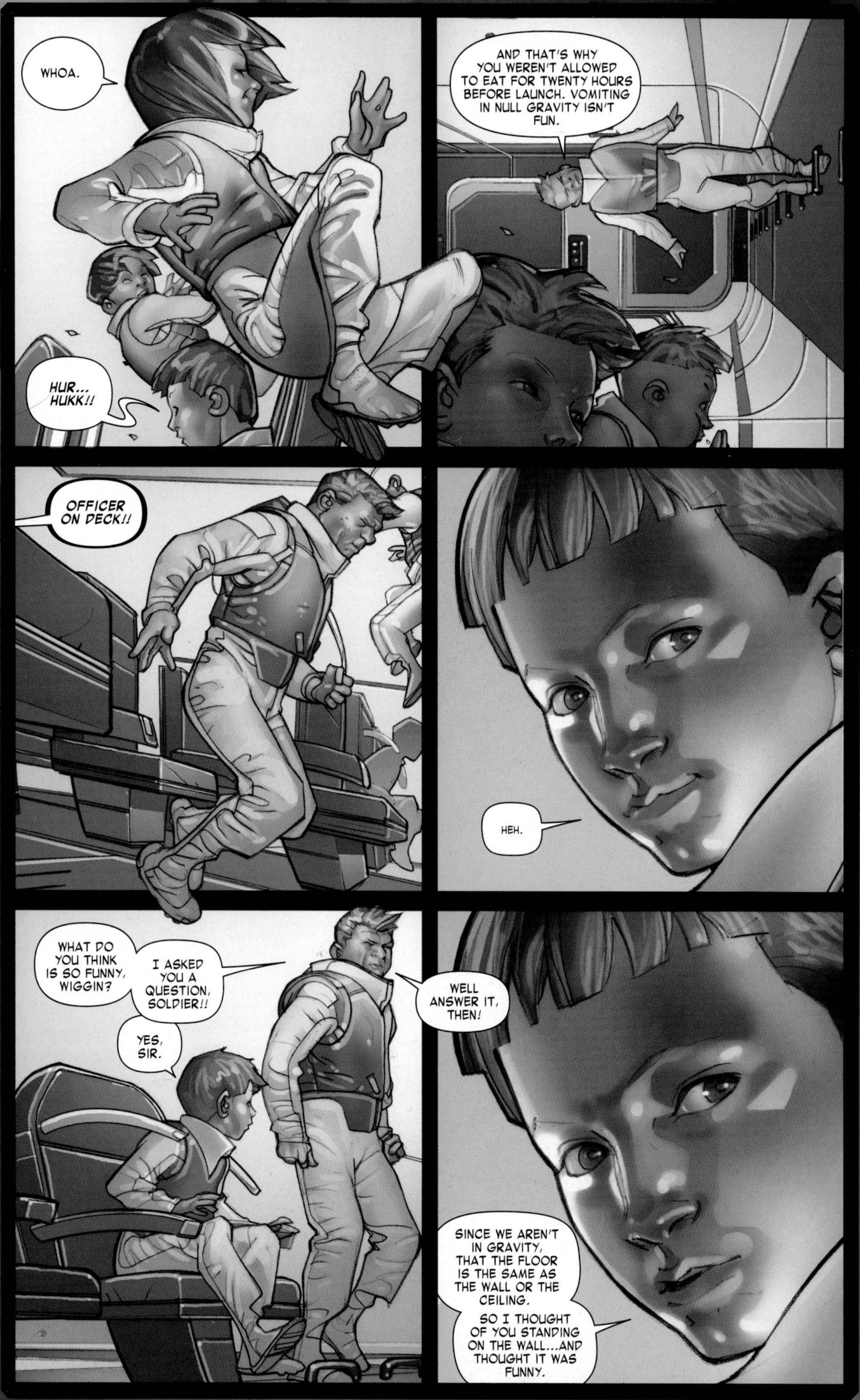
WHOA.
HUR... HUKK!!
AND THAT'S WHY YOU WEREN'T ALLOWED TO EAT FOR TWENTY HOURS BEFORE LAUNCH. VOMITING IN NULL GRAVITY ISN'T FUN.
OFFICER ON DECK!!
HEH.
WHAT DO YOU THINK IS SO FUNNY, WIGGIN?
I ASKED YOU A QUESTION, SOLDIER!!
YES, SIR.
WELL ANSWER IT, THEN!
SINCE WE AREN'T IN GRAVITY, THAT THE FLOOR IS THE SAME AS THE WALL OR THE CEILING.
SO I THOUGHT OF YOU STANDING ON THE WALL...AND THOUGHT IT WAS FUNNY.

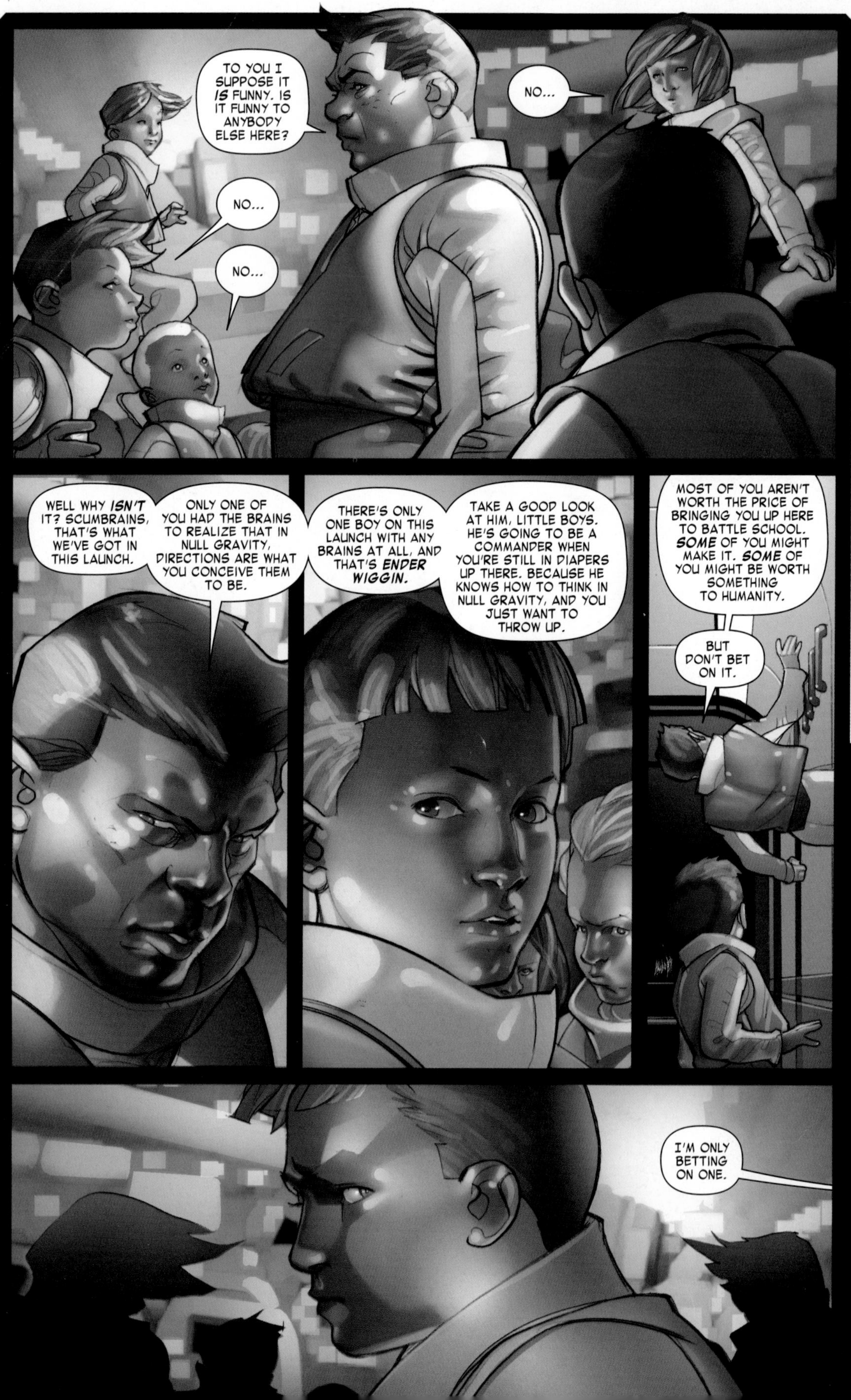
TO YOU I SUPPOSE IT *IS* FUNNY. IS IT FUNNY TO ANYBODY ELSE HERE?
NO...
NO...
NO...
WELL WHY *ISN'T* IT? SCUMBRAINS, THAT'S WHAT WE'VE GOT IN THIS LAUNCH.
ONLY ONE OF YOU HAD THE BRAINS TO REALIZE THAT IN NULL GRAVITY, DIRECTIONS ARE WHAT YOU CONCEIVE THEM TO BE.
THERE'S ONLY ONE BOY ON THIS LAUNCH WITH ANY BRAINS AT ALL, AND THAT'S *ENDER WIGGIN.*
TAKE A GOOD LOOK AT HIM, LITTLE BOYS. HE'S GOING TO BE A COMMANDER WHEN YOU'RE STILL IN DIAPERS UP THERE. BECAUSE HE KNOWS HOW TO THINK IN NULL GRAVITY, AND YOU JUST WANT TO THROW UP.
MOST OF YOU AREN'T WORTH THE PRICE OF BRINGING YOU UP HERE TO BATTLE SCHOOL. *SOME* OF YOU MIGHT MAKE IT. *SOME* OF YOU MIGHT BE WORTH SOMETHING TO HUMANITY.
BUT DON'T BET ON IT.
I'M ONLY BETTING ON ONE.

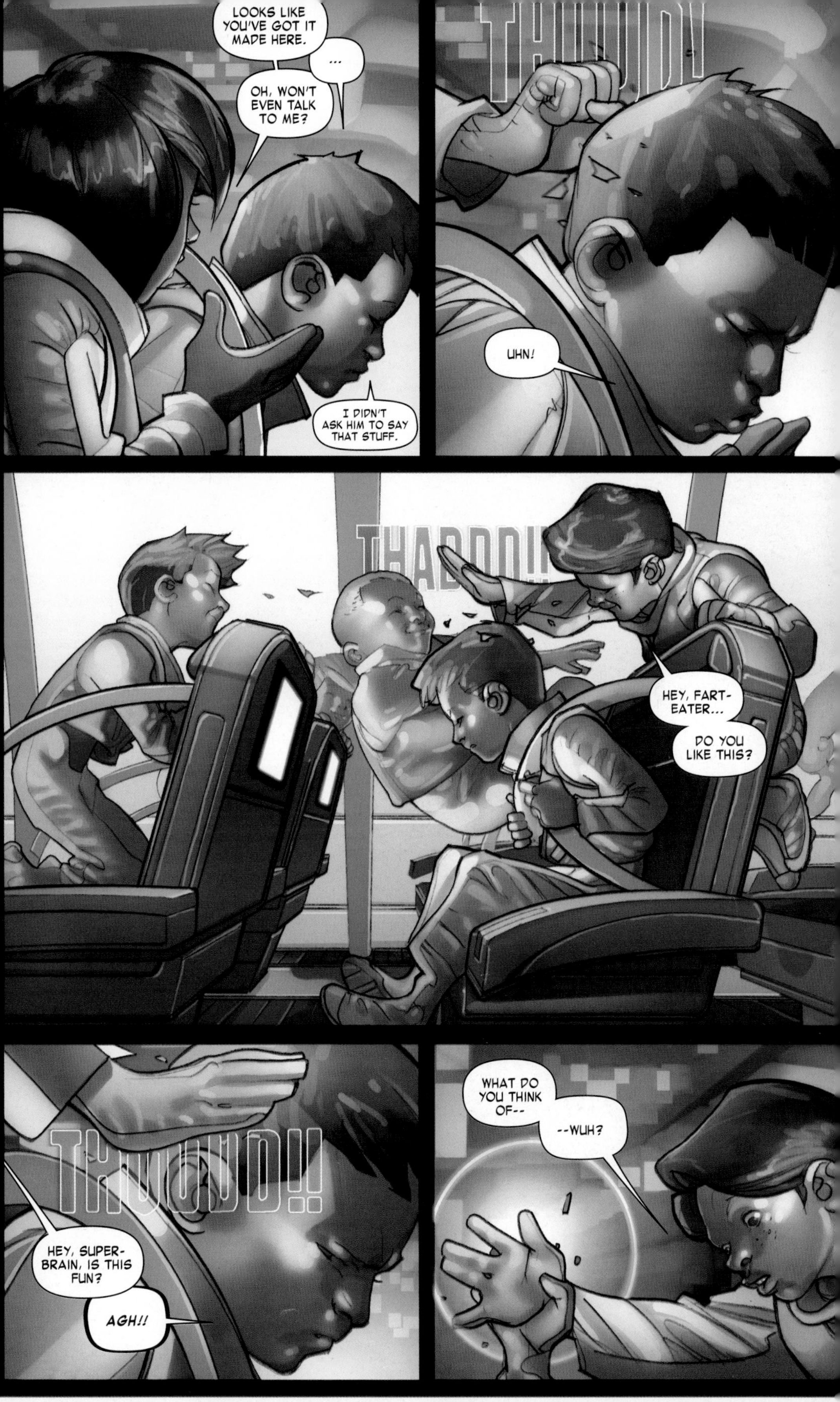
LOOKS LIKE YOU'VE GOT IT MADE HERE.
...
OH, WON'T EVEN TALK TO ME?
I DIDN'T ASK HIM TO SAY THAT STUFF.
UHN!
THADDD!!
HEY, FART-EATER...
DO YOU LIKE THIS?
THUUUD!!
HEY, SUPER-BRAIN, IS THIS FUN?
AGH!!
WHAT DO YOU THINK OF--
--WUH?

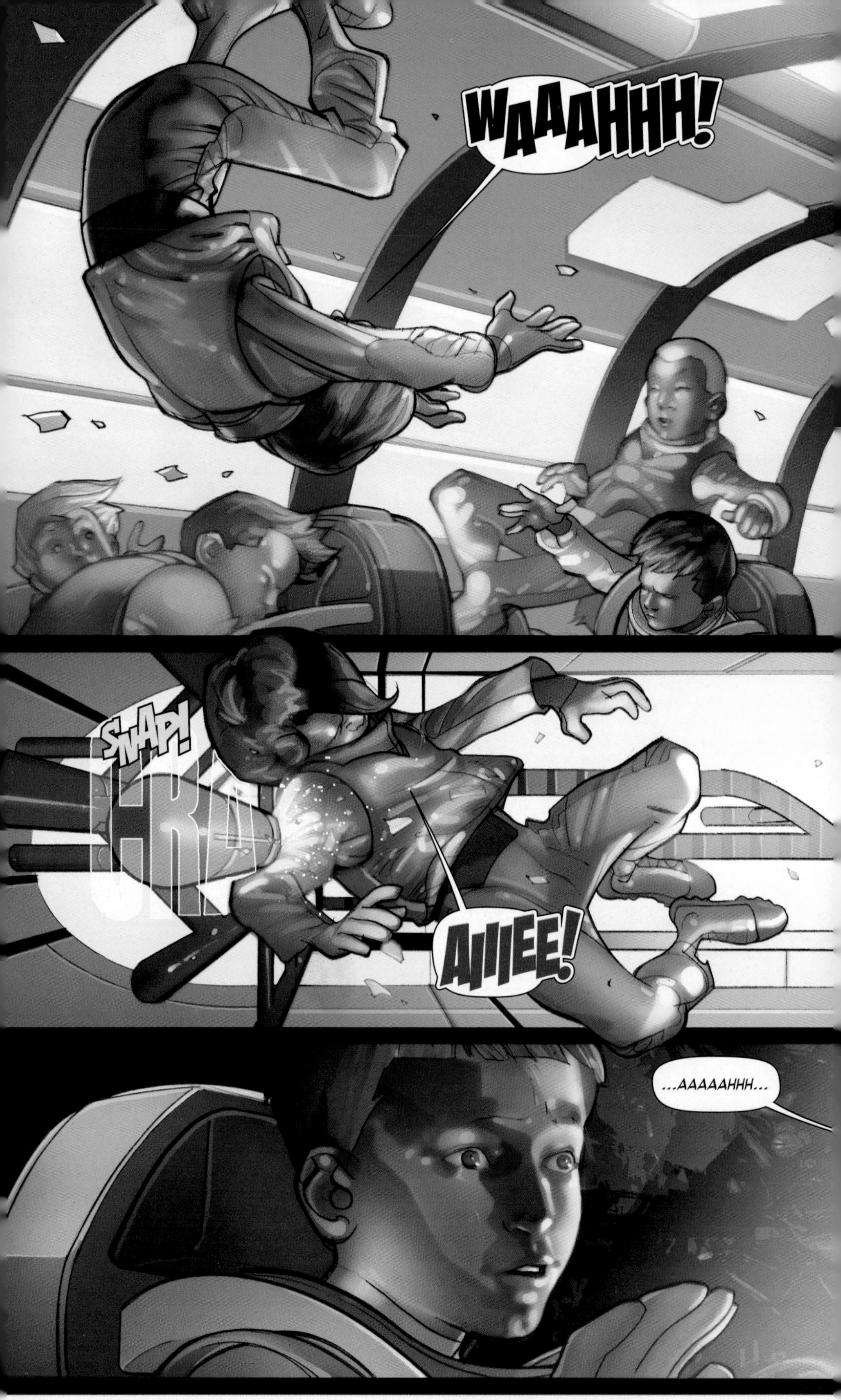
WAAAHHH!
SNAP!
AIIIEE!
...AAAAAHHH...

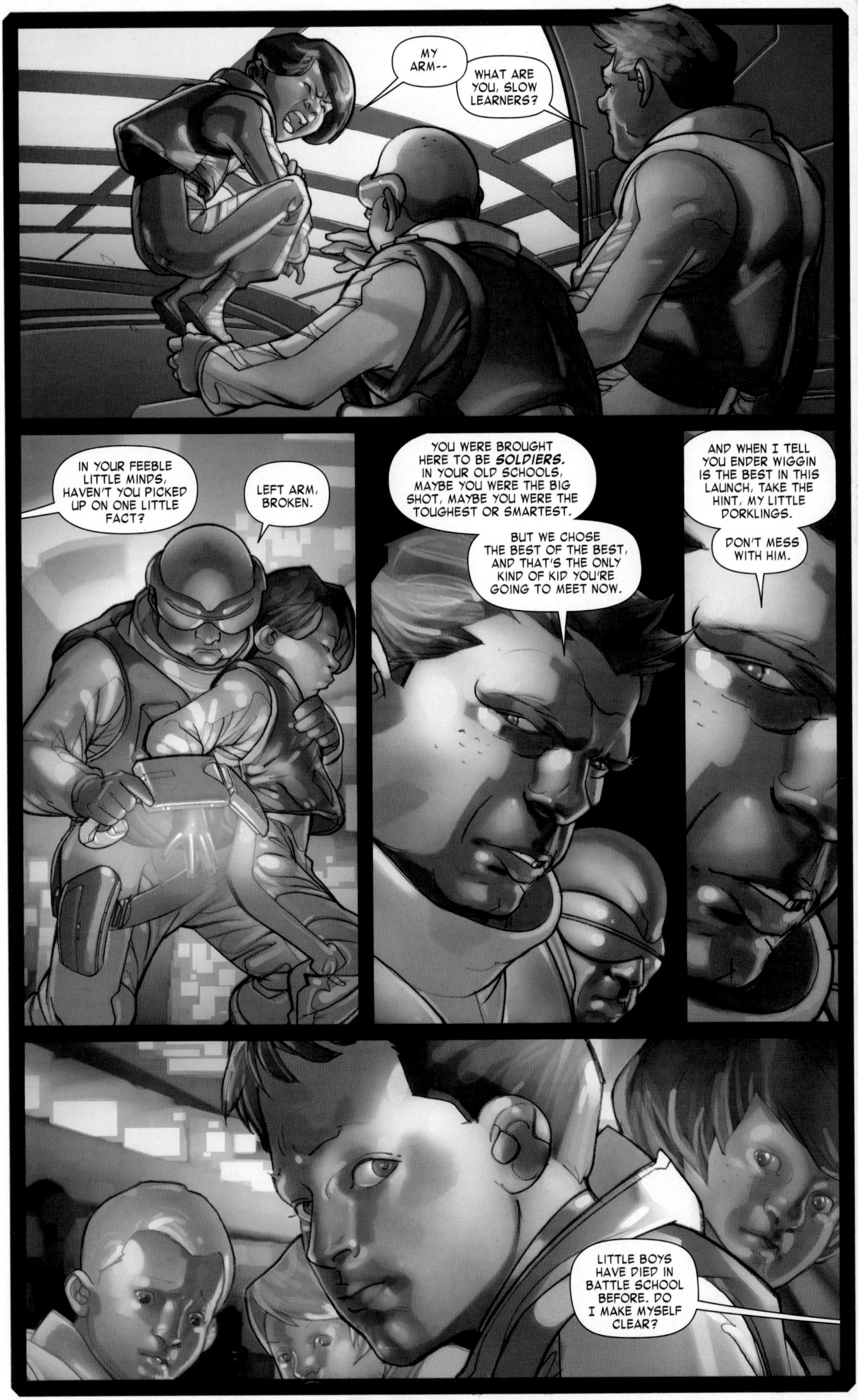
MY ARM--
WHAT ARE YOU, SLOW LEARNERS?
IN YOUR FEEBLE LITTLE MINDS, HAVEN'T YOU PICKED UP ON ONE LITTLE FACT?
LEFT ARM, BROKEN.
YOU WERE BROUGHT HERE TO BE SOLDIERS. IN YOUR OLD SCHOOLS, MAYBE YOU WERE THE BIG SHOT, MAYBE YOU WERE THE TOUGHEST OR SMARTEST.
BUT WE CHOSE THE BEST OF THE BEST, AND THAT'S THE ONLY KIND OF KID YOU'RE GOING TO MEET NOW.
AND WHEN I TELL YOU ENDER WIGGIN IS THE BEST IN THIS LAUNCH, TAKE THE HINT, MY LITTLE DORKLINGS.
DON'T MESS WITH HIM.
LITTLE BOYS HAVE DIED IN BATTLE SCHOOL BEFORE. DO I MAKE MYSELF CLEAR?

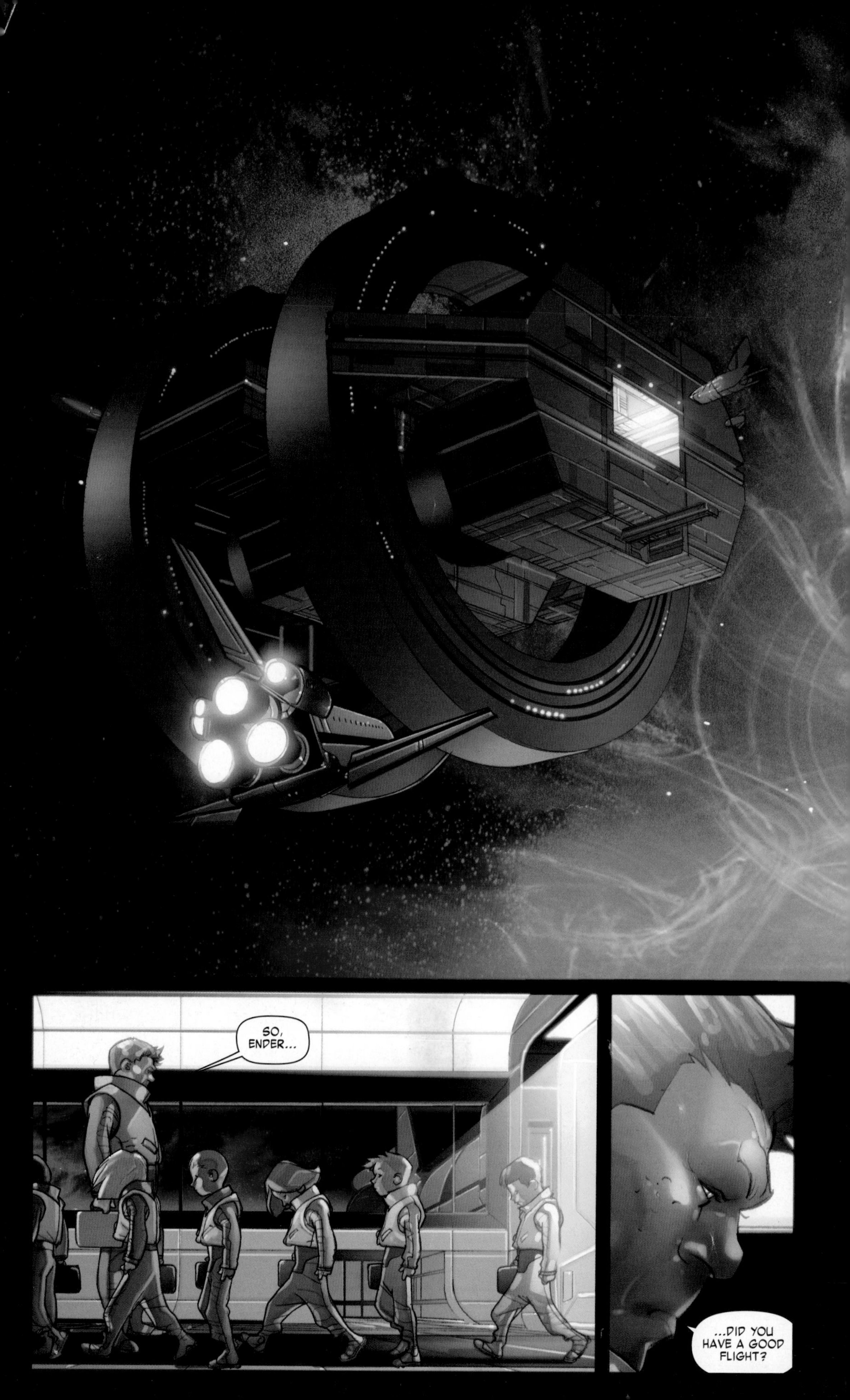
SO, ENDER...
...DID YOU HAVE A GOOD FLIGHT?

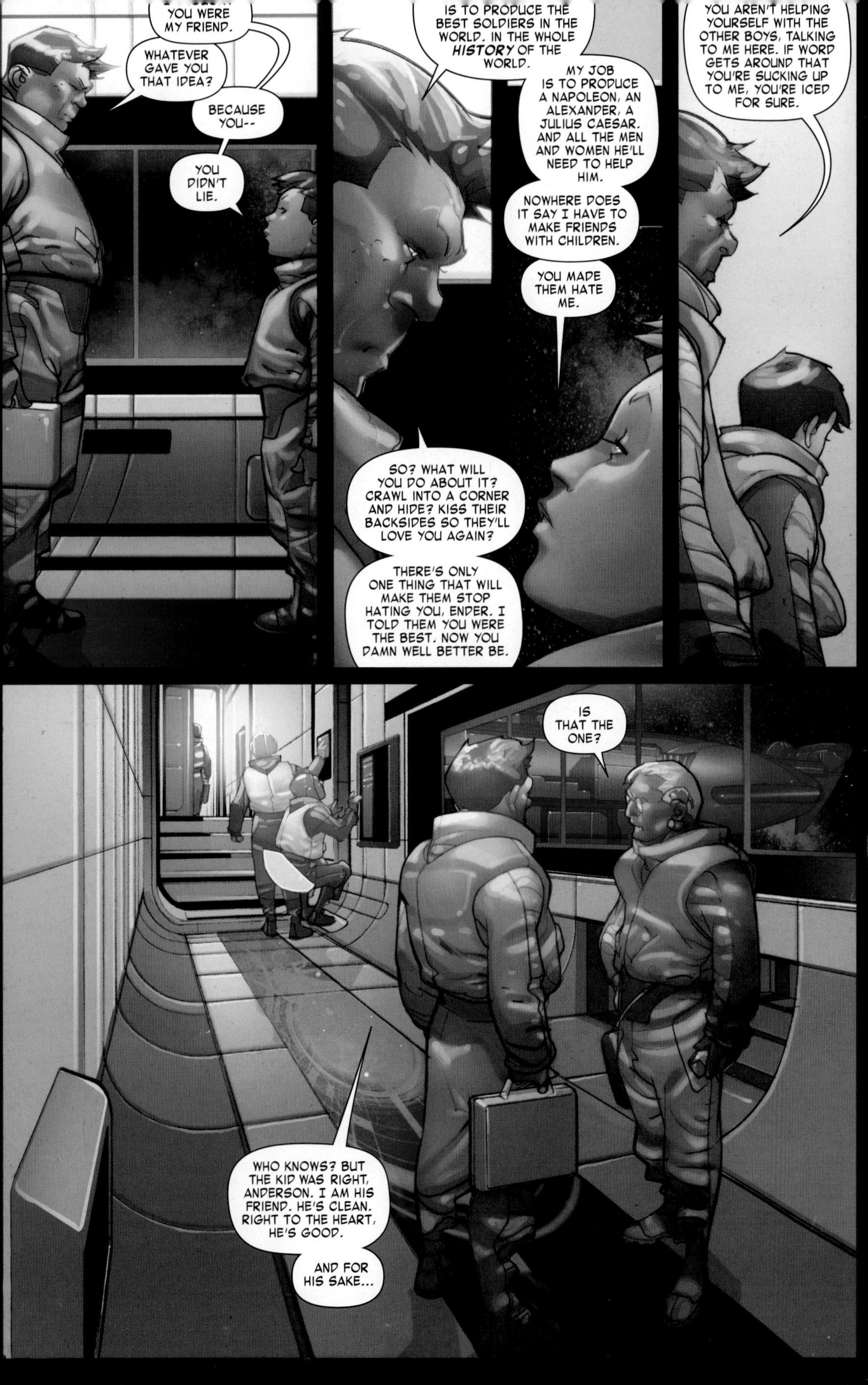
YOU WERE MY FRIEND.
WHATEVER GAVE YOU THAT IDEA?
BECAUSE YOU--
YOU DIDN'T LIE.
IS TO PRODUCE THE BEST SOLDIERS IN THE WORLD. IN THE WHOLE *HISTORY* OF THE WORLD.
MY JOB IS TO PRODUCE A NAPOLEON, AN ALEXANDER, A JULIUS CAESAR. AND ALL THE MEN AND WOMEN HE'LL NEED TO HELP HIM.
NOWHERE DOES IT SAY I HAVE TO MAKE FRIENDS WITH CHILDREN.
YOU MADE THEM HATE ME.
SO? WHAT WILL YOU DO ABOUT IT? CRAWL INTO A CORNER AND HIDE? KISS THEIR BACKSIDES SO THEY'LL LOVE YOU AGAIN?
THERE'S ONLY ONE THING THAT WILL MAKE THEM STOP HATING YOU, ENDER. I TOLD THEM YOU WERE THE BEST. NOW YOU DAMN WELL BETTER BE.
YOU AREN'T HELPING YOURSELF WITH THE OTHER BOYS, TALKING TO ME HERE. IF WORD GETS AROUND THAT YOU'RE SUCKING UP TO ME, YOU'RE ICED FOR SURE.
IS THAT THE ONE?
WHO KNOWS? BUT THE KID WAS RIGHT, ANDERSON. I AM HIS FRIEND. HE'S CLEAN. RIGHT TO THE HEART, HE'S GOOD.
AND FOR HIS SAKE...

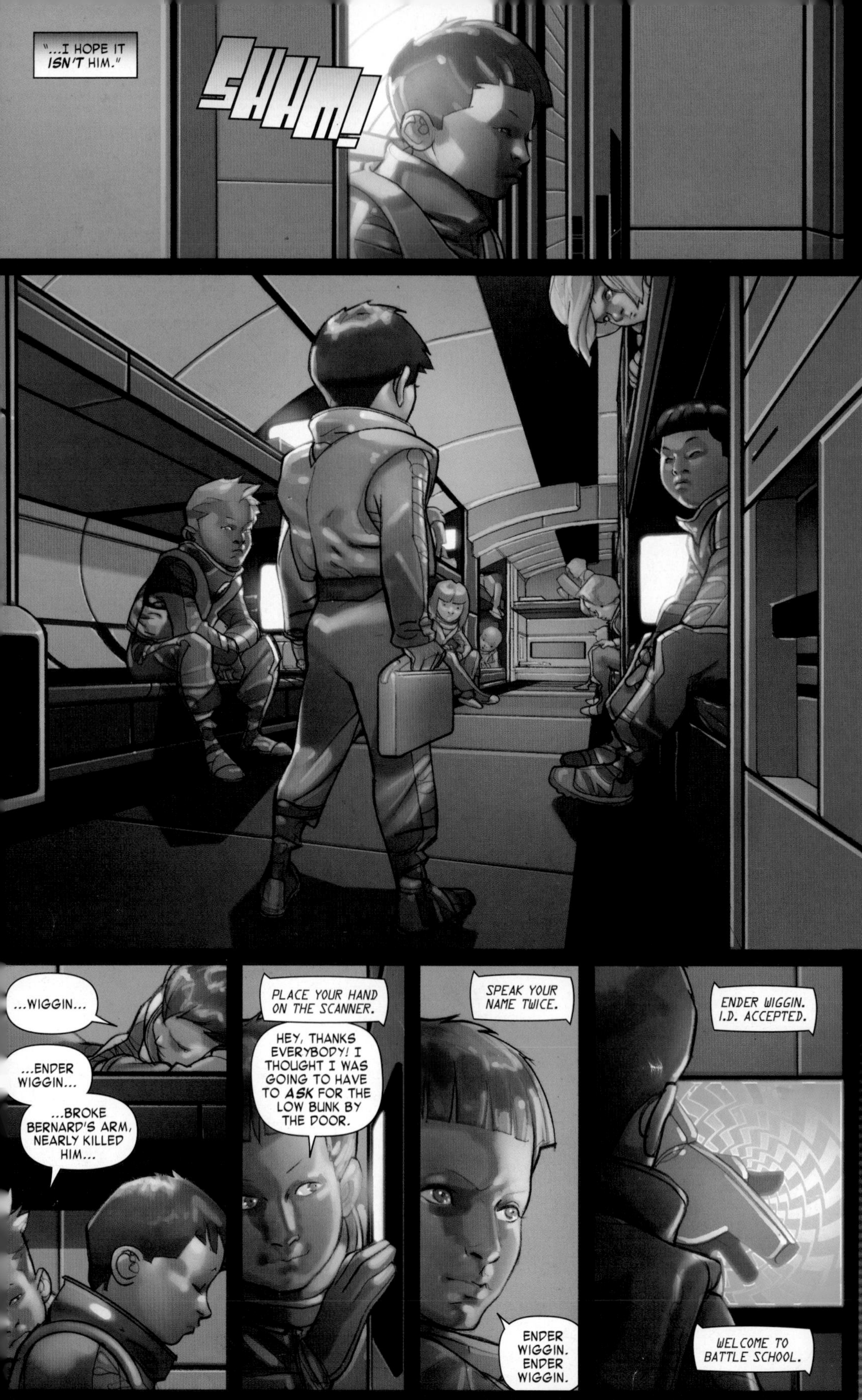
"...I HOPE IT ISN'T HIM."
SHHM!
...WIGGIN...
...ENDER WIGGIN...
...BROKE BERNARD'S ARM, NEARLY KILLED HIM...
PLACE YOUR HAND ON THE SCANNER.
HEY, THANKS EVERYBODY! I THOUGHT I WAS GOING TO HAVE TO ASK FOR THE LOW BUNK BY THE DOOR.
SPEAK YOUR NAME TWICE.
ENDER WIGGIN. ENDER WIGGIN.
ENDER WIGGIN. I.D. ACCEPTED.
WELCOME TO BATTLE SCHOOL.

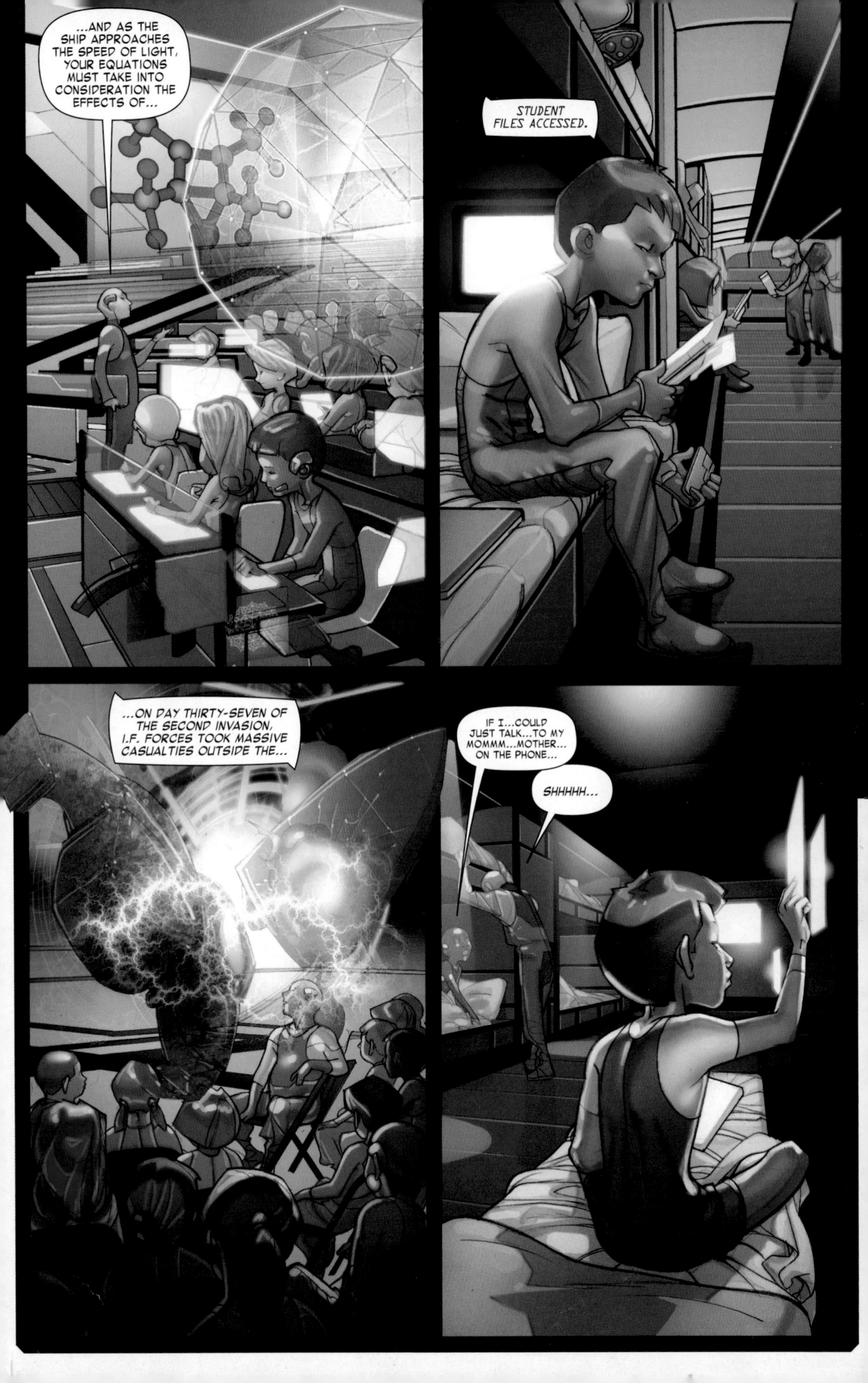
...AND AS THE SHIP APPROACHES THE SPEED OF LIGHT, YOUR EQUATIONS MUST TAKE INTO CONSIDERATION THE EFFECTS OF...
STUDENT FILES ACCESSED.
...ON DAY THIRTY-SEVEN OF THE SECOND INVASION, I.F. FORCES TOOK MASSIVE CASUALTIES OUTSIDE THE...
IF I...COULD JUST TALK...TO MY MOMMM...MOTHER... ON THE PHONE...
SHHHHH...

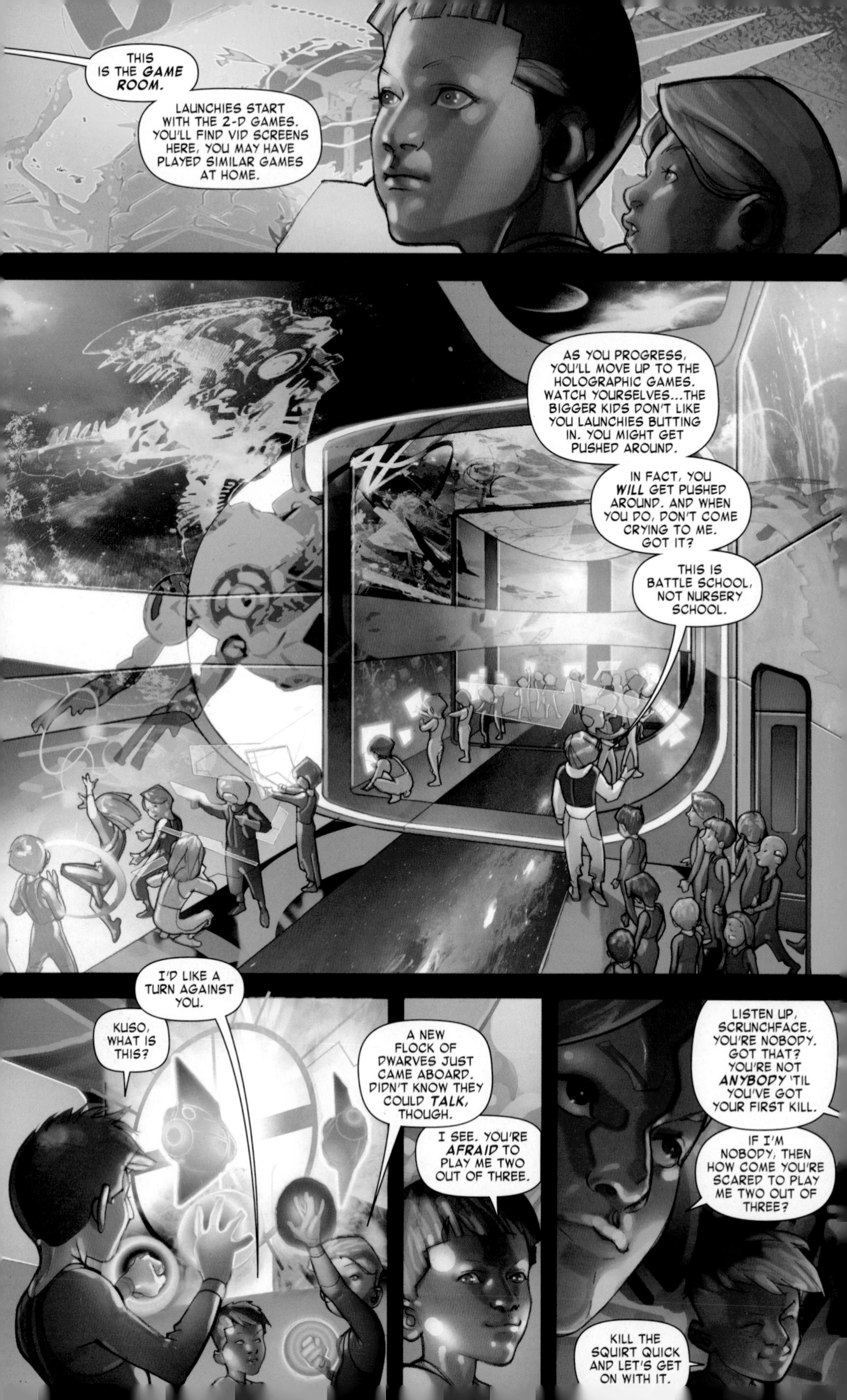
THIS IS THE GAME ROOM.
LAUNCHIES START WITH THE 2-D GAMES. YOU'LL FIND VID SCREENS HERE, YOU MAY HAVE PLAYED SIMILAR GAMES AT HOME.
AS YOU PROGRESS, YOU'LL MOVE UP TO THE HOLOGRAPHIC GAMES. WATCH YOURSELVES...THE BIGGER KIDS DON'T LIKE YOU LAUNCHIES BUTTING IN. YOU MIGHT GET PUSHED AROUND.
IN FACT, YOU WILL GET PUSHED AROUND. AND WHEN YOU DO, DON'T COME CRYING TO ME. GOT IT?
THIS IS BATTLE SCHOOL, NOT NURSERY SCHOOL.
KUSO, WHAT IS THIS?
I'D LIKE A TURN AGAINST YOU.
A NEW FLOCK OF DWARVES JUST CAME ABOARD. DIDN'T KNOW THEY COULD TALK, THOUGH.
I SEE. YOU'RE AFRAID TO PLAY ME TWO OUT OF THREE.
LISTEN UP, SCRUNCHFACE. YOU'RE NOBODY. GOT THAT? YOU'RE NOT ANYBODY 'TIL YOU'VE GOT YOUR FIRST KILL.
IF I'M NOBODY, THEN HOW COME YOU'RE SCARED TO PLAY ME TWO OUT OF THREE?
KILL THE SQUIRT QUICK AND LET'S GET ON WITH IT.

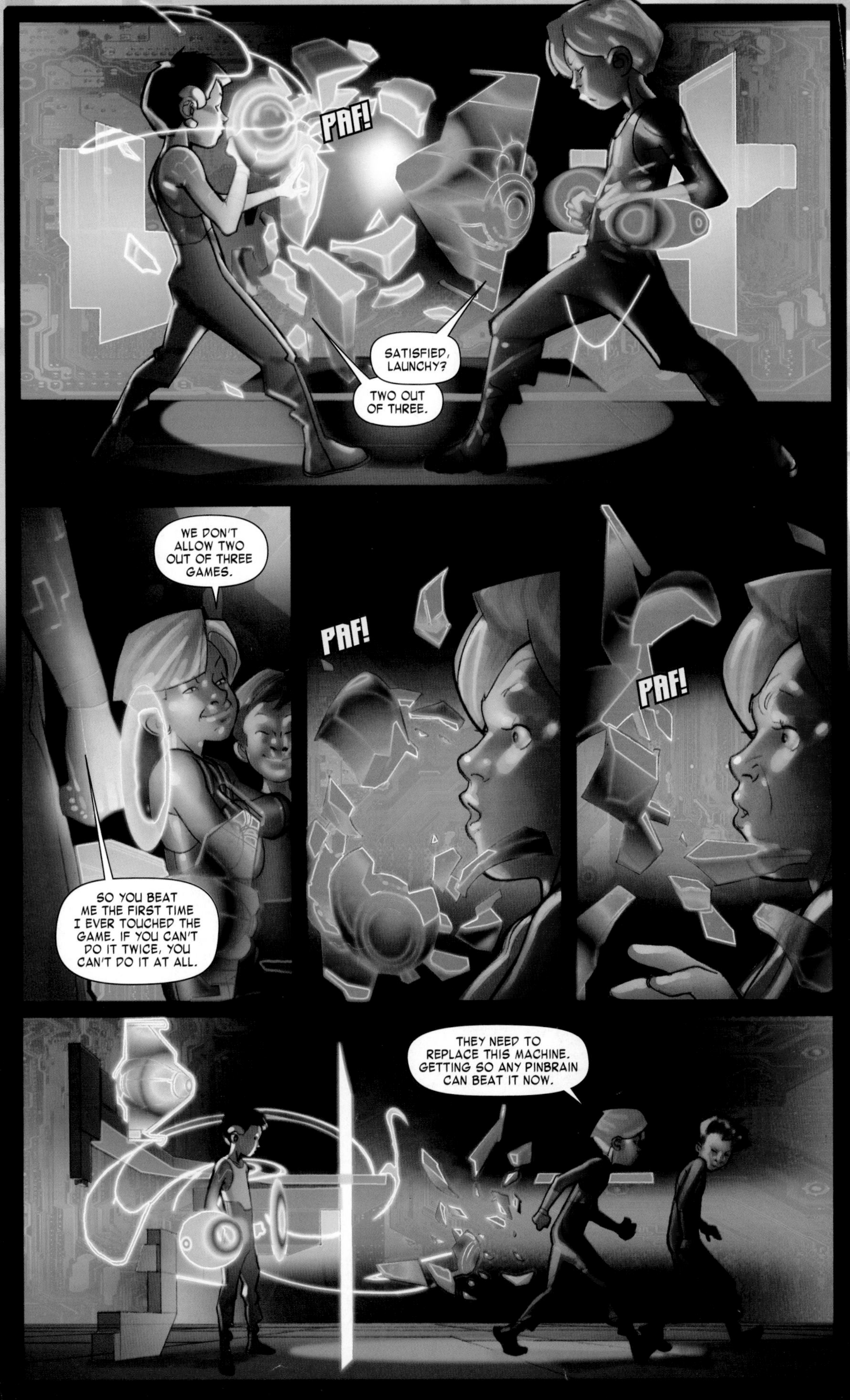
PAF!
SATISFIED, LAUNCHY?
TWO OUT OF THREE.
WE DON'T ALLOW TWO OUT OF THREE GAMES.
SO YOU BEAT ME THE FIRST TIME I EVER TOUCHED THE GAME. IF YOU CAN'T DO IT TWICE, YOU CAN'T DO IT AT ALL.
PAF!
PAF!
THEY NEED TO REPLACE THIS MACHINE. GETTING SO ANY PINBRAIN CAN BEAT IT NOW.

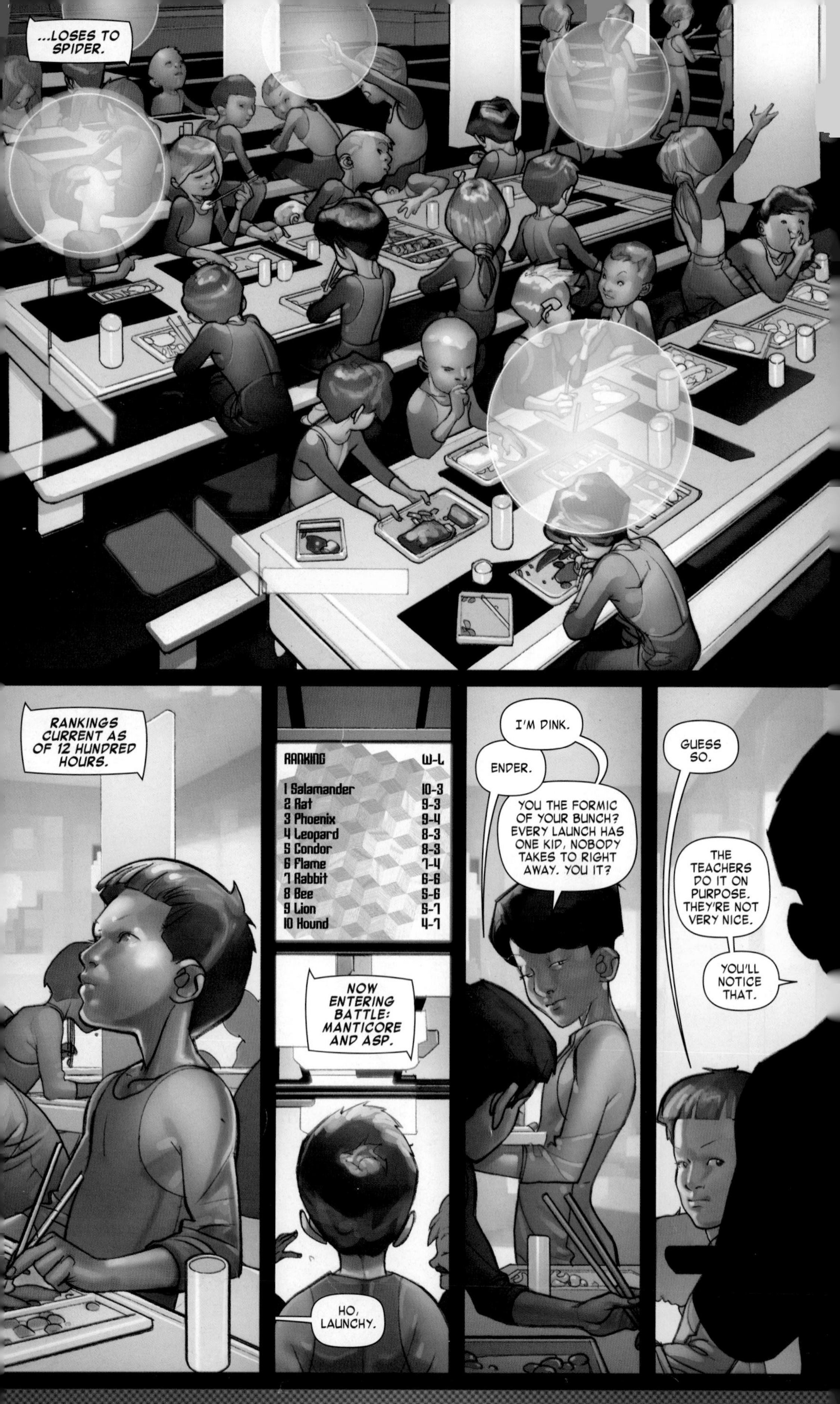
...LOSES TO SPIDER.
RANKINGS CURRENT AS OF 12 HUNDRED HOURS.
RANKING W-L
1 Salamander 10-3
2 Rat 9-3
3 Phoenix 9-4
4 Leopard 8-3
5 Condor 8-3
6 Flame 7-4
7 Rabbit 6-6
8 Bee 5-6
9 Lion 5-7
10 Hound 4-7
NOW ENTERING BATTLE: MANTICORE AND ASP.
HO, LAUNCHY.
I'M DINK.
ENDER.
YOU THE FORMIC OF YOUR BUNCH? EVERY LAUNCH HAS ONE KID, NOBODY TAKES TO RIGHT AWAY. YOU IT?
GUESS SO.
THE TEACHERS DO IT ON PURPOSE. THEY'RE NOT VERY NICE.
YOU'LL NOTICE THAT.

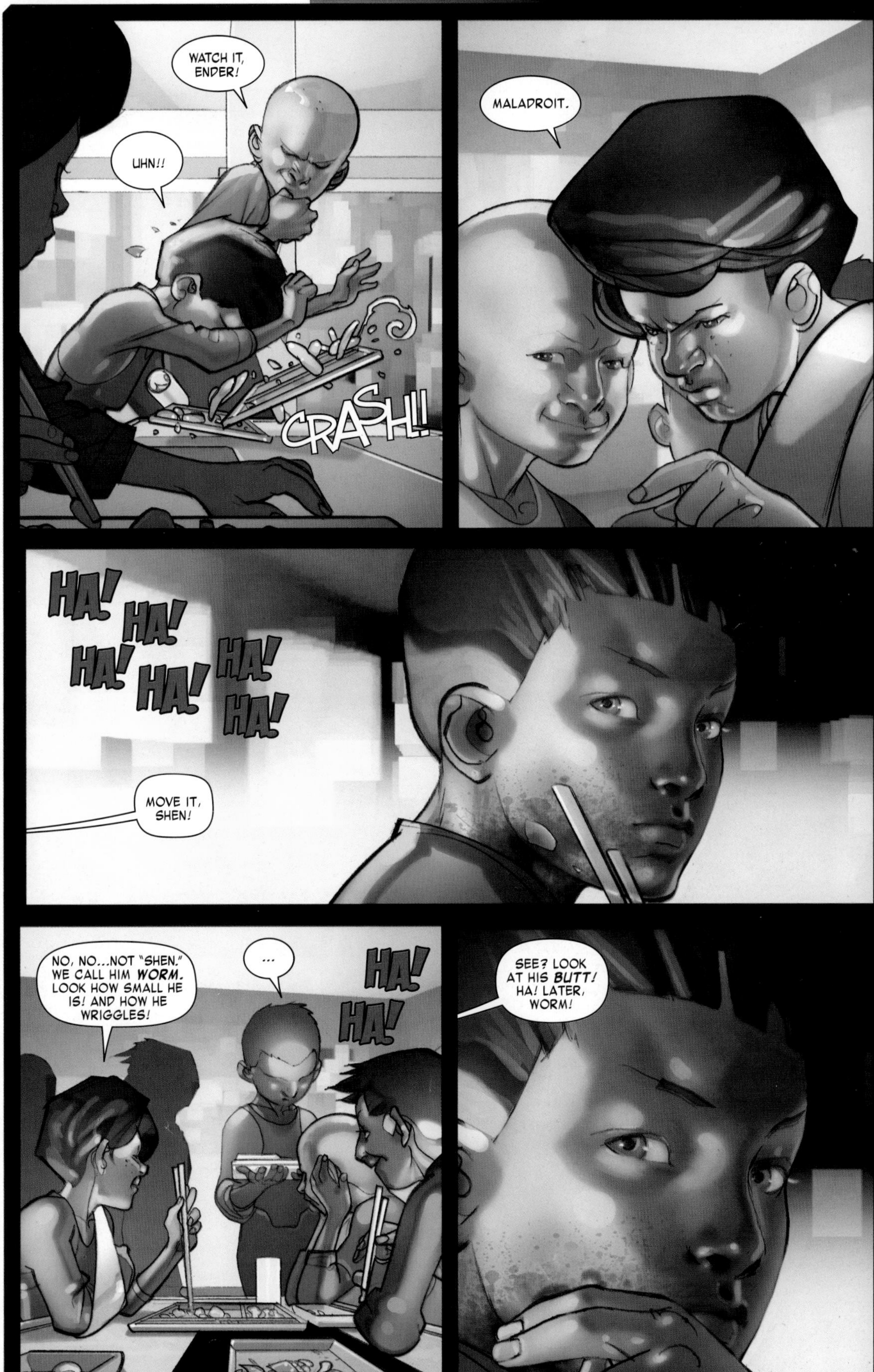
WATCH IT, ENDER!
UHN!!
CRASH!!
MALADROIT.
HA! HA! HA! HA! HA! HA!
MOVE IT, SHEN!
NO, NO...NOT "SHEN." WE CALL HIM WORM. LOOK HOW SMALL HE IS! AND HOW HE WRIGGLES!
...
HA! HA!
SEE? LOOK AT HIS BUTT! HA! LATER, WORM!

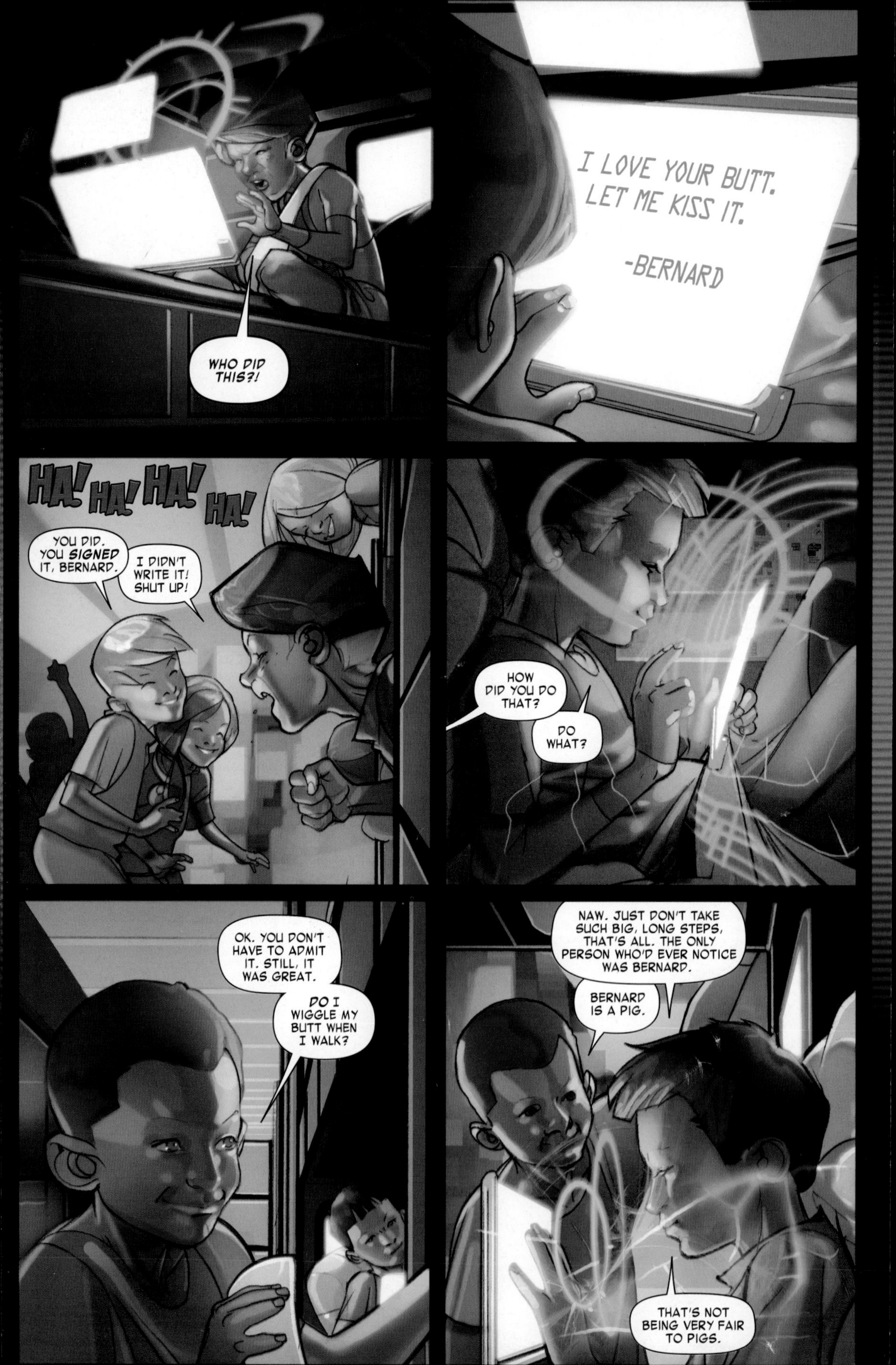
WHO DID THIS?!
I LOVE YOUR BUTT. LET ME KISS IT. -BERNARD
HA! HA! HA! HA!
YOU DID. YOU SIGNED IT, BERNARD.
I DIDN'T WRITE IT! SHUT UP!
HOW DID YOU DO THAT?
DO WHAT?
OK. YOU DON'T HAVE TO ADMIT IT. STILL, IT WAS GREAT.
DO I WIGGLE MY BUTT WHEN I WALK?
NAW. JUST DON'T TAKE SUCH BIG, LONG STEPS, THAT'S ALL. THE ONLY PERSON WHO'D EVER NOTICE WAS BERNARD.
BERNARD IS A PIG.
THAT'S NOT BEING VERY FAIR TO PIGS.

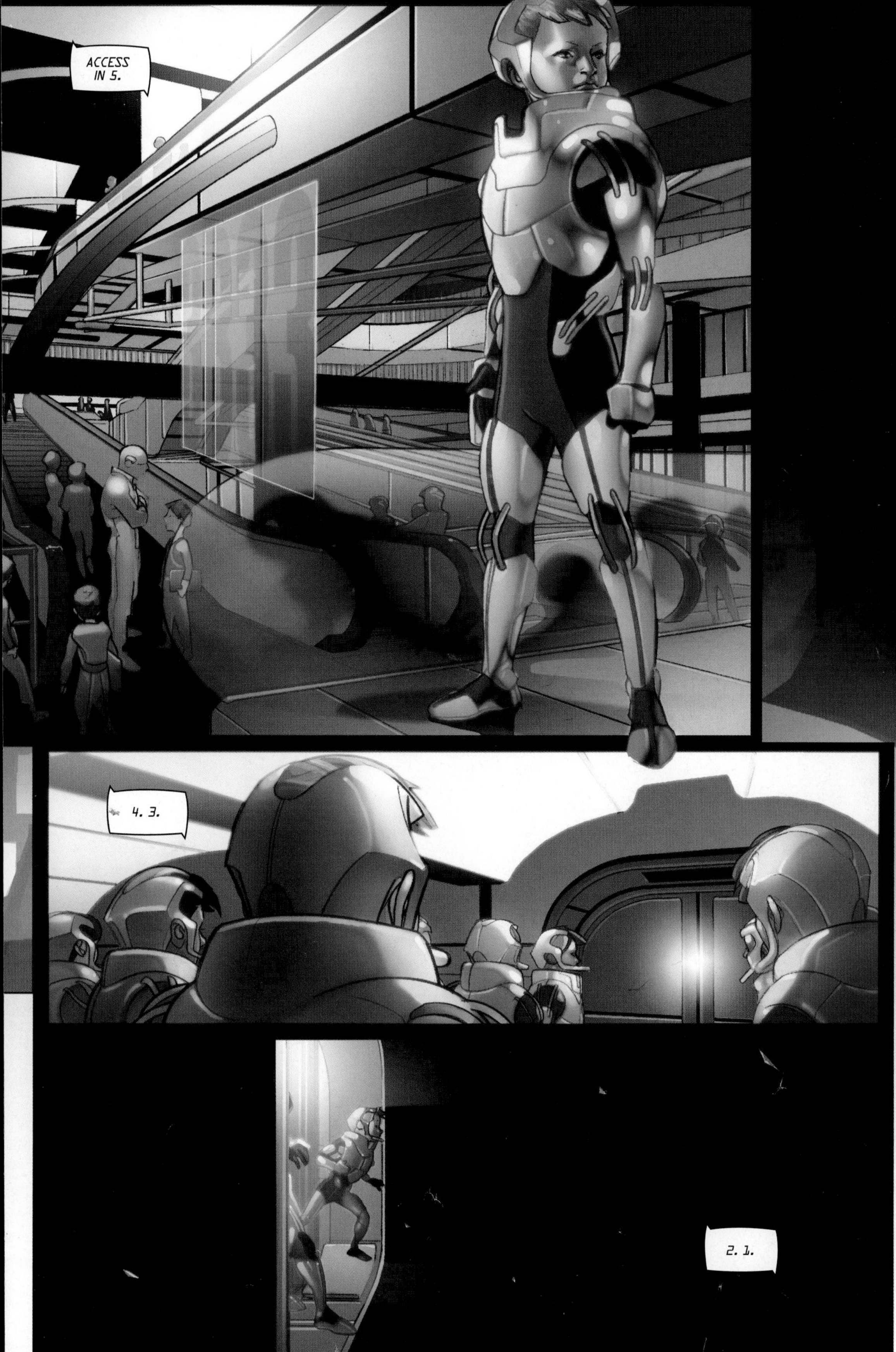
ACCESS IN 5.
4. 3.
2. 1.

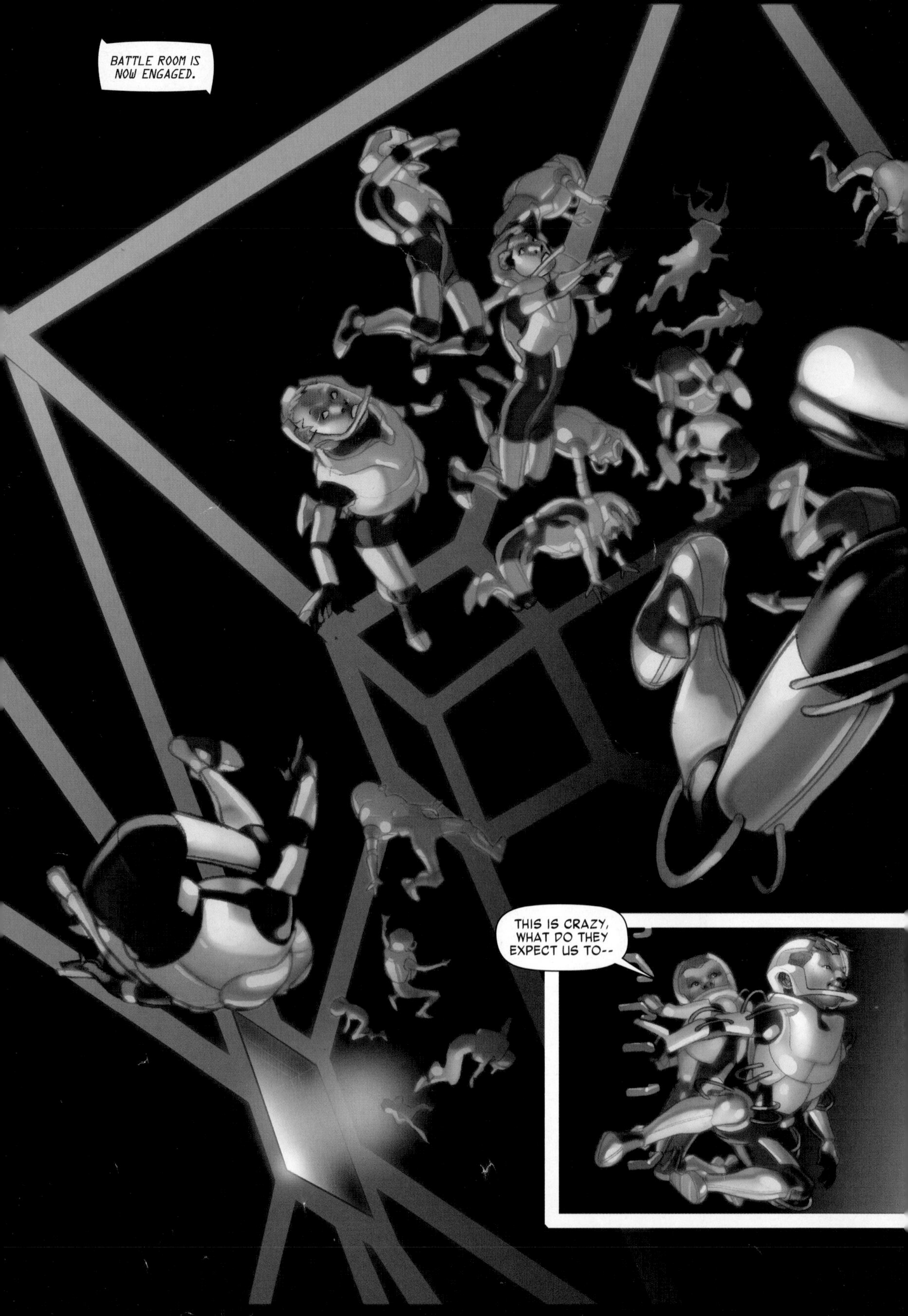
BATTLE ROOM IS NOW ENGAGED.
THIS IS CRAZY, WHAT DO THEY EXPECT US TO--

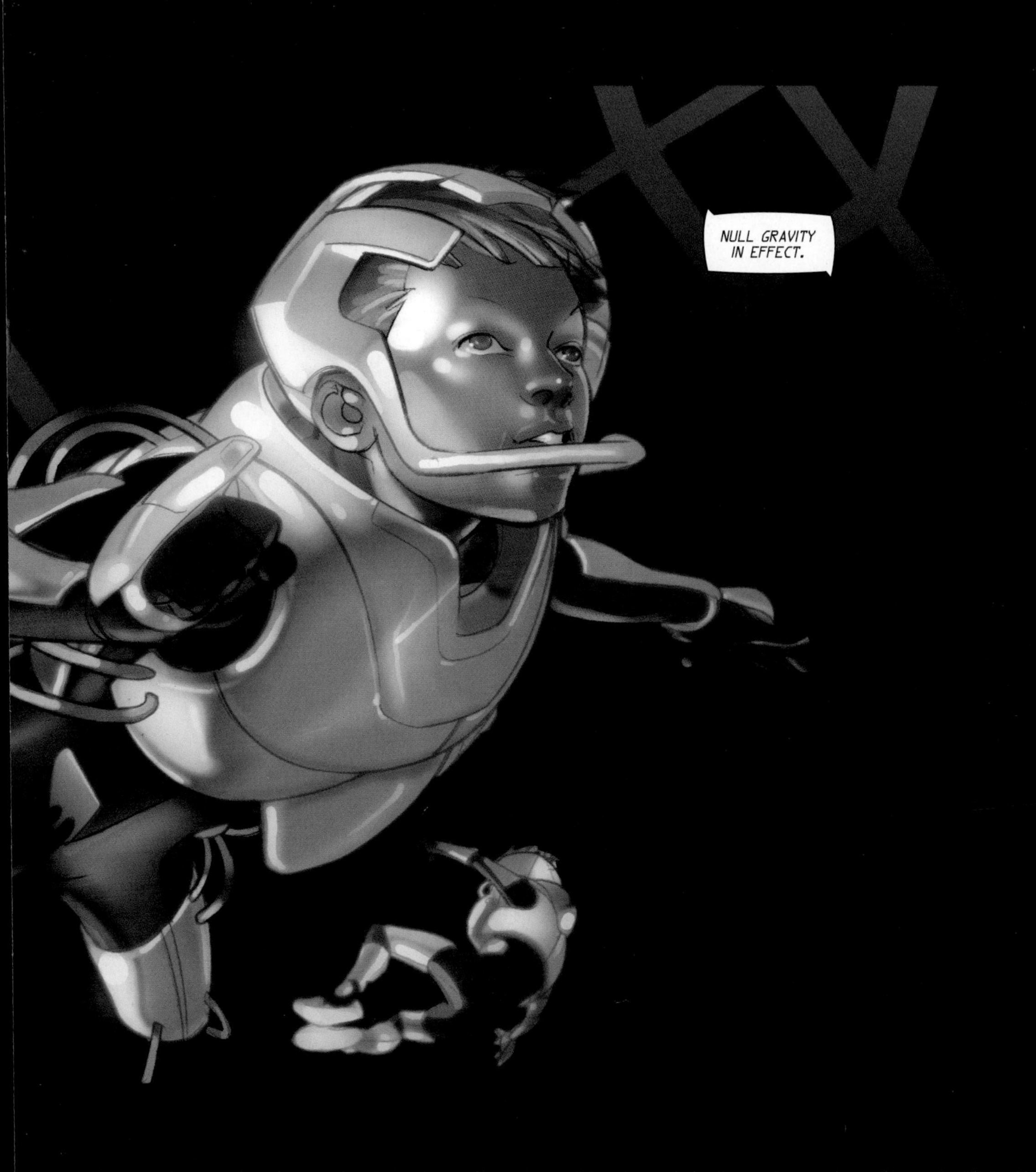
NULL GRAVITY IN EFFECT.

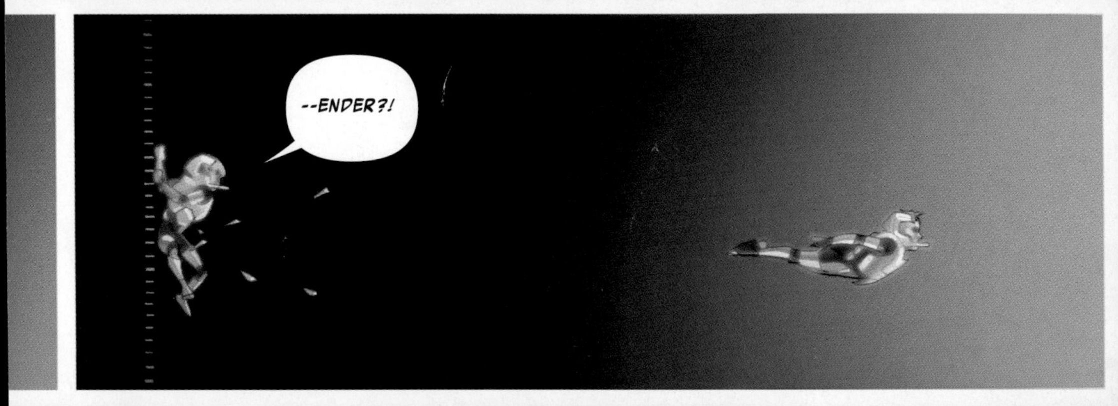
--ENDER?!

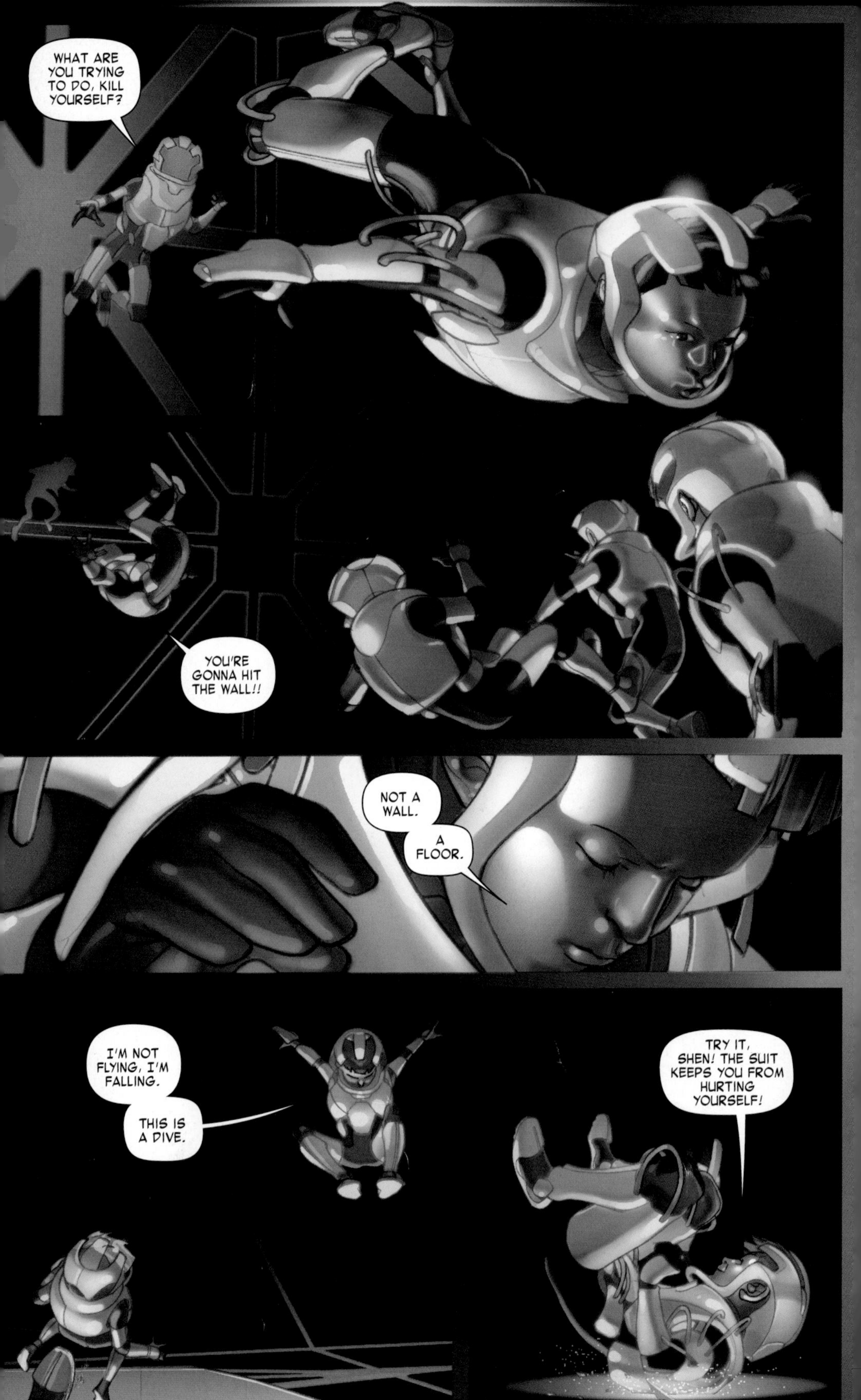
WHAT ARE YOU TRYING TO DO, KILL YOURSELF?
YOU'RE GONNA HIT THE WALL!!
NOT A WALL.
A FLOOR.
I'M NOT FLYING, I'M FALLING.
THIS IS A DIVE.
TRY IT, SHEN! THE SUIT KEEPS YOU FROM HURTING YOURSELF!

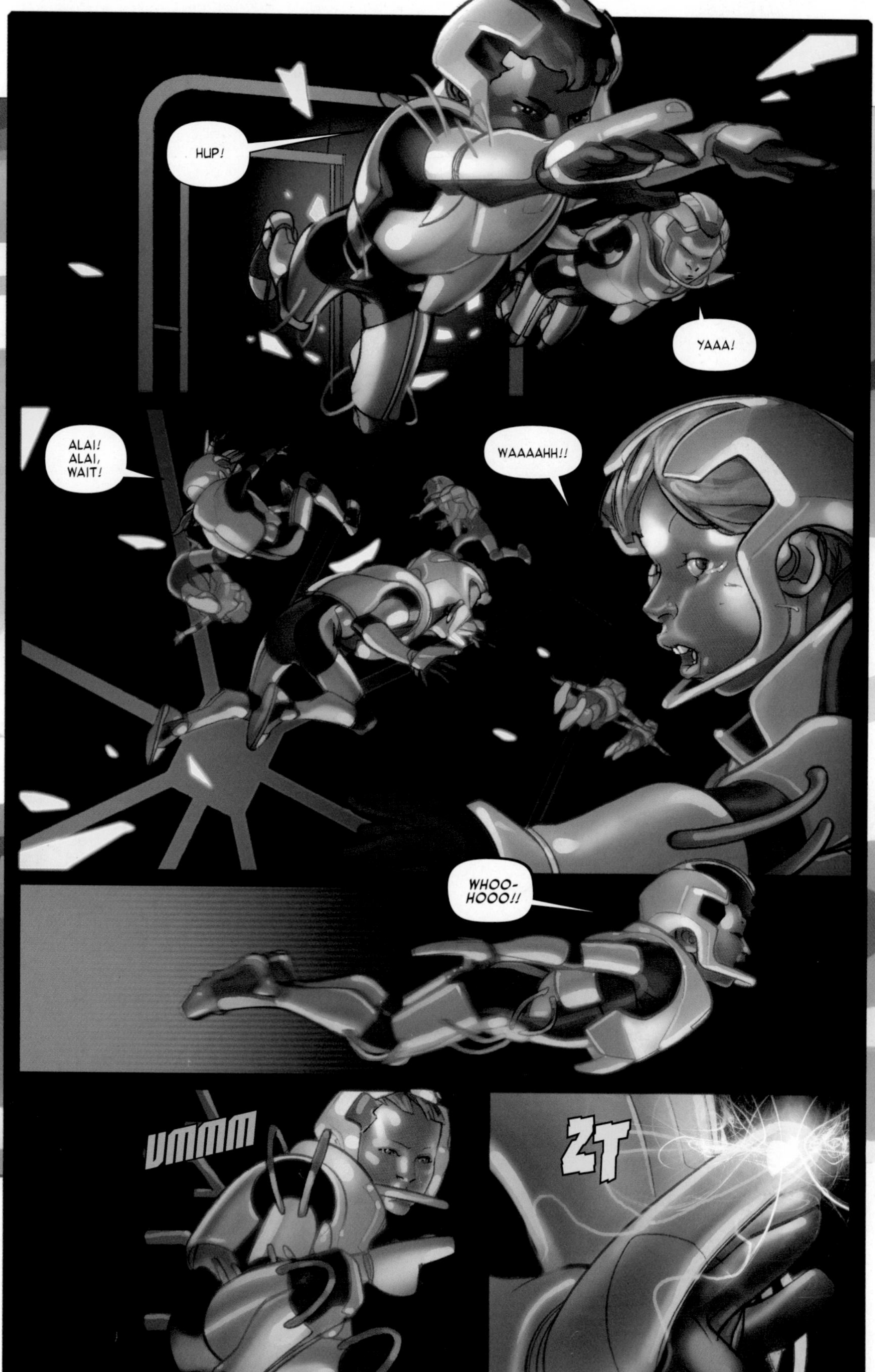
HUP!
YAAA!
ALAI! ALAI, WAIT!
WAAAAHH!!
WHOO-HOOO!!
VMMM
ZT

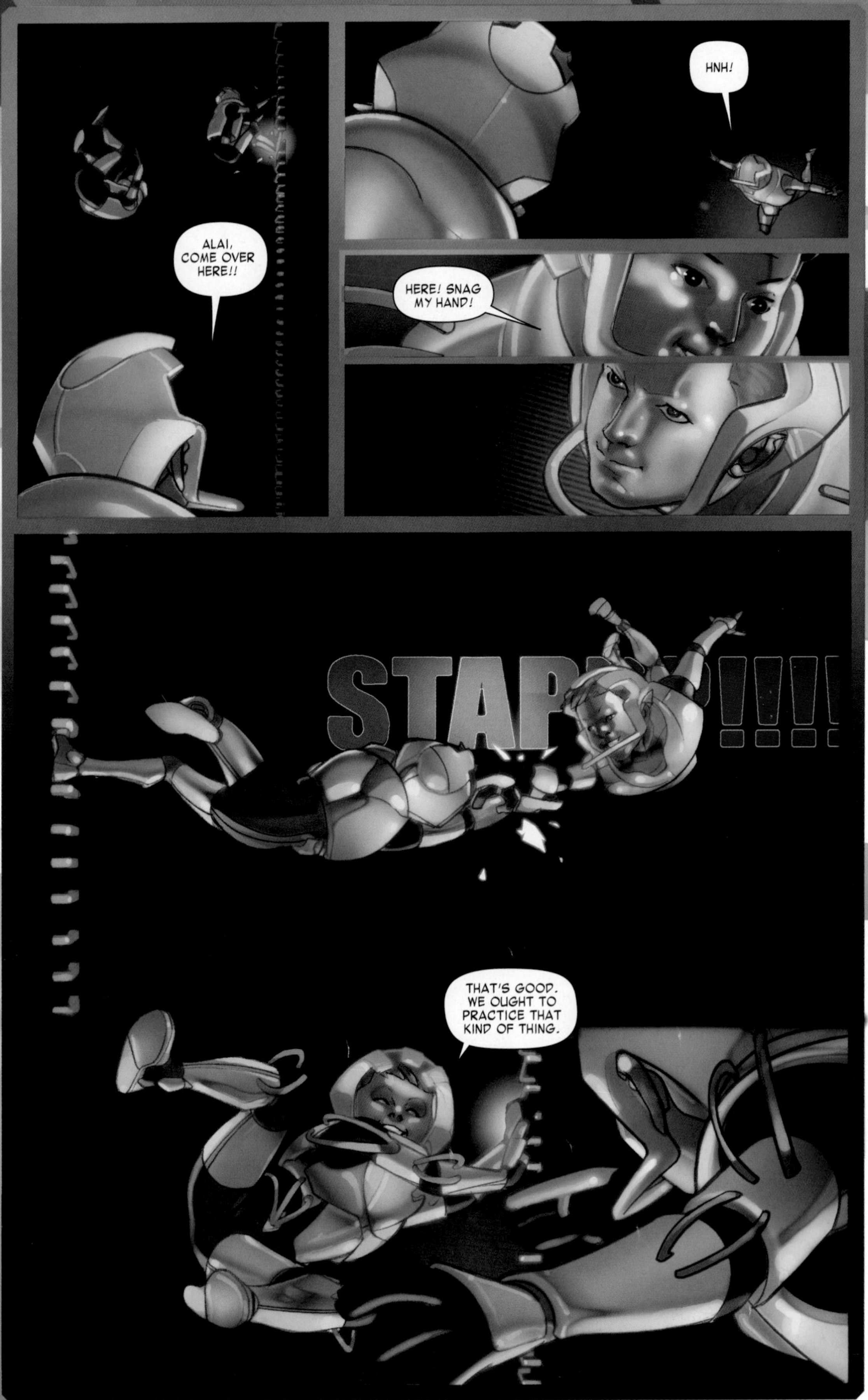
ALAI, COME OVER HERE!!
HNH!
HERE! SNAG MY HAND!
STAP!!!!
THAT'S GOOD. WE OUGHT TO PRACTICE THAT KIND OF THING.

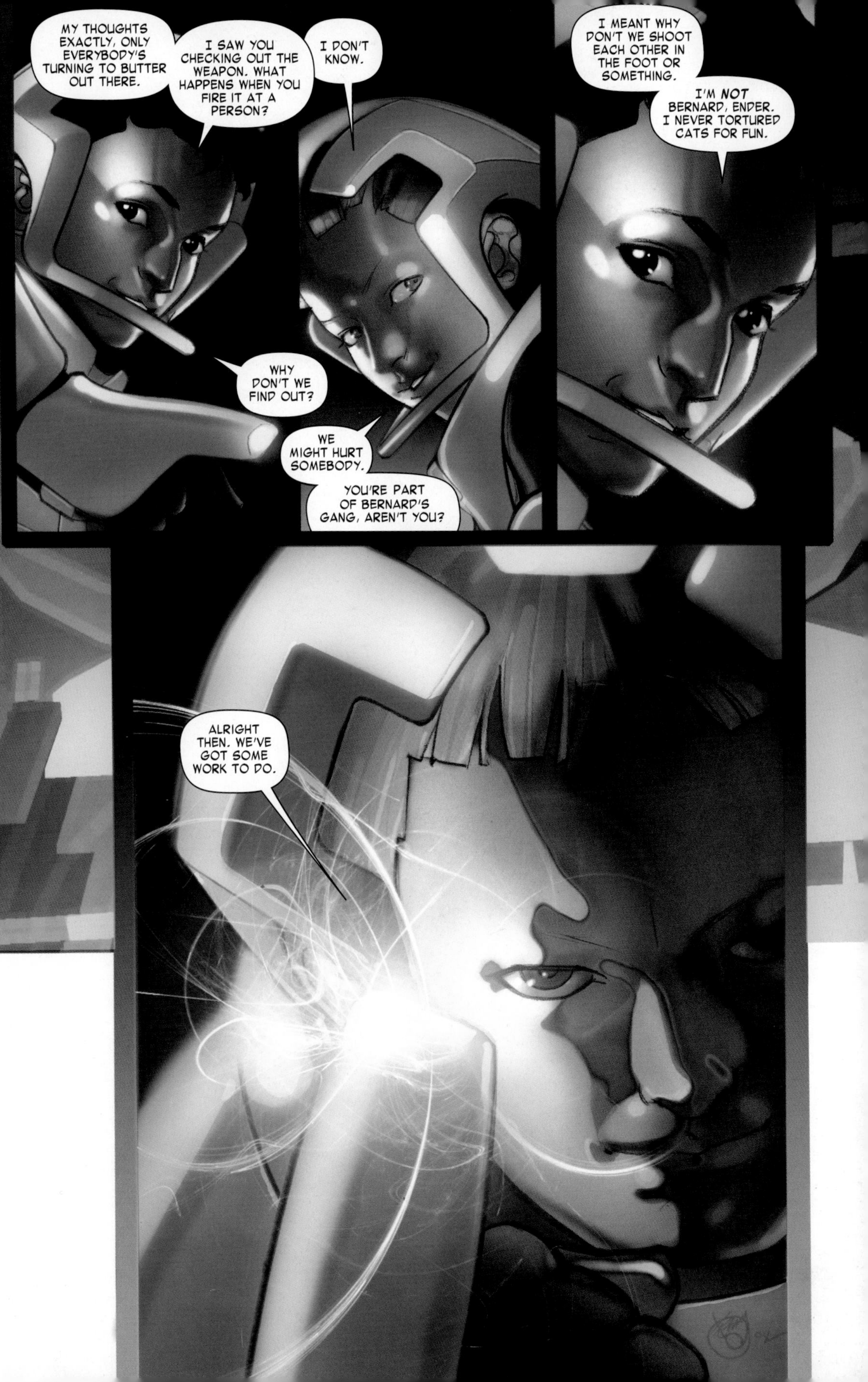
MY THOUGHTS EXACTLY, ONLY EVERYBODY'S TURNING TO BUTTER OUT THERE.
I SAW YOU CHECKING OUT THE WEAPON. WHAT HAPPENS WHEN YOU FIRE IT AT A PERSON?
I DON'T KNOW.
WHY DON'T WE FIND OUT?
WE MIGHT HURT SOMEBODY.
YOU'RE PART OF BERNARD'S GANG, AREN'T YOU?
I MEANT WHY DON'T WE SHOOT EACH OTHER IN THE FOOT OR SOMETHING.
I'M NOT BERNARD, ENDER. I NEVER TORTURED CATS FOR FUN.
ALRIGHT THEN. WE'VE GOT SOME WORK TO DO.

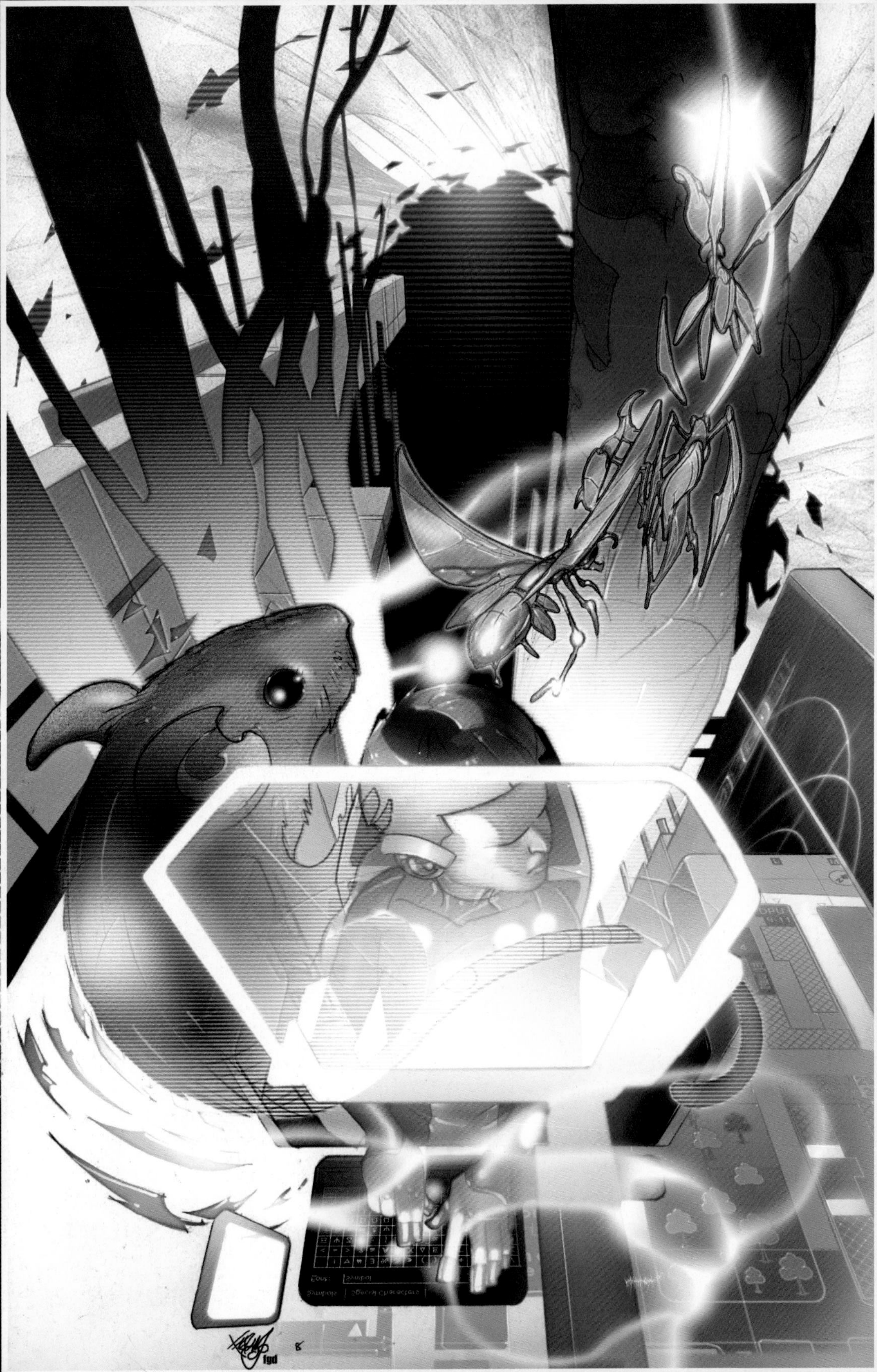

T H R E E

INTERNATIONAL FLEET MONITORED COMMUNICATIONS
PARTICIPANTS: COLONEL GRAFF, MAJOR ANDERSON
REF ID # 20909-24856, KEYWORD SEARCH: 'ENDER'

CONVERSATION RECORDED FOLLOWING THE ARRIVAL OF ANDREW WIGGIN AT THE BATTLE SCHOOL STATION.

ANDERSON: You have my admiration. Breaking an arm, that was a master stroke.

GRAFF: That was an accident. It's too strong. It makes that other little bastard into a hero. It could screw up training for a lot of the kids. I thought Ender might call for help.

ANDERSON: Call for help? I thought that was what you valued most in him–that he settles his own problems.

GRAFF: Who would have guessed the little sucker'd be out of his seat?

ANDERSON: See how Ender handles it. If we've already lost him, if he can't handle this, who's next? Who else?

GRAFF: I'll make up a list. But you're right about one thing. He can never come to believe that anybody will ever help him out, ever. If he once thinks there's an easy way out, he's wrecked.

ANDERSON: You're right. That would be terrible, if he believed he had a friend.

GRAFF: He can have friends. It's parents he can't have.

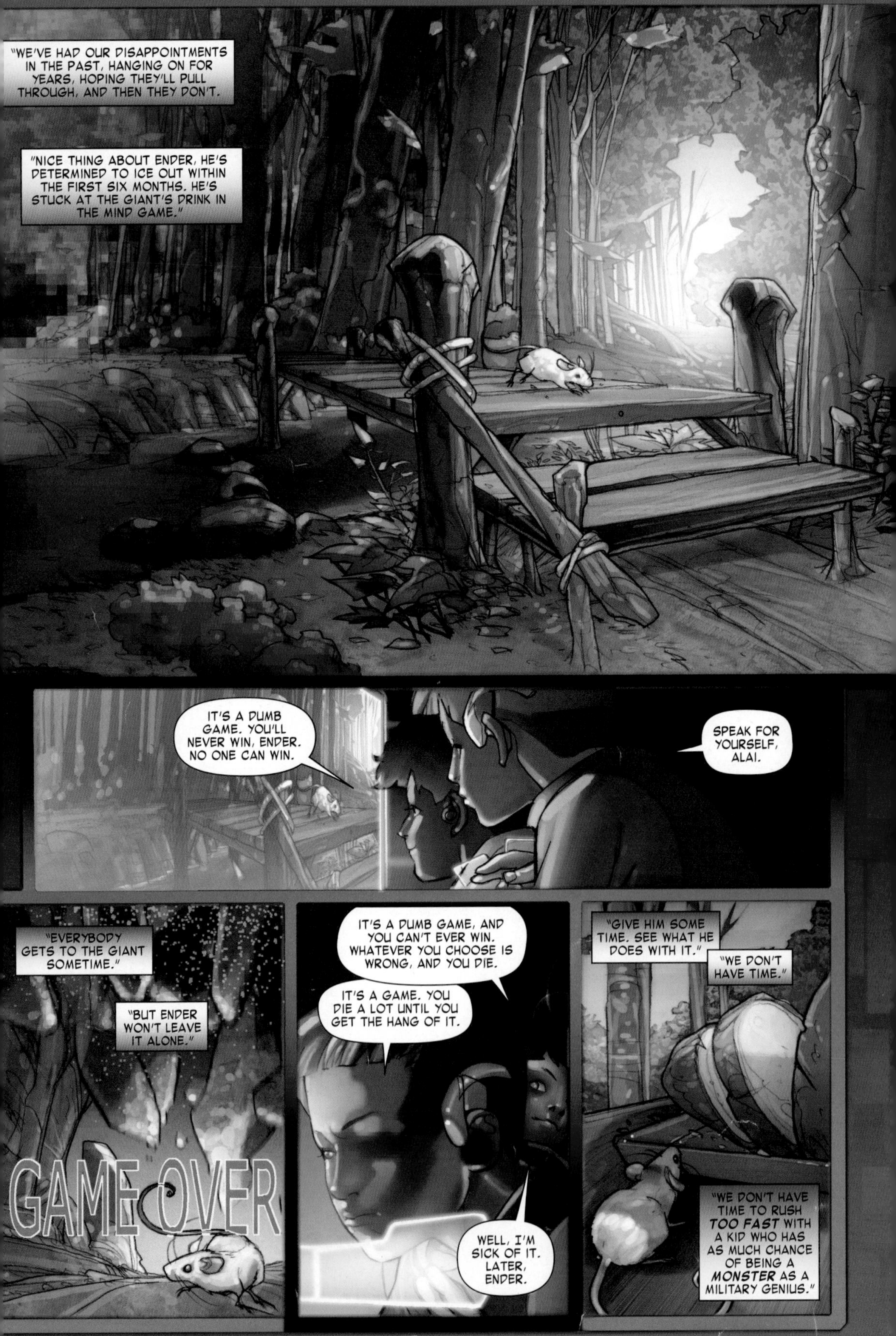
"WE'VE HAD OUR DISAPPOINTMENTS IN THE PAST, HANGING ON FOR YEARS, HOPING THEY'LL PULL THROUGH, AND THEN THEY DON'T.
"NICE THING ABOUT ENDER, HE'S DETERMINED TO ICE OUT WITHIN THE FIRST SIX MONTHS. HE'S STUCK AT THE GIANT'S DRINK IN THE MIND GAME."
IT'S A DUMB GAME. YOU'LL NEVER WIN, ENDER. NO ONE CAN WIN.
SPEAK FOR YOURSELF, ALAI.
"EVERYBODY GETS TO THE GIANT SOMETIME."
"BUT ENDER WON'T LEAVE IT ALONE."
GAME OVER
IT'S A DUMB GAME, AND YOU CAN'T EVER WIN. WHATEVER YOU CHOOSE IS WRONG, AND YOU DIE.
IT'S A GAME. YOU DIE A LOT UNTIL YOU GET THE HANG OF IT.
WELL, I'M SICK OF IT. LATER, ENDER.
"GIVE HIM SOME TIME. SEE WHAT HE DOES WITH IT."
"WE DON'T HAVE TIME."
"WE DON'T HAVE TIME TO RUSH ***TOO FAST*** WITH A KID WHO HAS AS MUCH CHANCE OF BEING A ***MONSTER*** AS A MILITARY GENIUS."

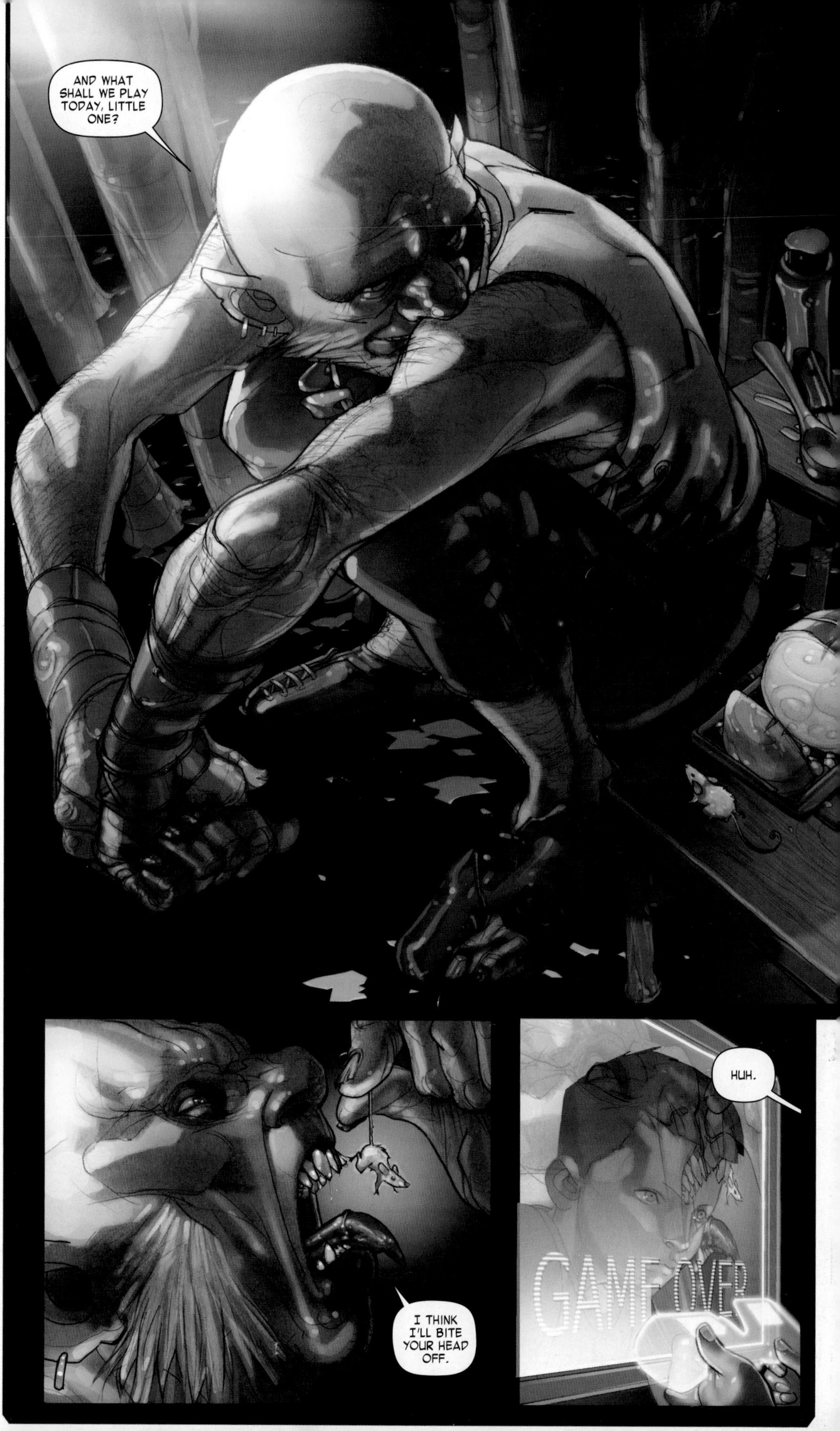
AND WHAT SHALL WE PLAY TODAY, LITTLE ONE?
I THINK I'LL BITE YOUR HEAD OFF.
HUH.
GAME OVER

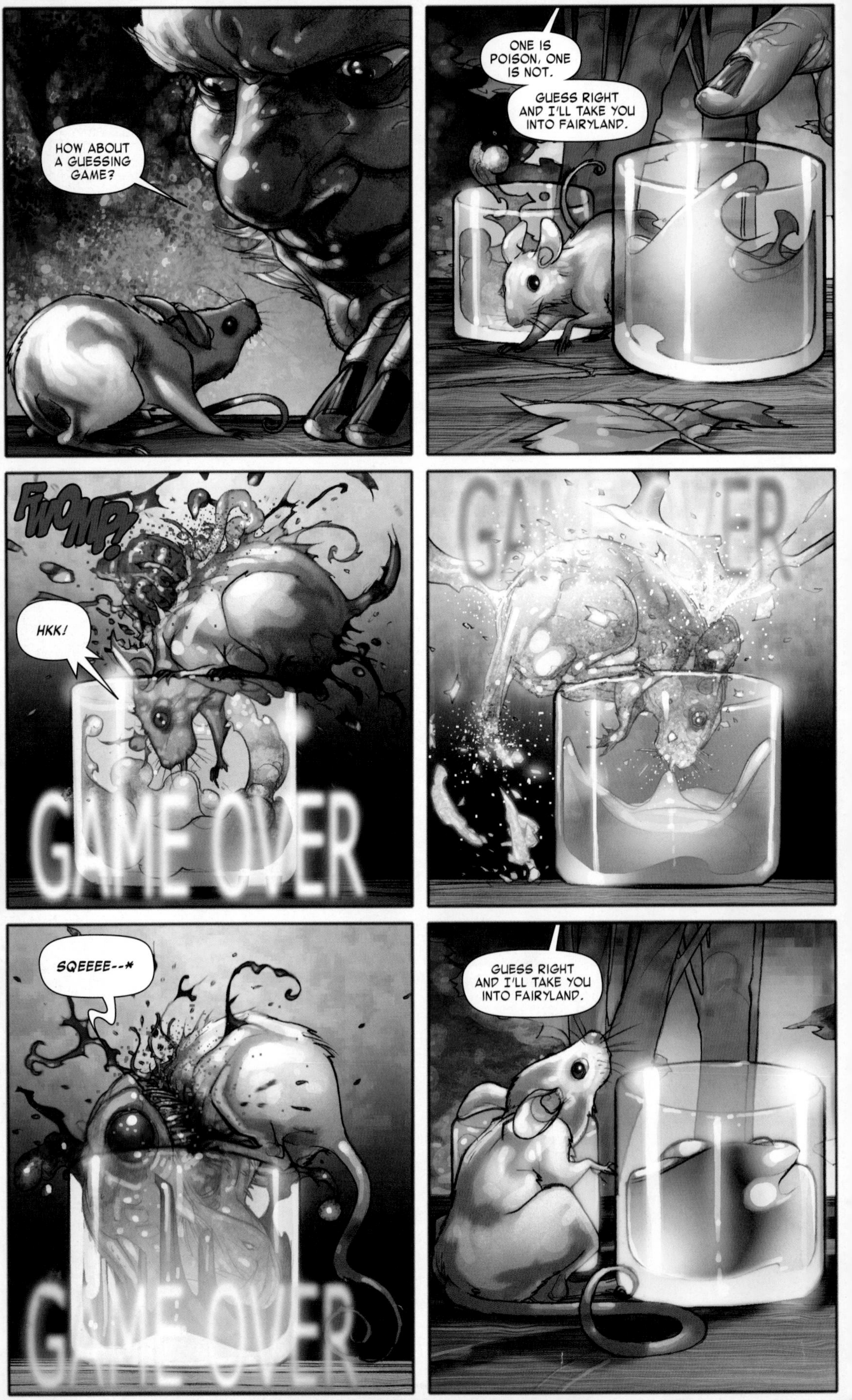
HOW ABOUT A GUESSING GAME?
ONE IS POISON, ONE IS NOT.
GUESS RIGHT AND I'LL TAKE YOU INTO FAIRYLAND.
FWOMP!
HKK!
GAME OVER
GAME OVER
SQEEEE--*
GAME OVER
GUESS RIGHT AND I'LL TAKE YOU INTO FAIRYLAND.

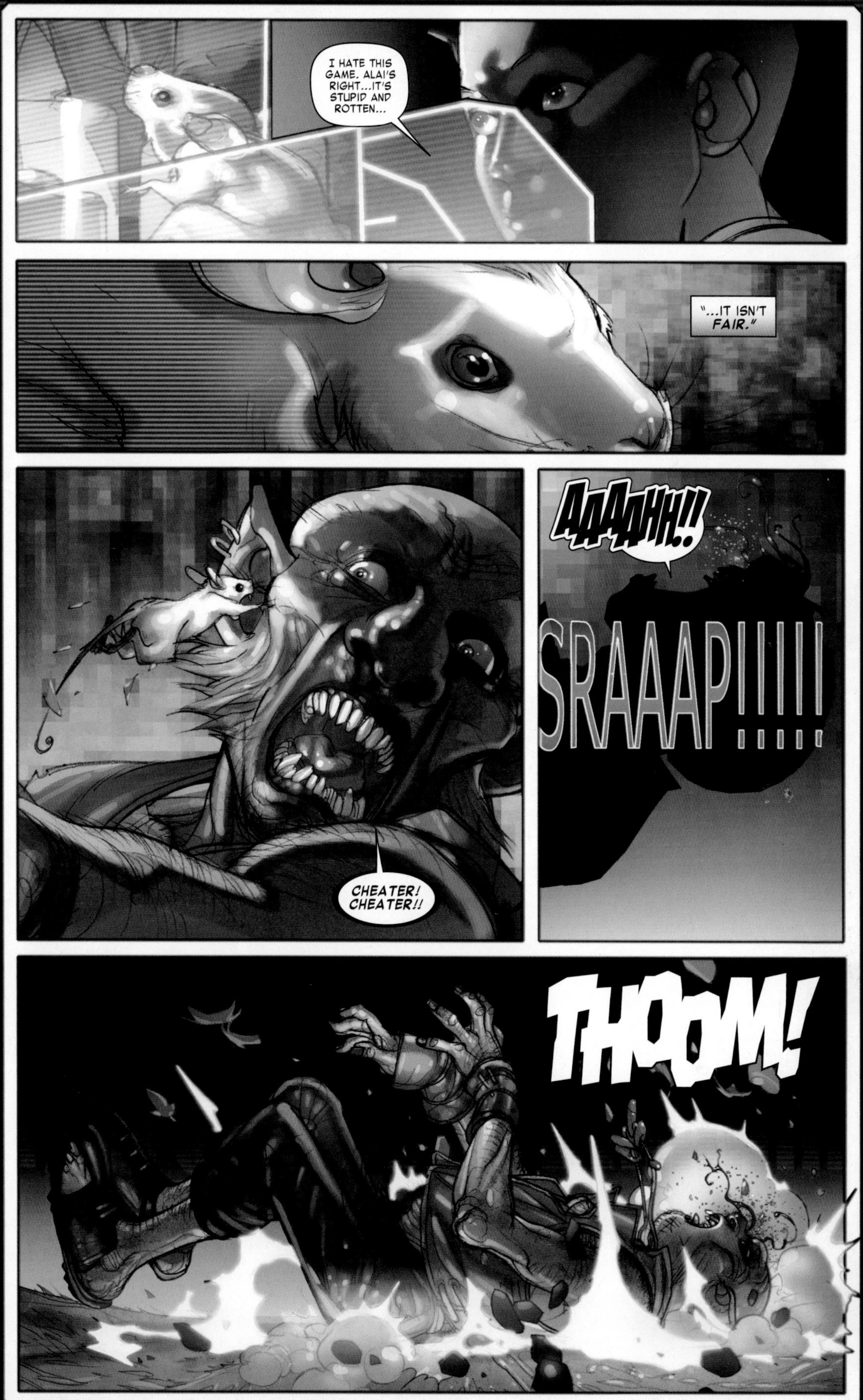
I HATE THIS GAME. ALAI'S RIGHT...IT'S STUPID AND ROTTEN...
"...IT ISN'T FAIR."
CHEATER! CHEATER!!
AAAAHH!!
SRAAAP!!!!!
THOOM!

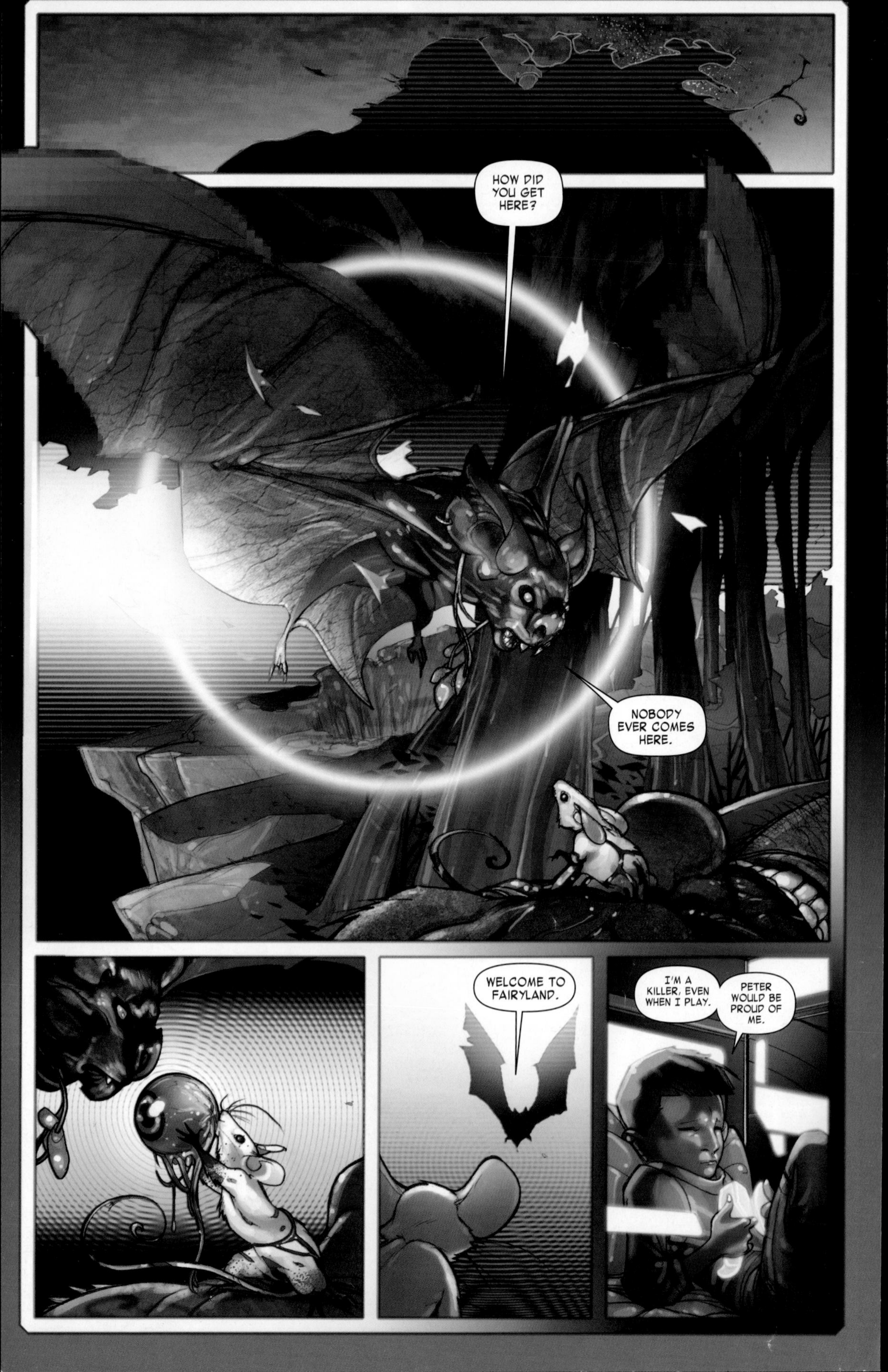
HOW DID YOU GET HERE?
NOBODY EVER COMES HERE.
WELCOME TO FAIRYLAND.
I'M A KILLER, EVEN WHEN I PLAY.
PETER WOULD BE PROUD OF ME.

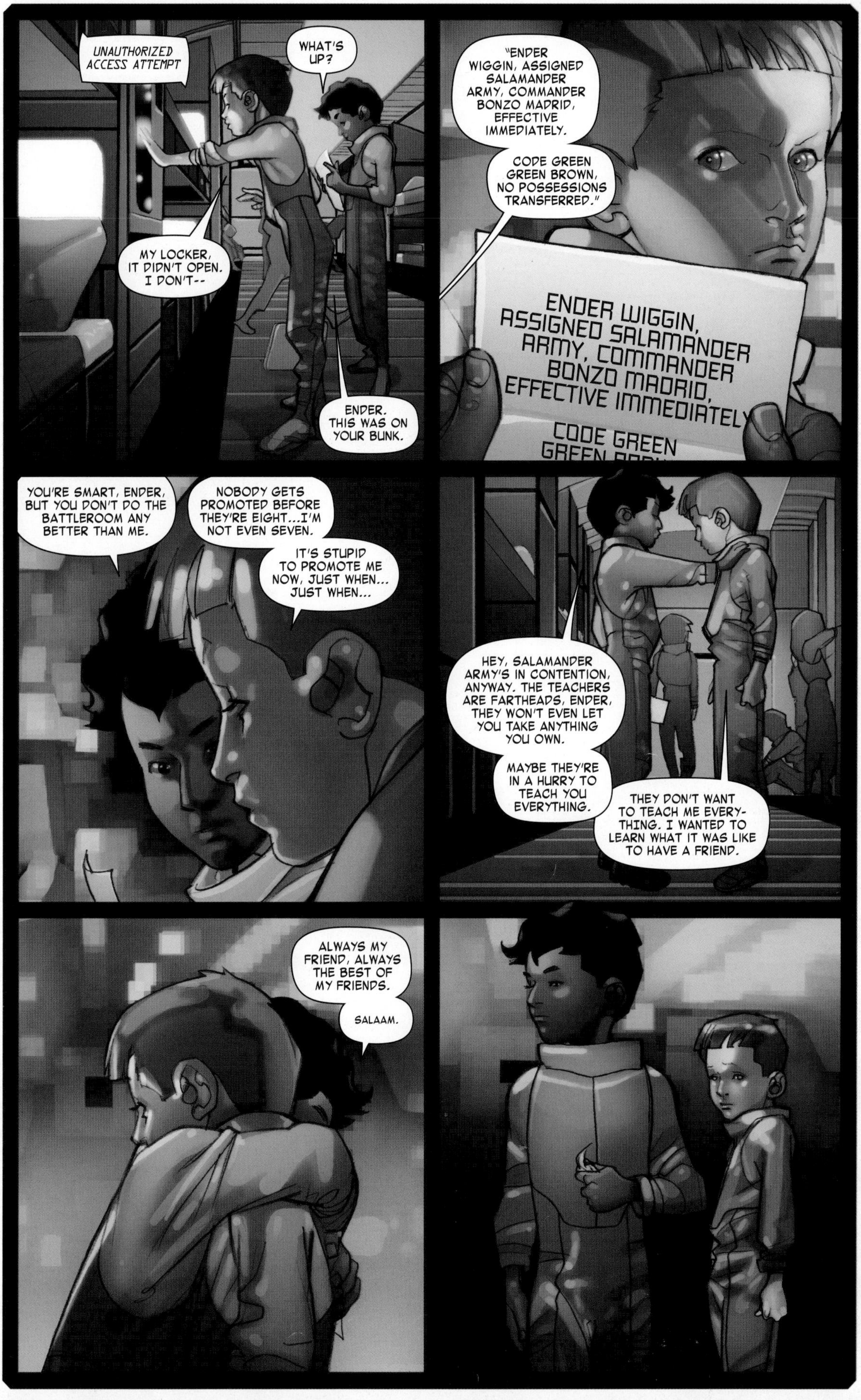
UNAUTHORIZED ACCESS ATTEMPT
WHAT'S UP?
MY LOCKER, IT DIDN'T OPEN. I DON'T--
ENDER. THIS WAS ON YOUR BUNK.
"ENDER WIGGIN, ASSIGNED SALAMANDER ARMY, COMMANDER BONZO MADRID, EFFECTIVE IMMEDIATELY.
CODE GREEN GREEN BROWN, NO POSSESSIONS TRANSFERRED."
ENDER WIGGIN, ASSIGNED SALAMANDER ARMY, COMMANDER BONZO MADRID, EFFECTIVE IMMEDIATEL
CODE GREEN
YOU'RE SMART, ENDER, BUT YOU DON'T DO THE BATTLEROOM ANY BETTER THAN ME.
NOBODY GETS PROMOTED BEFORE THEY'RE EIGHT...I'M NOT EVEN SEVEN.
IT'S STUPID TO PROMOTE ME NOW, JUST WHEN... JUST WHEN...
HEY, SALAMANDER ARMY'S IN CONTENTION, ANYWAY. THE TEACHERS ARE FARTHEADS, ENDER, THEY WON'T EVEN LET YOU TAKE ANYTHING YOU OWN.
MAYBE THEY'RE IN A HURRY TO TEACH YOU EVERYTHING.
THEY DON'T WANT TO TEACH ME EVERY-THING. I WANTED TO LEARN WHAT IT WAS LIKE TO HAVE A FRIEND.
ALWAYS MY FRIEND, ALWAYS THE BEST OF MY FRIENDS.
SALAAM.

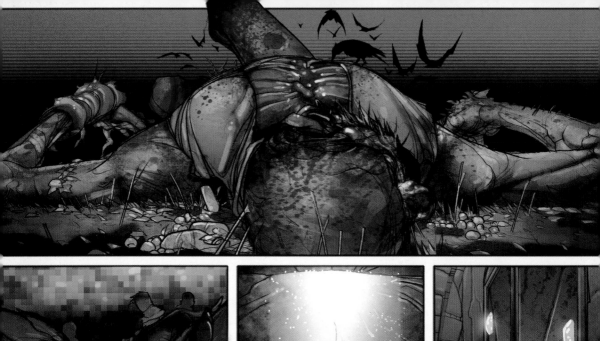

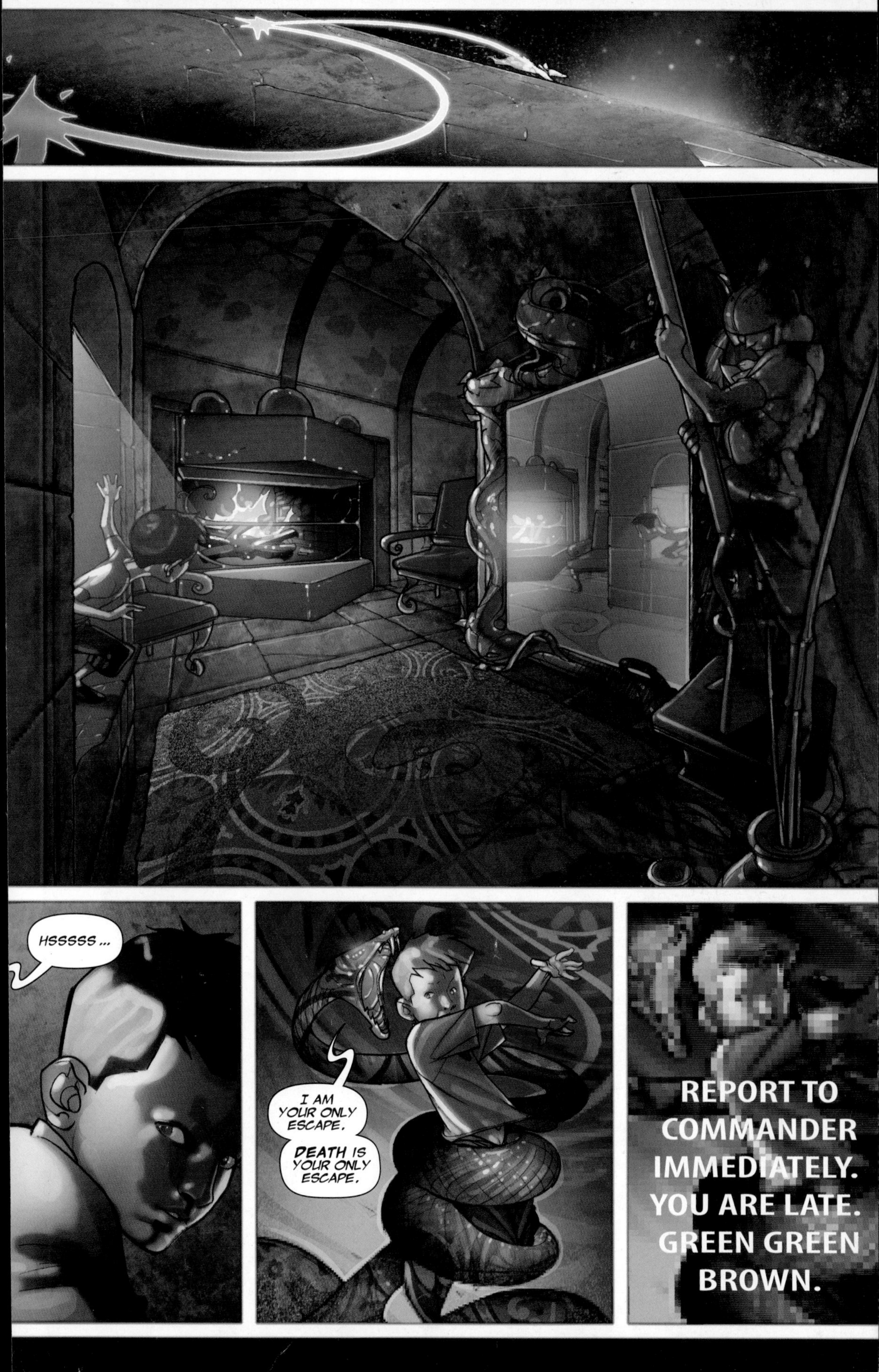
HSSSSS...
I AM YOUR ONLY ESCAPE.
DEATH IS YOUR ONLY ESCAPE.
REPORT TO COMMANDER IMMEDIATELY. YOU ARE LATE. GREEN GREEN BROWN.

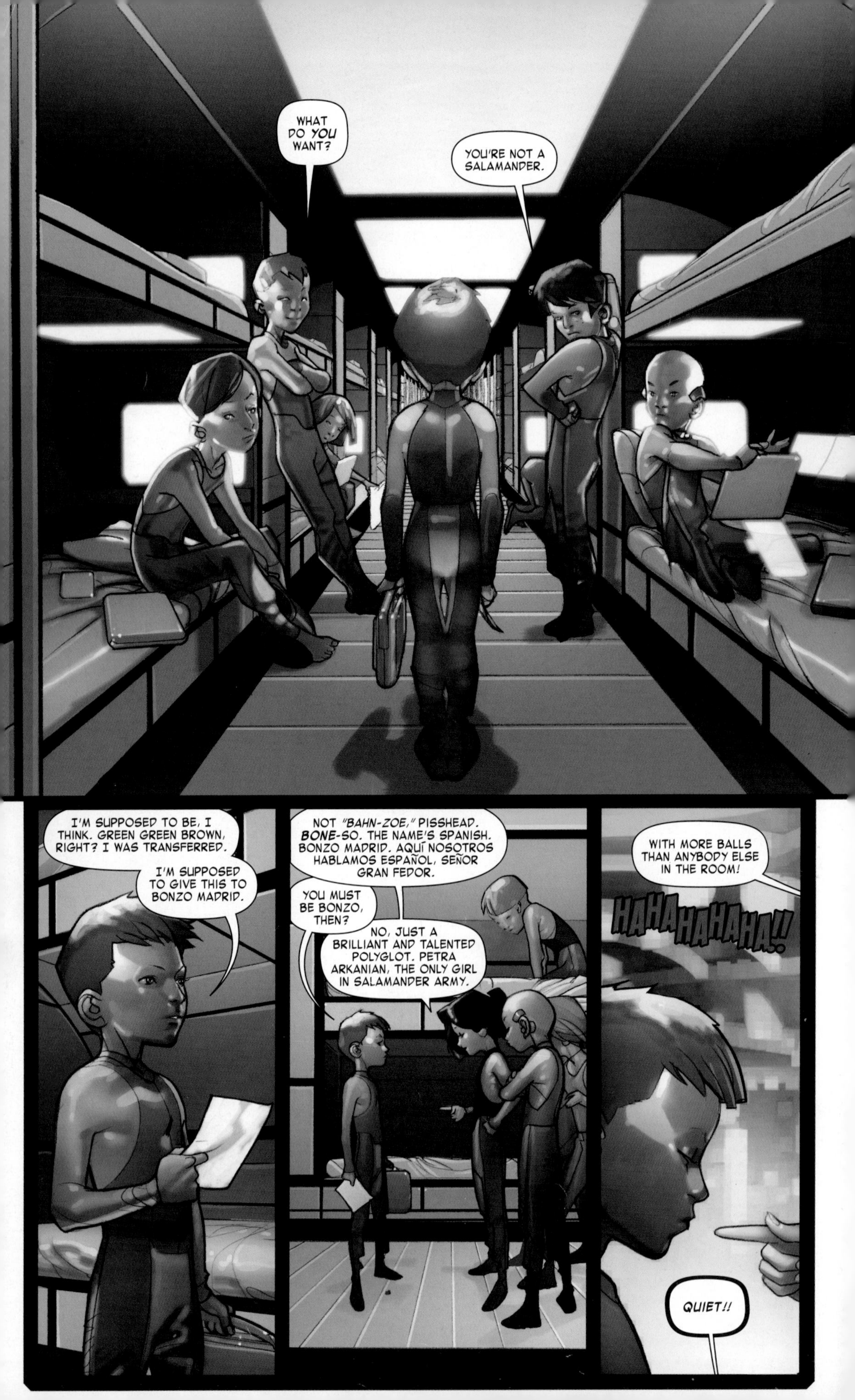
WHAT DO *YOU* WANT?
YOU'RE NOT A SALAMANDER.
I'M SUPPOSED TO BE, I THINK. GREEN GREEN BROWN, RIGHT? I WAS TRANSFERRED.
I'M SUPPOSED TO GIVE THIS TO BONZO MADRID.
NOT *"BAHN-ZOE,"* PISSHEAD. ***BONE***-SO. THE NAME'S SPANISH. BONZO MADRID. AQUÍ NOSOTROS HABLAMOS ESPAÑOL, SEÑOR GRAN FEDOR.
YOU MUST BE BONZO, THEN?
NO, JUST A BRILLIANT AND TALENTED POLYGLOT. PETRA ARKANIAN, THE ONLY GIRL IN SALAMANDER ARMY.
WITH MORE BALLS THAN ANYBODY ELSE IN THE ROOM!
HAHAHAHAHA!!
QUIET!!

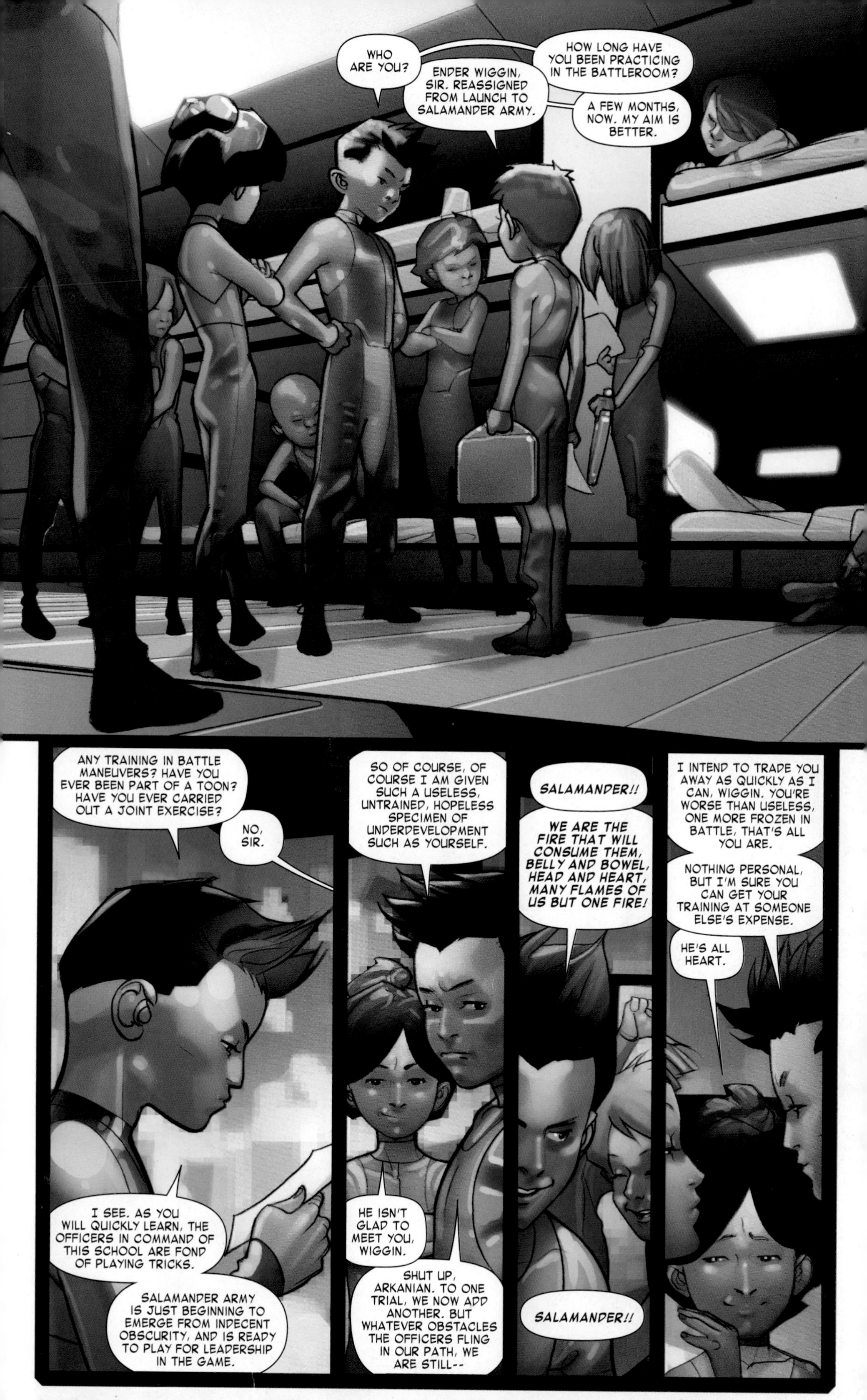
WHO ARE YOU?
ENDER WIGGIN, SIR. REASSIGNED FROM LAUNCH TO SALAMANDER ARMY.
HOW LONG HAVE YOU BEEN PRACTICING IN THE BATTLEROOM?
A FEW MONTHS, NOW. MY AIM IS BETTER.
ANY TRAINING IN BATTLE MANEUVERS? HAVE YOU EVER BEEN PART OF A TOON? HAVE YOU EVER CARRIED OUT A JOINT EXERCISE?
NO, SIR.
I SEE. AS YOU WILL QUICKLY LEARN, THE OFFICERS IN COMMAND OF THIS SCHOOL ARE FOND OF PLAYING TRICKS.
SALAMANDER ARMY IS JUST BEGINNING TO EMERGE FROM INDECENT OBSCURITY, AND IS READY TO PLAY FOR LEADERSHIP IN THE GAME.
SO OF COURSE, OF COURSE I AM GIVEN SUCH A USELESS, UNTRAINED, HOPELESS SPECIMEN OF UNDERDEVELOPMENT SUCH AS YOURSELF.
HE ISN'T GLAD TO MEET YOU, WIGGIN.
SHUT UP, ARKANIAN. TO ONE TRIAL, WE NOW ADD ANOTHER. BUT WHATEVER OBSTACLES THE OFFICERS FLING IN OUR PATH, WE ARE STILL--
SALAMANDER!!
WE ARE THE FIRE THAT WILL CONSUME THEM, BELLY AND BOWEL, HEAD AND HEART, MANY FLAMES OF US BUT ONE FIRE!
SALAMANDER!!
I INTEND TO TRADE YOU AWAY AS QUICKLY AS I CAN, WIGGIN. YOU'RE WORSE THAN USELESS, ONE MORE FROZEN IN BATTLE, THAT'S ALL YOU ARE.
NOTHING PERSONAL, BUT I'M SURE YOU CAN GET YOUR TRAINING AT SOMEONE ELSE'S EXPENSE.
HE'S ALL HEART.

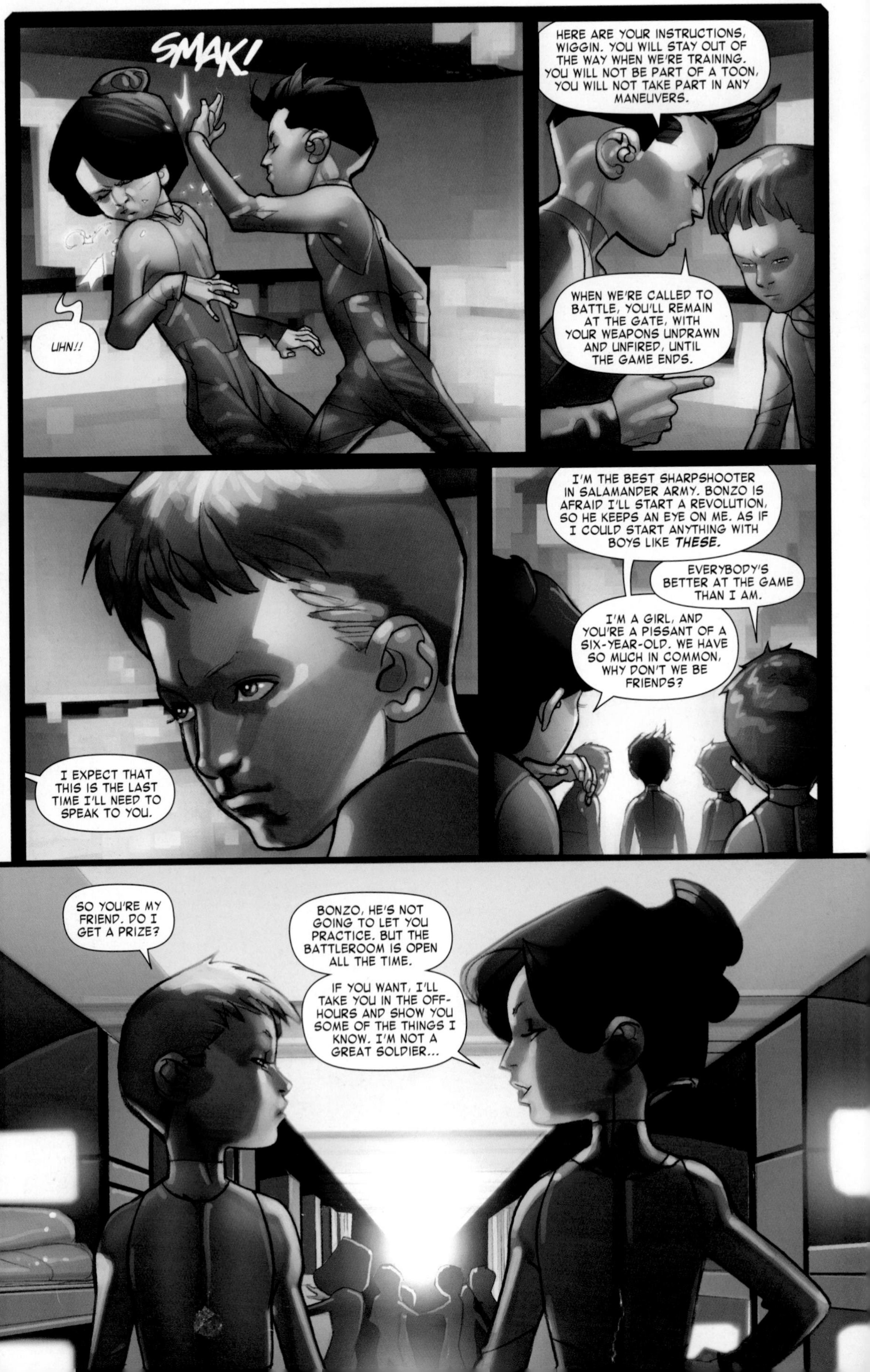
SMAK!
UHN!!
HERE ARE YOUR INSTRUCTIONS, WIGGIN. YOU WILL STAY OUT OF THE WAY WHEN WE'RE TRAINING. YOU WILL NOT BE PART OF A TOON, YOU WILL NOT TAKE PART IN ANY MANEUVERS.
WHEN WE'RE CALLED TO BATTLE, YOU'LL REMAIN AT THE GATE, WITH YOUR WEAPONS UNDRAWN AND UNFIRED, UNTIL THE GAME ENDS.
I EXPECT THAT THIS IS THE LAST TIME I'LL NEED TO SPEAK TO YOU.
I'M THE BEST SHARPSHOOTER IN SALAMANDER ARMY. BONZO IS AFRAID I'LL START A REVOLUTION, SO HE KEEPS AN EYE ON ME. AS IF I COULD START ANYTHING WITH BOYS LIKE *THESE.*
EVERYBODY'S BETTER AT THE GAME THAN I AM.
I'M A GIRL, AND YOU'RE A PISSANT OF A SIX-YEAR-OLD. WE HAVE SO MUCH IN COMMON, WHY DON'T WE BE FRIENDS?
SO YOU'RE MY FRIEND. DO I GET A PRIZE?
BONZO, HE'S NOT GOING TO LET YOU PRACTICE. BUT THE BATTLEROOM IS OPEN ALL THE TIME.
IF YOU WANT, I'LL TAKE YOU IN THE OFF-HOURS AND SHOW YOU SOME OF THE THINGS I KNOW. I'M NOT A GREAT SOLDIER...

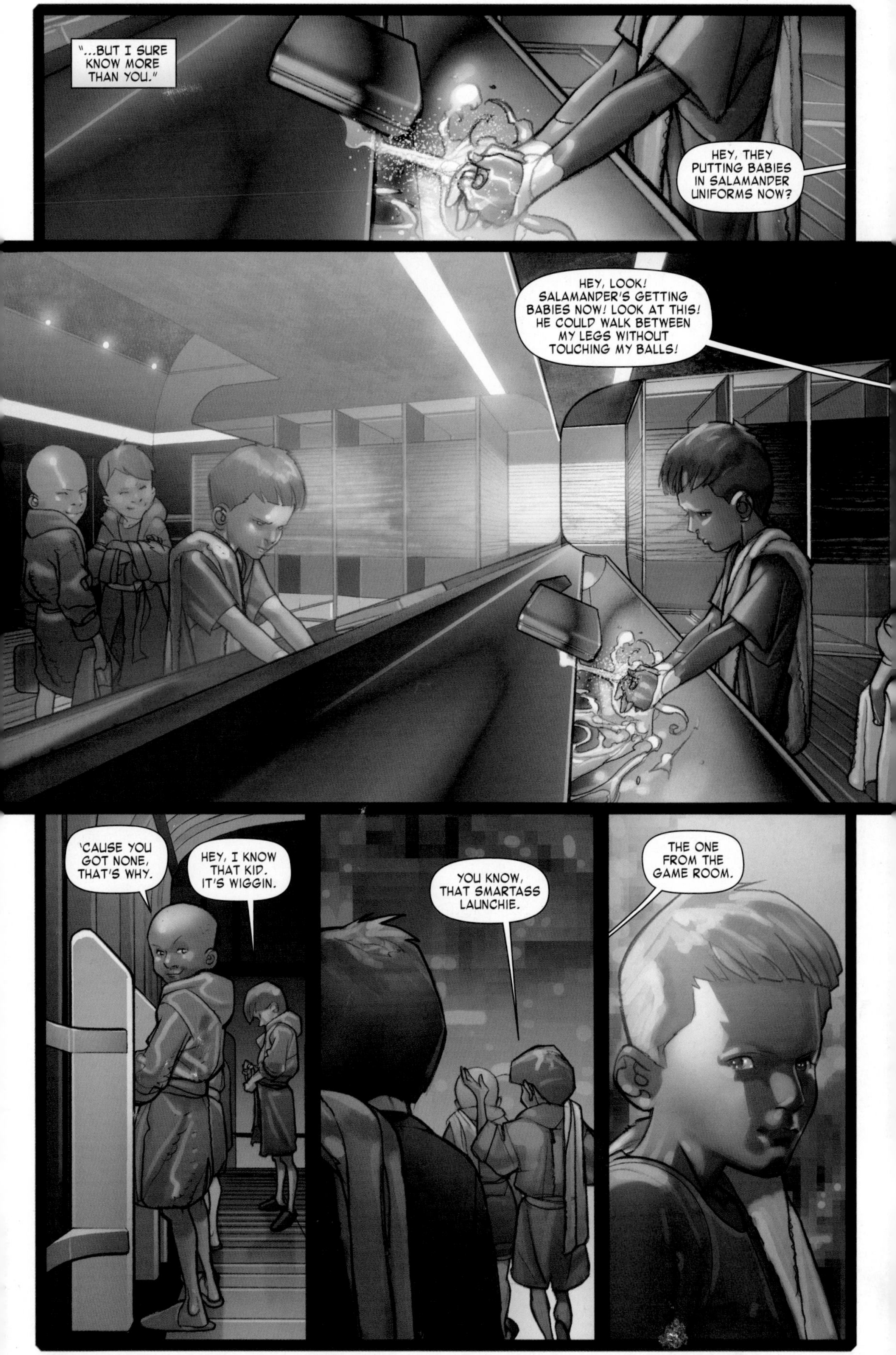
"...BUT I SURE KNOW MORE THAN YOU."
HEY, THEY PUTTING BABIES IN SALAMANDER UNIFORMS NOW?
HEY, LOOK! SALAMANDER'S GETTING BABIES NOW! LOOK AT THIS! HE COULD WALK BETWEEN MY LEGS WITHOUT TOUCHING MY BALLS!
'CAUSE YOU GOT NONE, THAT'S WHY.
HEY, I KNOW THAT KID. IT'S WIGGIN.
YOU KNOW, THAT SMARTASS LAUNCHIE.
THE ONE FROM THE GAME ROOM.

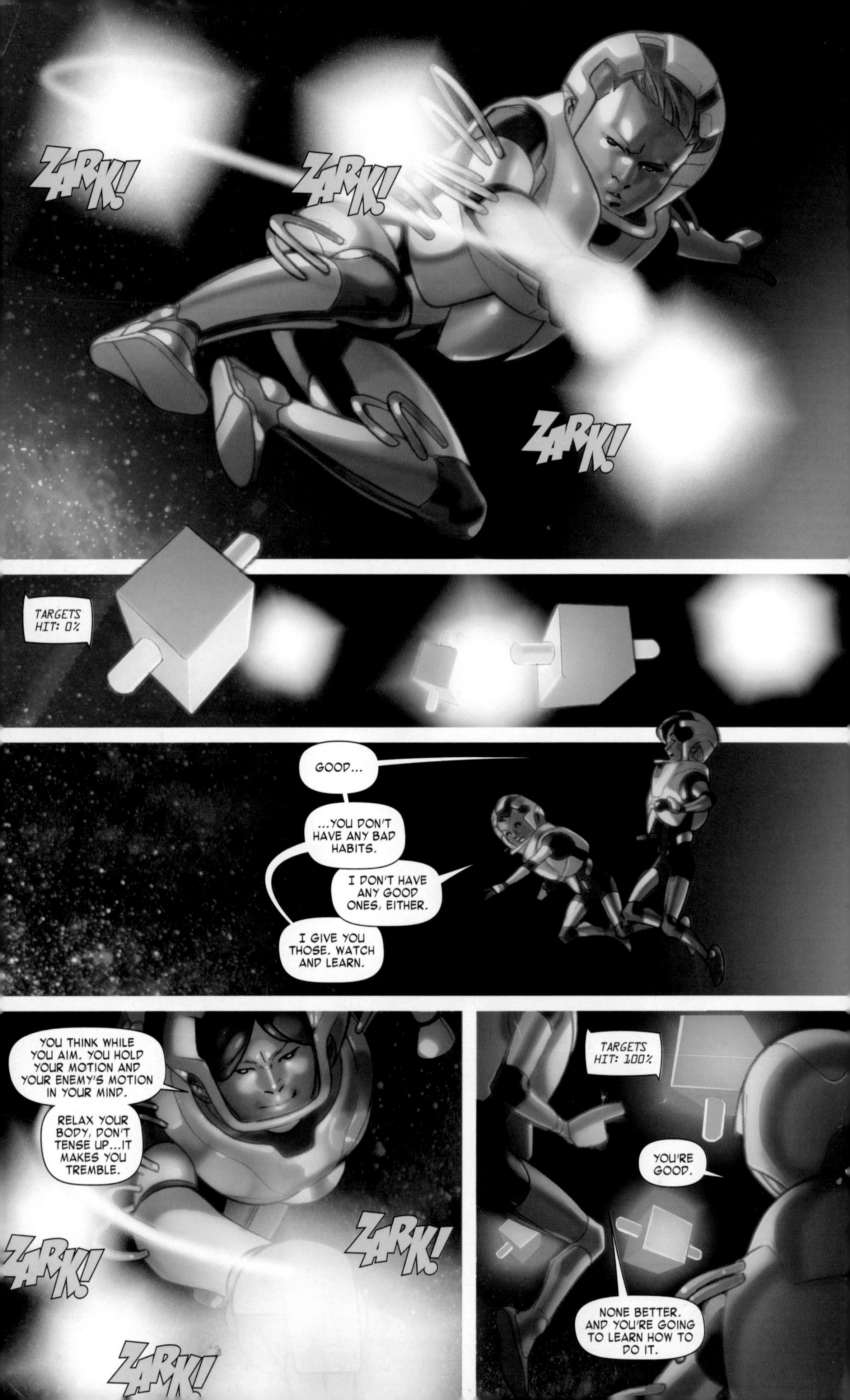
ZARK!
ZARK!
ZARK!
TARGETS HIT: 0%
GOOD...
...YOU DON'T HAVE ANY BAD HABITS.
I DON'T HAVE ANY GOOD ONES, EITHER.
I GIVE YOU THOSE. WATCH AND LEARN.
YOU THINK WHILE YOU AIM. YOU HOLD YOUR MOTION AND YOUR ENEMY'S MOTION IN YOUR MIND.
RELAX YOUR BODY, DON'T TENSE UP...IT MAKES YOU TREMBLE.
ZARK!
ZARK!
ZARK!
TARGETS HIT: 100%
YOU'RE GOOD.
NONE BETTER. AND YOU'RE GOING TO LEARN HOW TO DO IT.

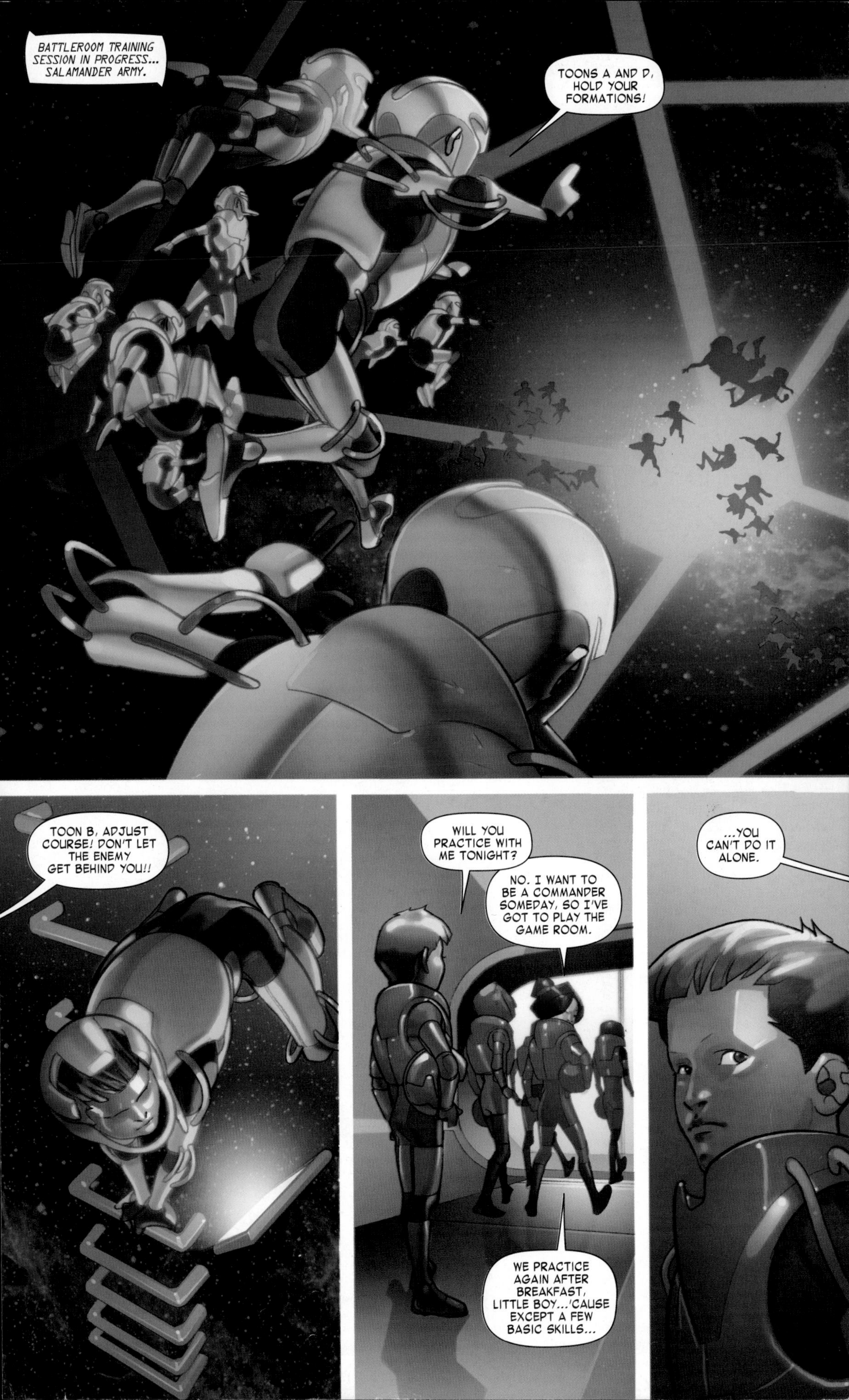
BATTLEROOM TRAINING SESSION IN PROGRESS... SALAMANDER ARMY.
TOONS A AND D, HOLD YOUR FORMATIONS!
TOON B, ADJUST COURSE! DON'T LET THE ENEMY GET BEHIND YOU!!
WILL YOU PRACTICE WITH ME TONIGHT?
NO. I WANT TO BE A COMMANDER SOMEDAY, SO I'VE GOT TO PLAY THE GAME ROOM.
WE PRACTICE AGAIN AFTER BREAKFAST, LITTLE BOY...'CAUSE EXCEPT A FEW BASIC SKILLS...
...YOU CAN'T DO IT ALONE.

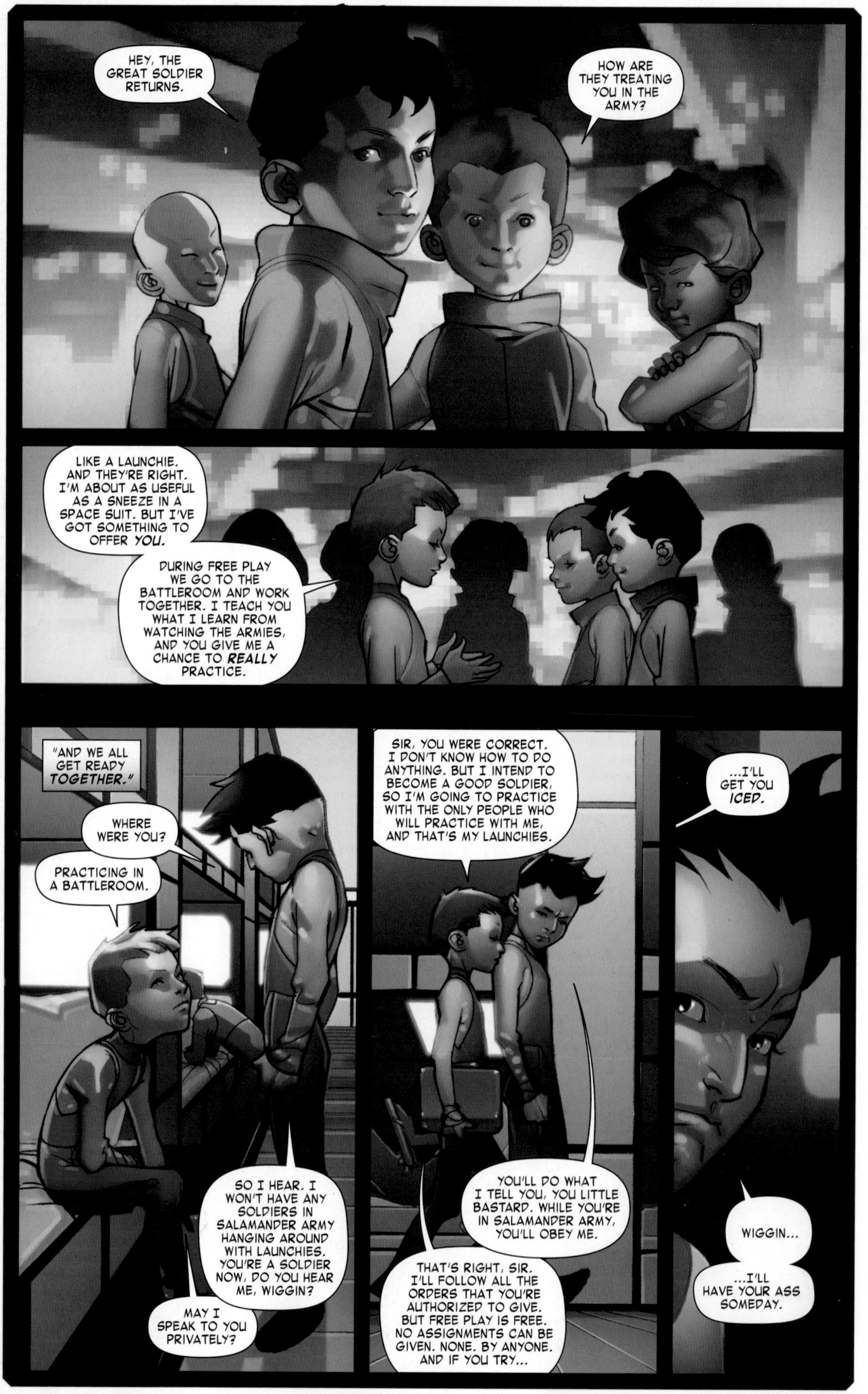
HEY, THE GREAT SOLDIER RETURNS.
HOW ARE THEY TREATING YOU IN THE ARMY?
LIKE A LAUNCHIE. AND THEY'RE RIGHT. I'M ABOUT AS USEFUL AS A SNEEZE IN A SPACE SUIT. BUT I'VE GOT SOMETHING TO OFFER YOU.
DURING FREE PLAY WE GO TO THE BATTLEROOM AND WORK TOGETHER. I TEACH YOU WHAT I LEARN FROM WATCHING THE ARMIES, AND YOU GIVE ME A CHANCE TO REALLY PRACTICE.
"AND WE ALL GET READY TOGETHER."
WHERE WERE YOU?
PRACTICING IN A BATTLEROOM.
SO I HEAR. I WON'T HAVE ANY SOLDIERS IN SALAMANDER ARMY HANGING AROUND WITH LAUNCHIES. YOU'RE A SOLDIER NOW, DO YOU HEAR ME, WIGGIN?
MAY I SPEAK TO YOU PRIVATELY?
SIR, YOU WERE CORRECT. I DON'T KNOW HOW TO DO ANYTHING. BUT I INTEND TO BECOME A GOOD SOLDIER, SO I'M GOING TO PRACTICE WITH THE ONLY PEOPLE WHO WILL PRACTICE WITH ME, AND THAT'S MY LAUNCHIES.
YOU'LL DO WHAT I TELL YOU, YOU LITTLE BASTARD. WHILE YOU'RE IN SALAMANDER ARMY, YOU'LL OBEY ME.
THAT'S RIGHT, SIR. I'LL FOLLOW ALL THE ORDERS THAT YOU'RE AUTHORIZED TO GIVE. BUT FREE PLAY IS FREE. NO ASSIGNMENTS CAN BE GIVEN. NONE. BY ANYONE. AND IF YOU TRY...
...I'LL GET YOU ICED.
WIGGIN...
...I'LL HAVE YOUR ASS SOMEDAY.

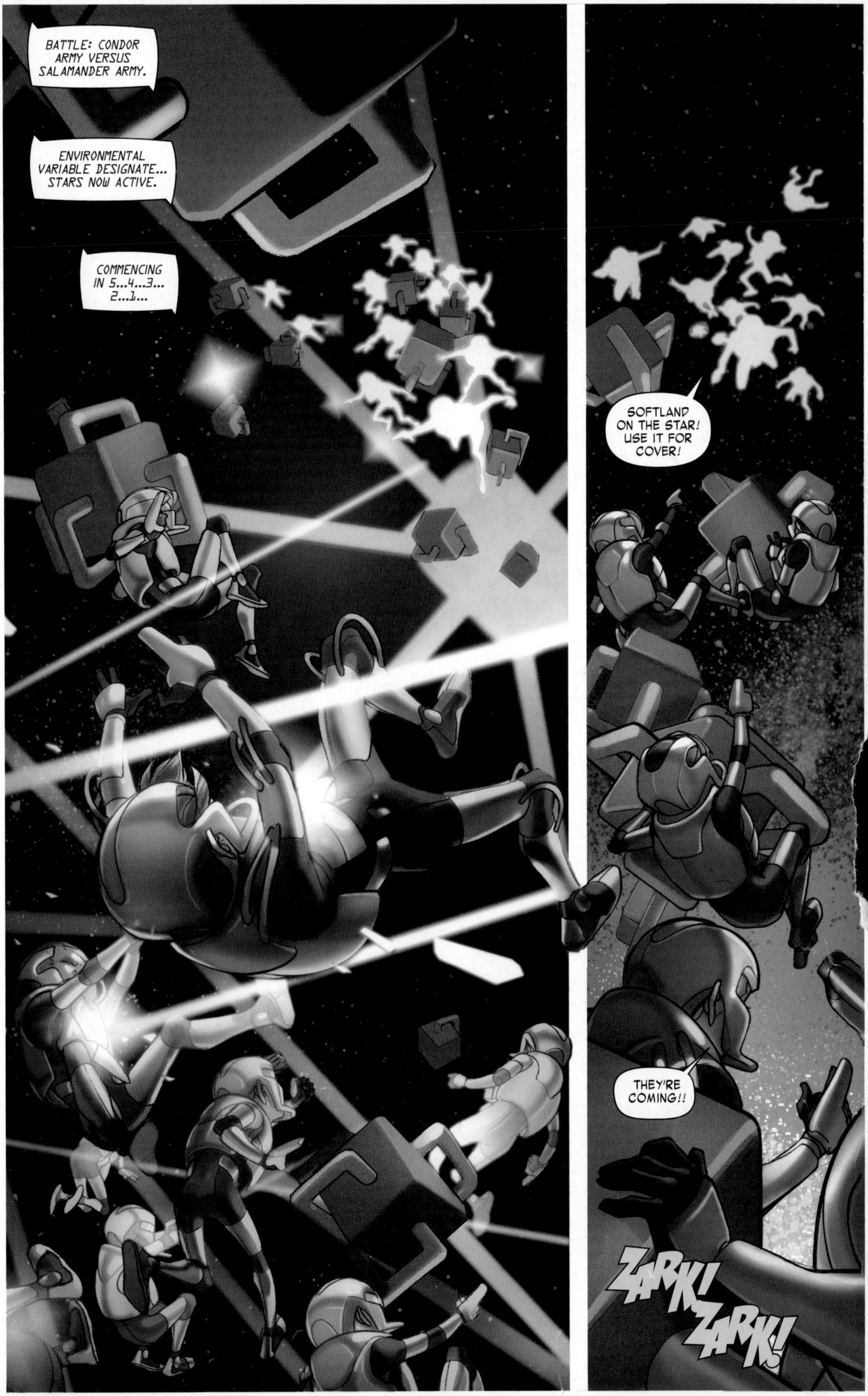
BATTLE: CONDOR ARMY VERSUS SALAMANDER ARMY.
ENVIRONMENTAL VARIABLE DESIGNATE... STARS NOW ACTIVE.
COMMENCING IN 5...4...3... 2...1...
SOFTLAND ON THE STAR! USE IT FOR COVER!
THEY'RE COMING!!
ZARK! ZARK!

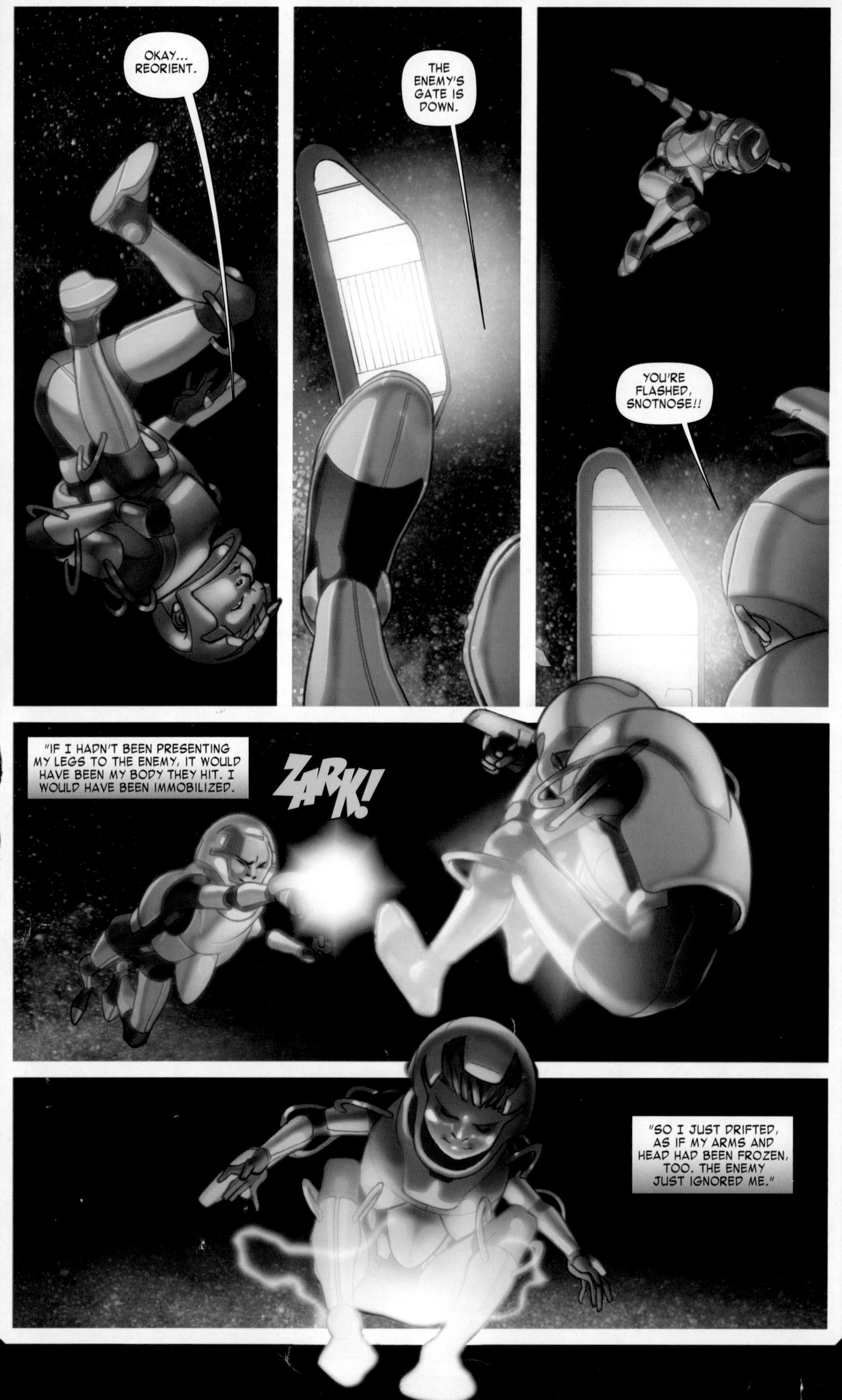
OKAY... REORIENT.
THE ENEMY'S GATE IS DOWN.
YOU'RE FLASHED, SNOTNOSE!!
"IF I HADN'T BEEN PRESENTING MY LEGS TO THE ENEMY, IT WOULD HAVE BEEN MY BODY THEY HIT. I WOULD HAVE BEEN IMMOBILIZED.
ZARK!
"SO I JUST DRIFTED, AS IF MY ARMS AND HEAD HAD BEEN FROZEN, TOO. THE ENEMY JUST IGNORED ME."

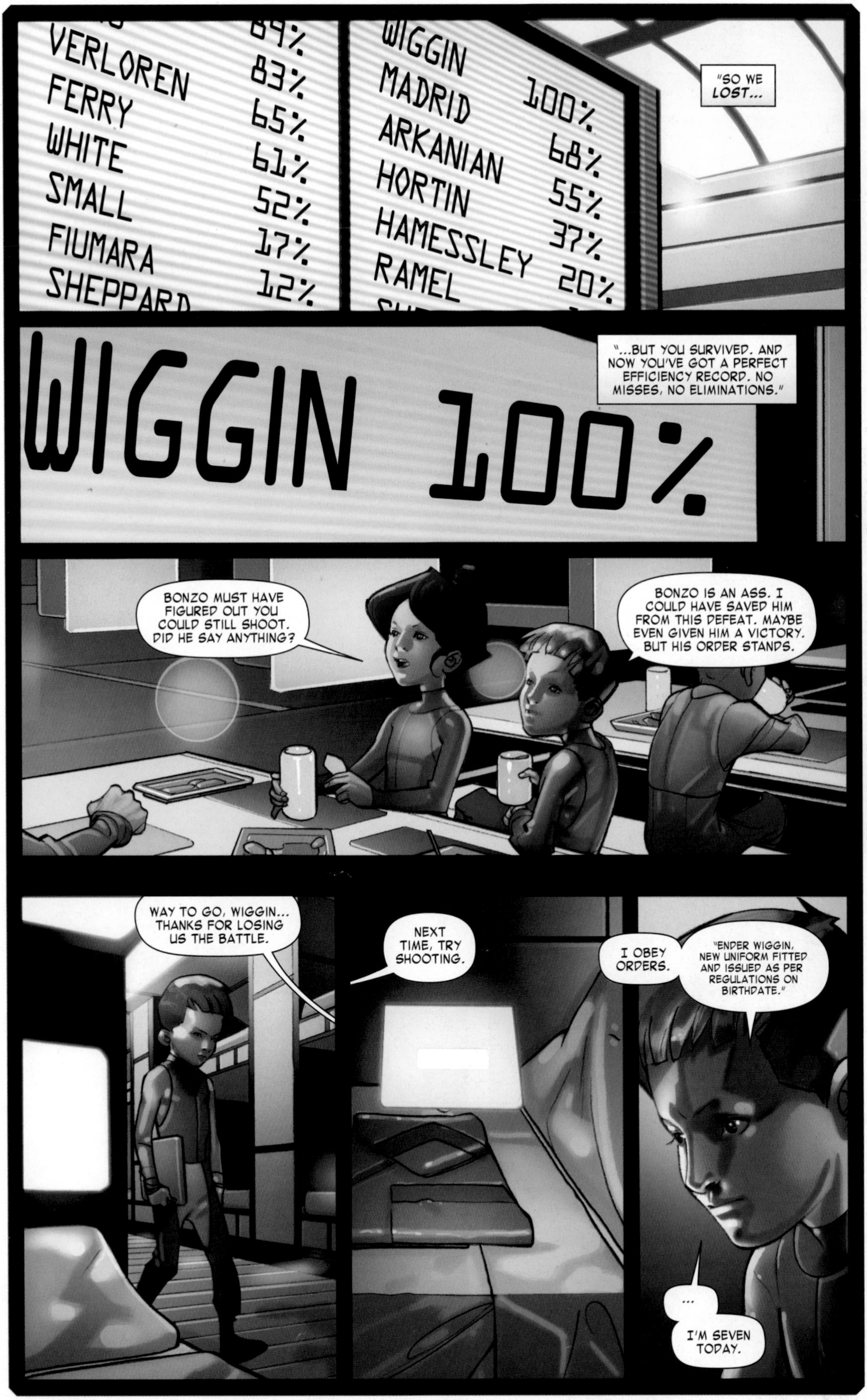
VERLOREN 83%
FERRY 65%
WHITE 61%
SMALL 52%
FIUMARA 17%
SHEPPARD 12%
WIGGIN
MADRID 100%
ARKANIAN 68%
HORTIN 55%
HAMESSLEY 37%
RAMEL 20%
"SO WE LOST...
WIGGIN 100%
"...BUT YOU SURVIVED. AND NOW YOU'VE GOT A PERFECT EFFICIENCY RECORD. NO MISSES, NO ELIMINATIONS."
BONZO MUST HAVE FIGURED OUT YOU COULD STILL SHOOT. DID HE SAY ANYTHING?
BONZO IS AN ASS. I COULD HAVE SAVED HIM FROM THIS DEFEAT. MAYBE EVEN GIVEN HIM A VICTORY. BUT HIS ORDER STANDS.
WAY TO GO, WIGGIN... THANKS FOR LOSING US THE BATTLE.
NEXT TIME, TRY SHOOTING.
I OBEY ORDERS.
"ENDER WIGGIN, NEW UNIFORM FITTED AND ISSUED AS PER REGULATIONS ON BIRTHDATE."
...
I'M SEVEN TODAY.

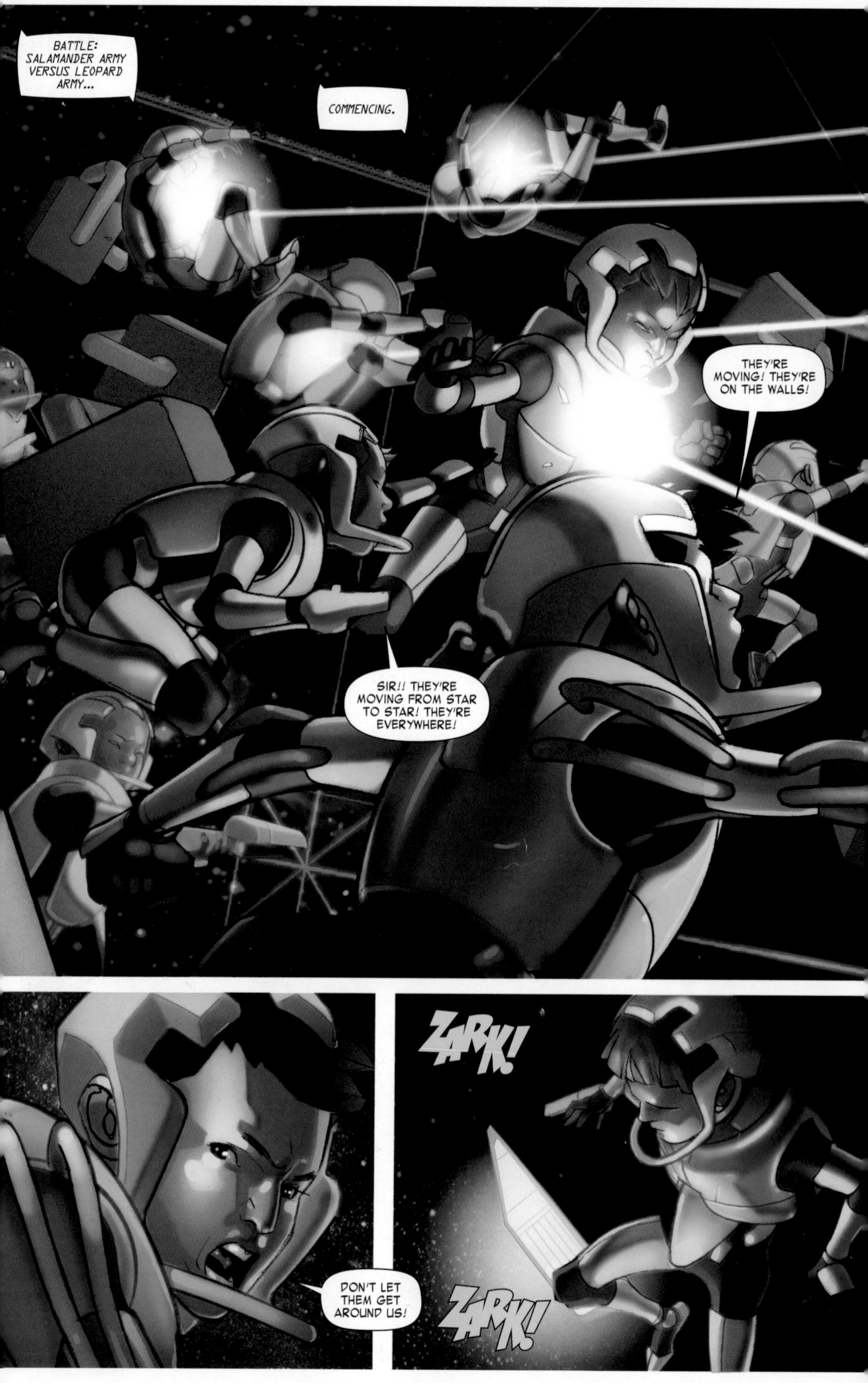

BATTLE: SALAMANDER ARMY VERSUS LEOPARD ARMY...
COMMENCING.
THEY'RE MOVING! THEY'RE ON THE WALLS!
SIR!! THEY'RE MOVING FROM STAR TO STAR! THEY'RE EVERYWHERE!
DON'T LET THEM GET AROUND US!
ZARK!
ZARK!

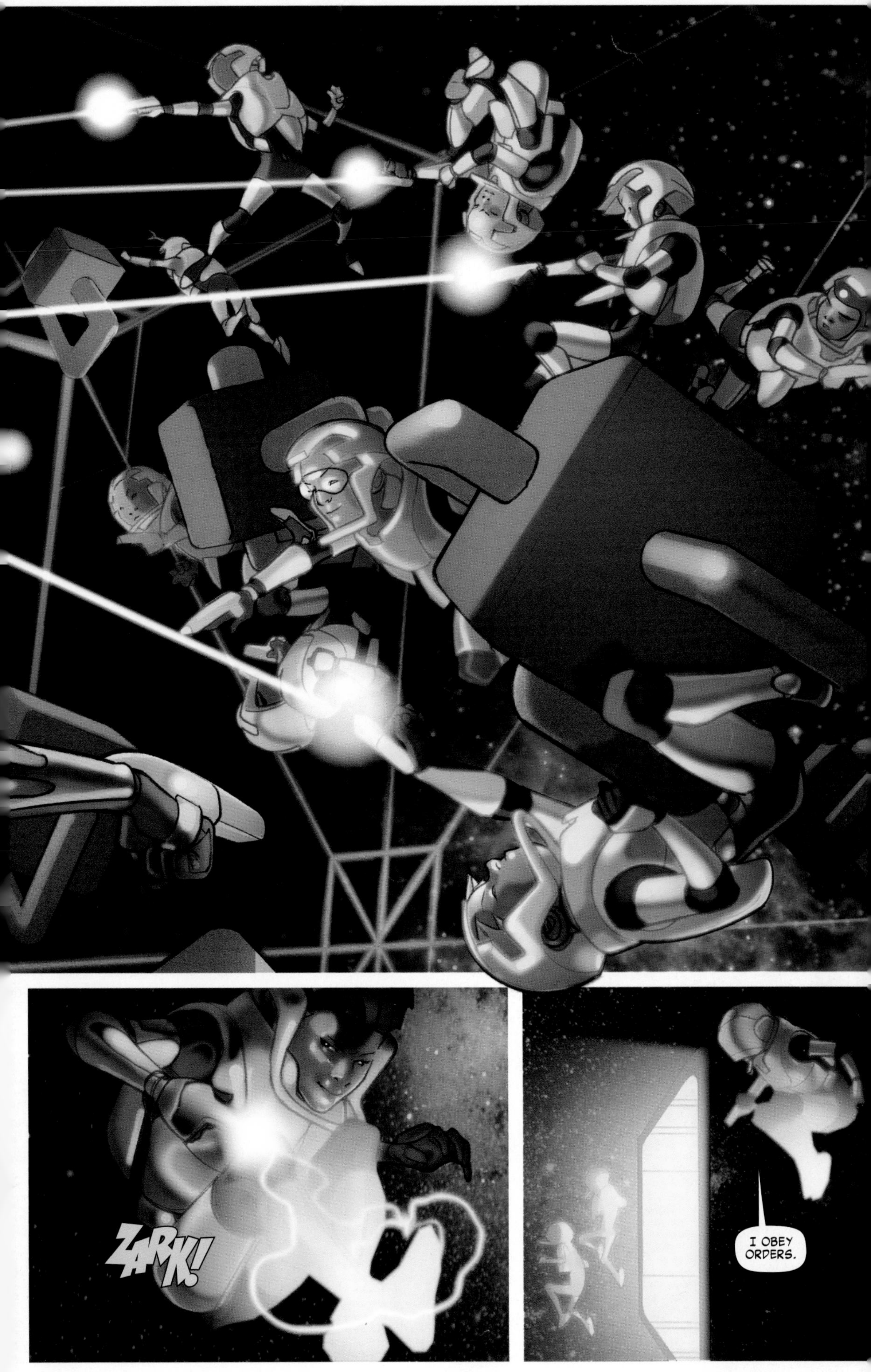
ZARK!
I OBEY ORDERS.

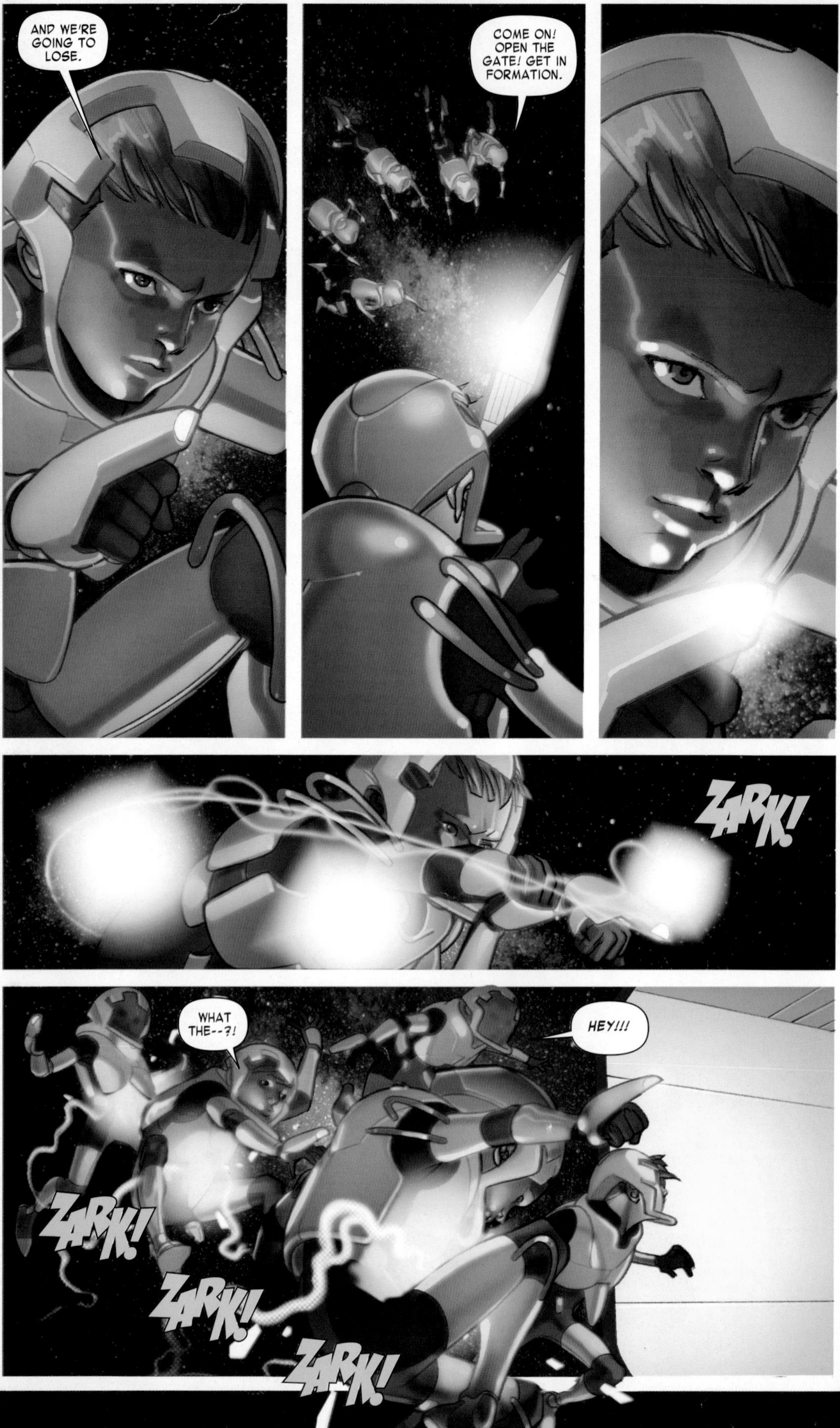
AND WE'RE GOING TO LOSE.
COME ON! OPEN THE GATE! GET IN FORMATION.
ZARK!
WHAT THE--?!
HEY!!!
ZARK!
ZARK!
ZARK!

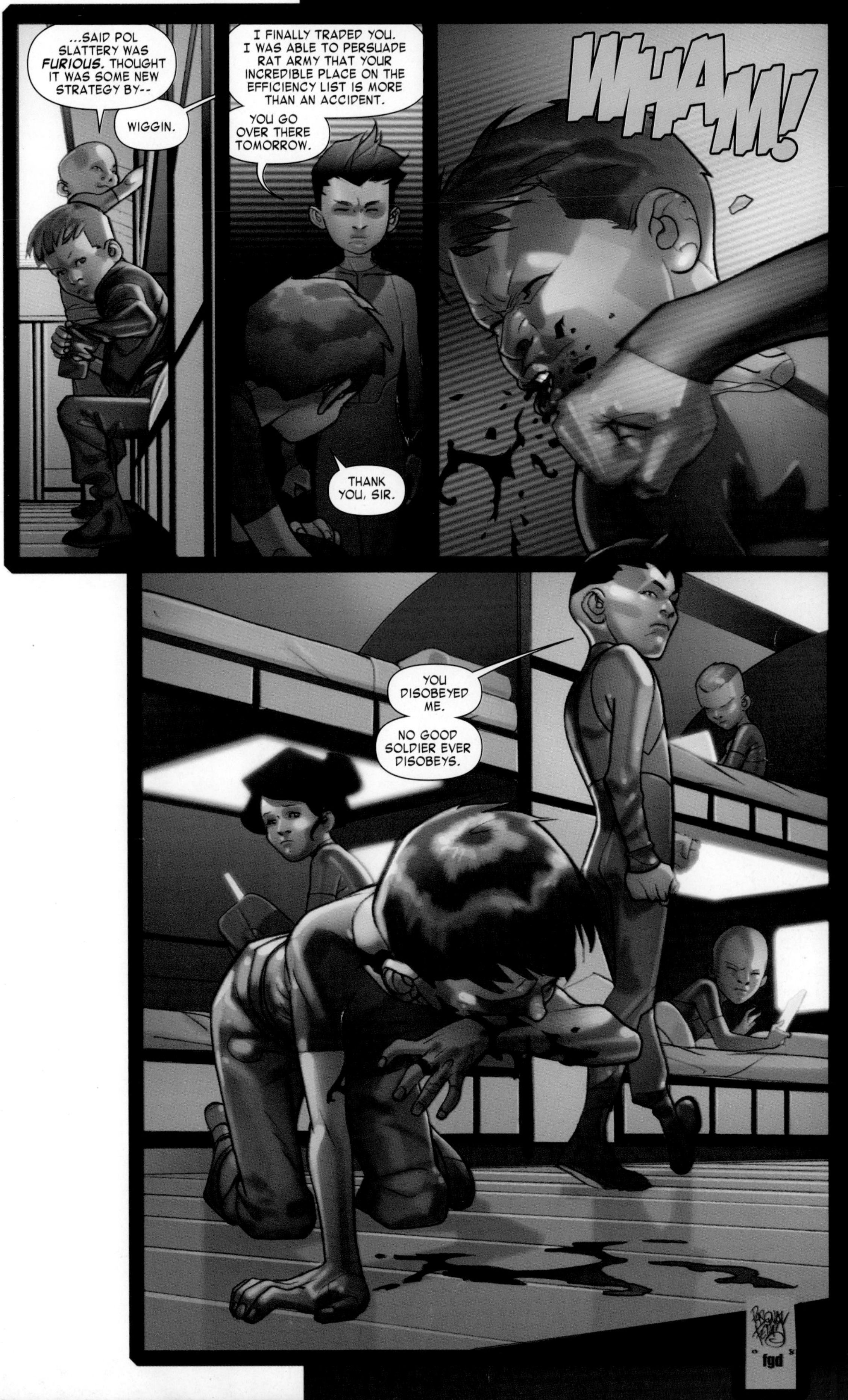
...SAID POL SLATTERY WAS FURIOUS. THOUGHT IT WAS SOME NEW STRATEGY BY--
WIGGIN.
I FINALLY TRADED YOU. I WAS ABLE TO PERSUADE RAT ARMY THAT YOUR INCREDIBLE PLACE ON THE EFFICIENCY LIST IS MORE THAN AN ACCIDENT.
YOU GO OVER THERE TOMORROW.
THANK YOU, SIR.
WHAM!
YOU DISOBEYED ME.
NO GOOD SOLDIER EVER DISOBEYS.

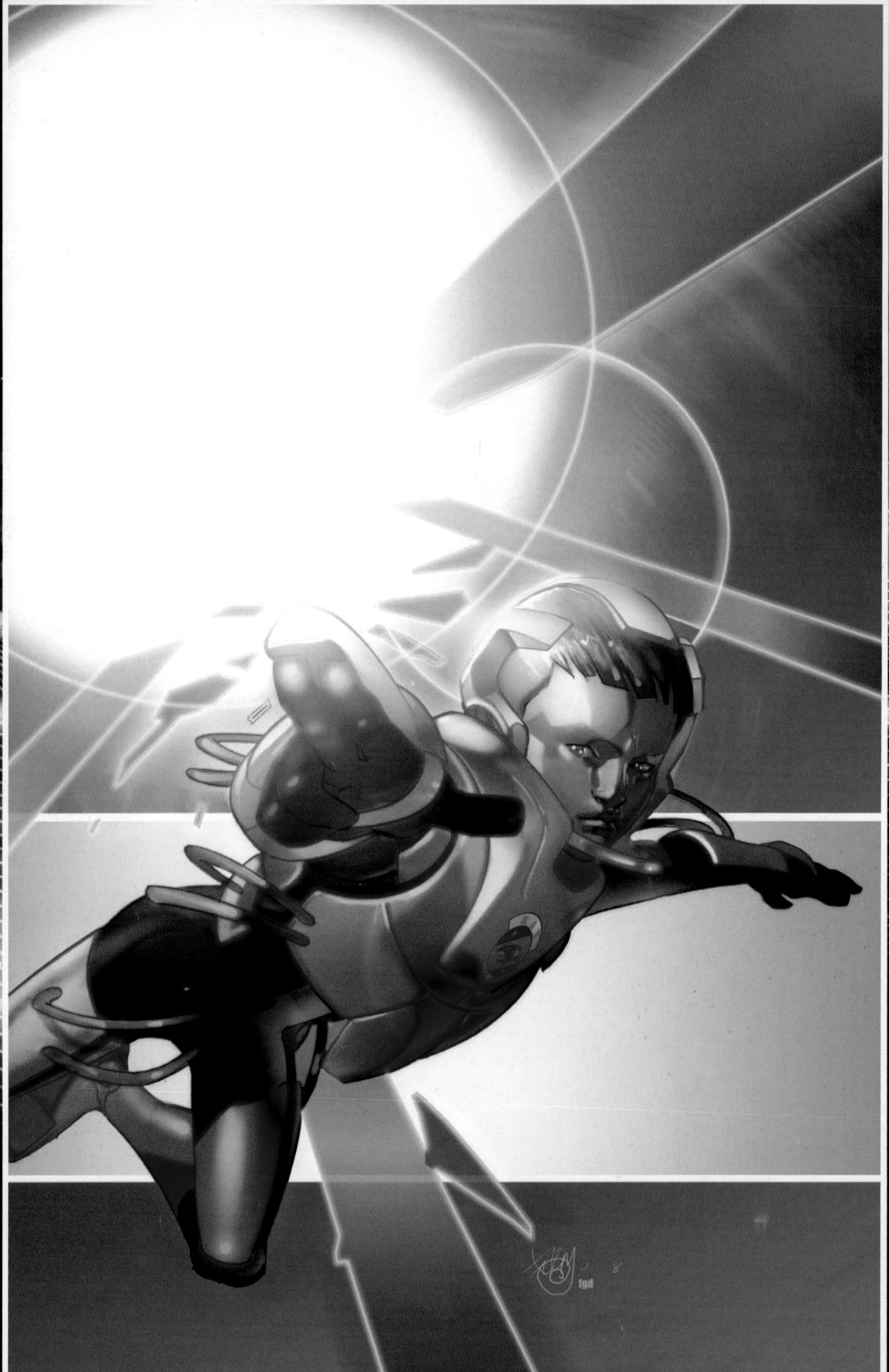

F O U R

INTERNATIONAL FLEET MONITORED COMMUNICATIONS
PARTICIPANTS: COLONEL GRAFF, MAJOR ANDERSON
REF ID # 21953-34954, KEYWORD SEARCH: 'MIND GAME'

CONVERSATION RECORDED FOLLOWING THE SUCCESSFUL COMPLETION OF MIND GAME LEVEL 'GIANT'S DRINK.'

GRAFF: Isn't it nice to know that Ender can do the impossible?

ANDERSON: The players' deaths have always been sickening, I've always thought the Giant's Drink was the most perverted part of the whole mind game, but going for the eye like that– this is the one we want to put in command of our fleet?

GRAFF: What matters is that he won the game that couldn't be won.

ANDERSON: Does it ever seem to you that these boys aren't children? Look at what they do, the way they talk, and they don't seem like little kids.

GRAFF: They're the most brilliant children in the world, each in his own way.

ANDERSON: But shouldn't they still act like children? They aren't normal. They act like– history. Napoleon and Wellington. Caesar and Brutus.

GRAFF: We're trying to save the world not heal the wounded heart. You're too compassionate.

ANDERSON: Don't hurt this boy.

GRAFF: Are you joking?

ANDERSON: I mean, don't hurt him more than you have to.

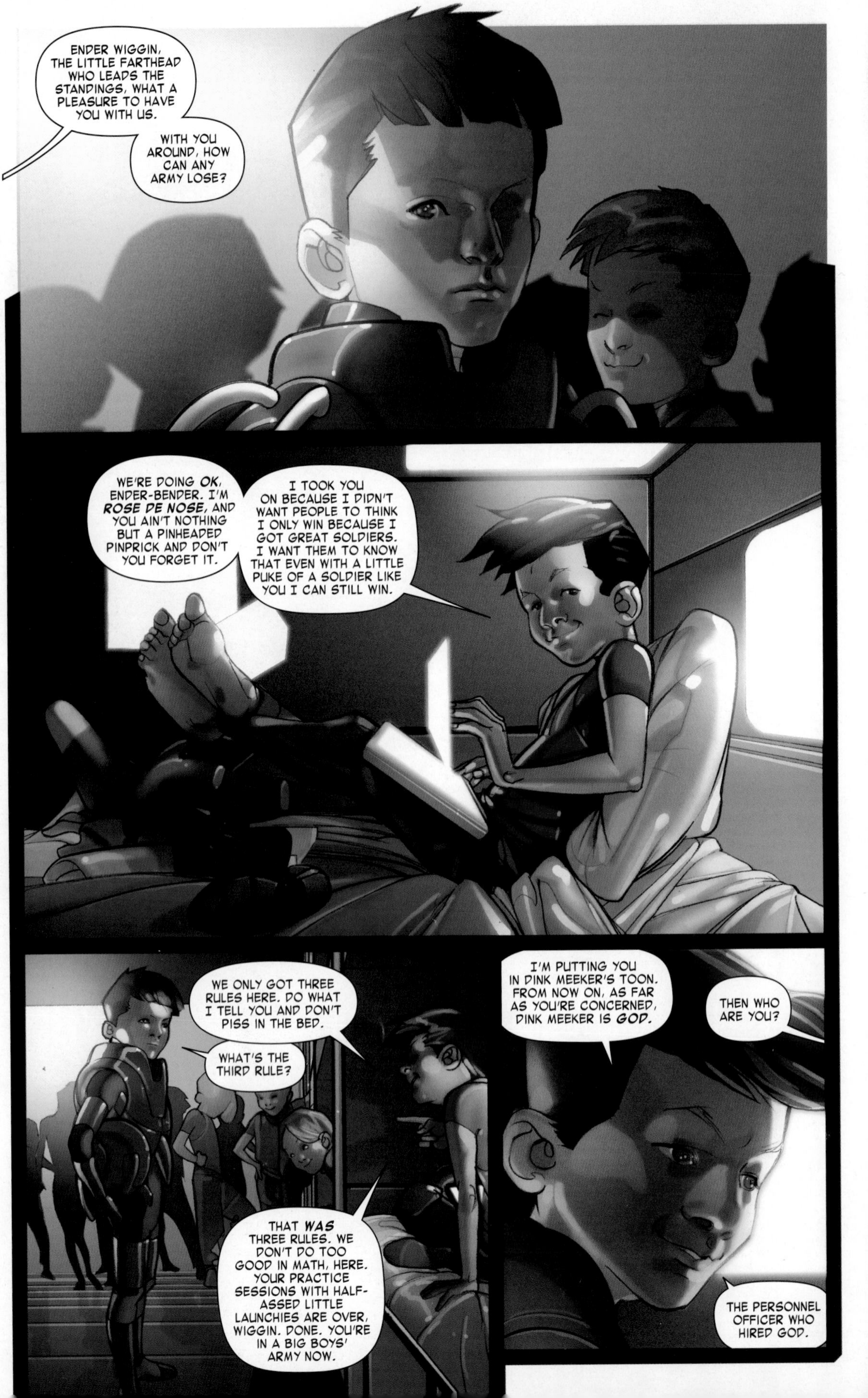
ENDER WIGGIN, THE LITTLE FARTHEAD WHO LEADS THE STANDINGS, WHAT A PLEASURE TO HAVE YOU WITH US.
WITH YOU AROUND, HOW CAN ANY ARMY LOSE?
WE'RE DOING OK, ENDER-BENDER. I'M ROSE DE NOSE, AND YOU AIN'T NOTHING BUT A PINHEADED PINPRICK AND DON'T YOU FORGET IT.
I TOOK YOU ON BECAUSE I DIDN'T WANT PEOPLE TO THINK I ONLY WIN BECAUSE I GOT GREAT SOLDIERS. I WANT THEM TO KNOW THAT EVEN WITH A LITTLE PUKE OF A SOLDIER LIKE YOU I CAN STILL WIN.
WE ONLY GOT THREE RULES HERE. DO WHAT I TELL YOU AND DON'T PISS IN THE BED.
WHAT'S THE THIRD RULE?
THAT WAS THREE RULES. WE DON'T DO TOO GOOD IN MATH, HERE. YOUR PRACTICE SESSIONS WITH HALF-ASSED LITTLE LAUNCHIES ARE OVER, WIGGIN. DONE. YOU'RE IN A BIG BOYS' ARMY NOW.
I'M PUTTING YOU IN DINK MEEKER'S TOON. FROM NOW ON, AS FAR AS YOU'RE CONCERNED, DINK MEEKER IS GOD.
THEN WHO ARE YOU?
THE PERSONNEL OFFICER WHO HIRED GOD.

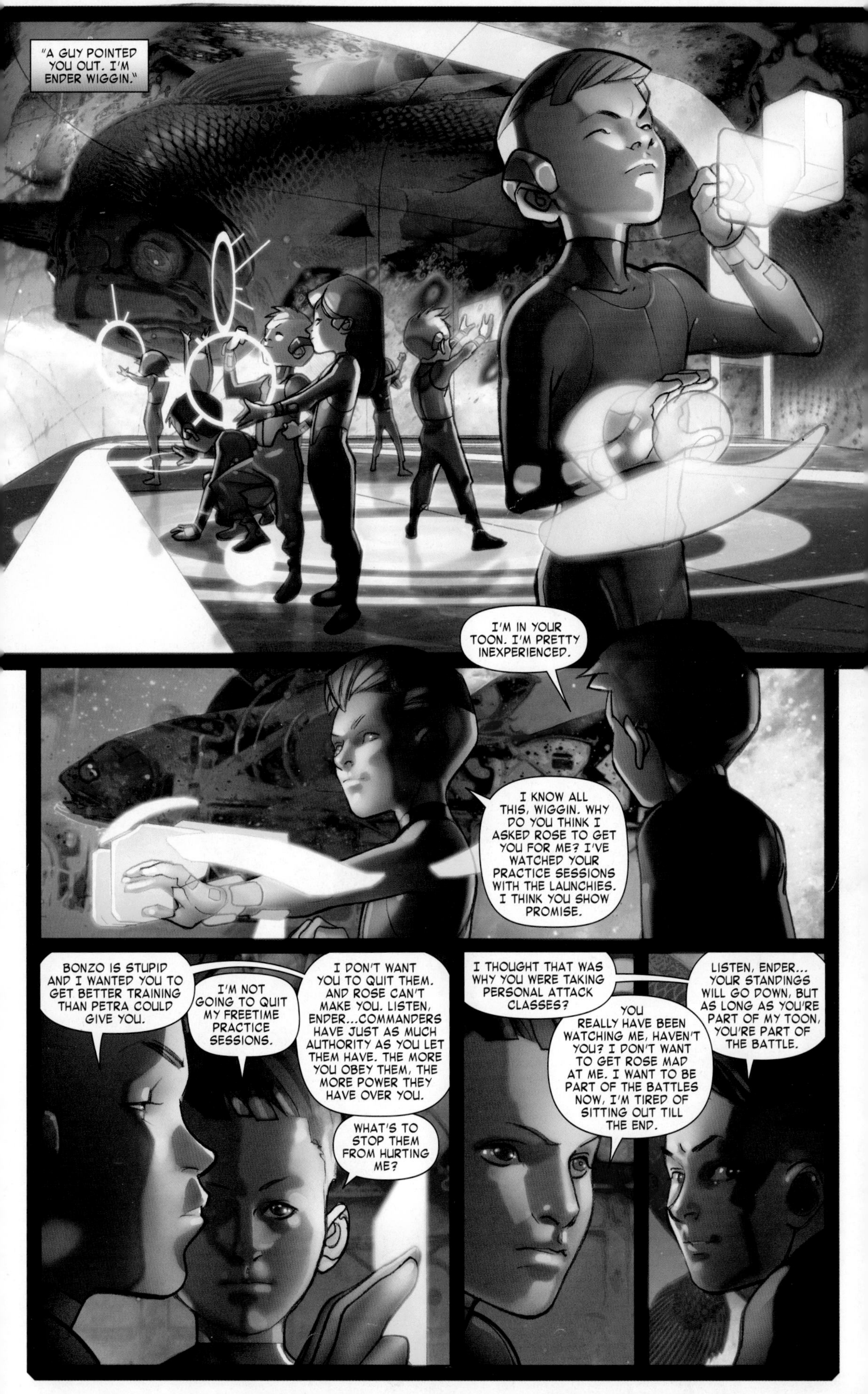
"A GUY POINTED YOU OUT. I'M ENDER WIGGIN."
I'M IN YOUR TOON. I'M PRETTY INEXPERIENCED.
I KNOW ALL THIS, WIGGIN. WHY DO YOU THINK I ASKED ROSE TO GET YOU FOR ME? I'VE WATCHED YOUR PRACTICE SESSIONS WITH THE LAUNCHIES. I THINK YOU SHOW PROMISE.
BONZO IS STUPID AND I WANTED YOU TO GET BETTER TRAINING THAN PETRA COULD GIVE YOU.
I'M NOT GOING TO QUIT MY FREETIME PRACTICE SESSIONS.
I DON'T WANT YOU TO QUIT THEM. AND ROSE CAN'T MAKE YOU. LISTEN, ENDER...COMMANDERS HAVE JUST AS MUCH AUTHORITY AS YOU LET THEM HAVE. THE MORE YOU OBEY THEM, THE MORE POWER THEY HAVE OVER YOU.
WHAT'S TO STOP THEM FROM HURTING ME?
I THOUGHT THAT WAS WHY YOU WERE TAKING PERSONAL ATTACK CLASSES?
YOU REALLY HAVE BEEN WATCHING ME, HAVEN'T YOU? I DON'T WANT TO GET ROSE MAD AT ME. I WANT TO BE PART OF THE BATTLES NOW, I'M TIRED OF SITTING OUT TILL THE END.
LISTEN, ENDER... YOUR STANDINGS WILL GO DOWN, BUT AS LONG AS YOU'RE PART OF MY TOON, YOU'RE PART OF THE BATTLE.

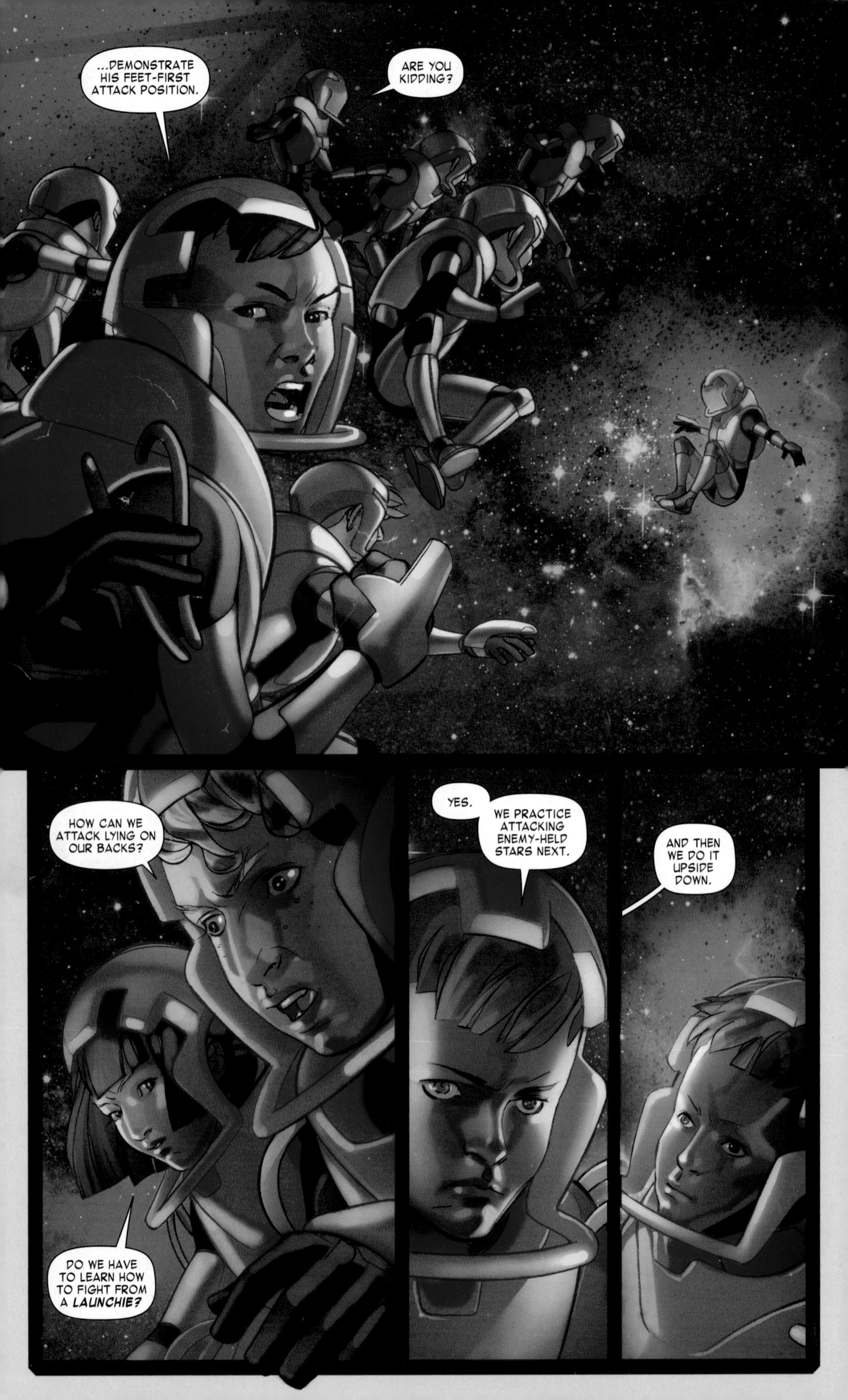
...DEMONSTRATE HIS FEET-FIRST ATTACK POSITION.
ARE YOU KIDDING?
HOW CAN WE ATTACK LYING ON OUR BACKS?
DO WE HAVE TO LEARN HOW TO FIGHT FROM A LAUNCHIE?
YES.
WE PRACTICE ATTACKING ENEMY-HELD STARS NEXT.
AND THEN WE DO IT UPSIDE DOWN.

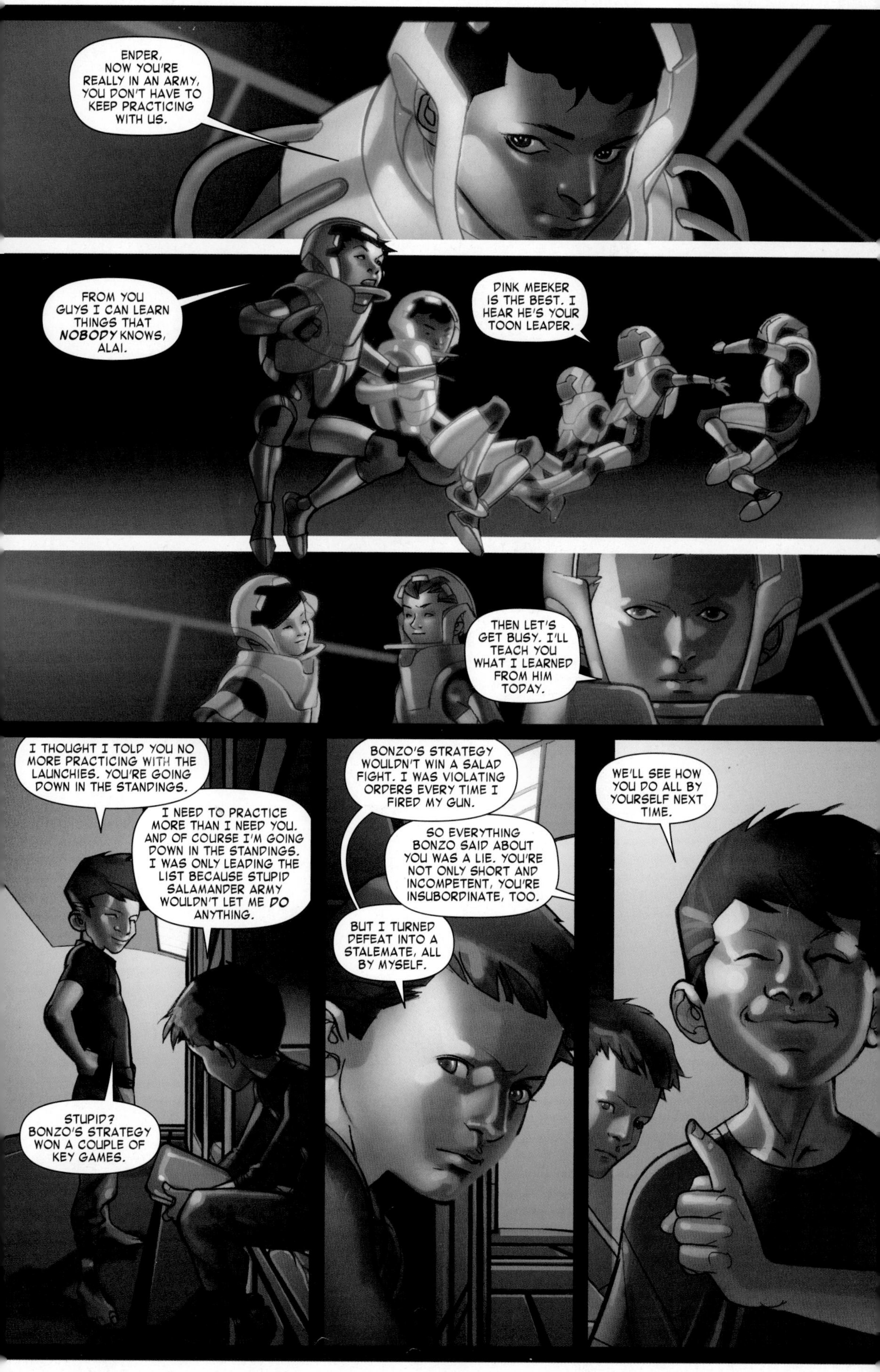
ENDER, NOW YOU'RE REALLY IN AN ARMY, YOU DON'T HAVE TO KEEP PRACTICING WITH US.
FROM YOU GUYS I CAN LEARN THINGS THAT *NOBODY* KNOWS, ALAI.
DINK MEEKER IS THE BEST. I HEAR HE'S YOUR TOON LEADER.
THEN LET'S GET BUSY. I'LL TEACH YOU WHAT I LEARNED FROM HIM TODAY.
I THOUGHT I TOLD YOU NO MORE PRACTICING WITH THE LAUNCHIES. YOU'RE GOING DOWN IN THE STANDINGS.
I NEED TO PRACTICE MORE THAN I NEED YOU. AND OF COURSE I'M GOING DOWN IN THE STANDINGS. I WAS ONLY LEADING THE LIST BECAUSE STUPID SALAMANDER ARMY WOULDN'T LET ME *DO* ANYTHING.
STUPID? BONZO'S STRATEGY WON A COUPLE OF KEY GAMES.
BONZO'S STRATEGY WOULDN'T WIN A SALAD FIGHT. I WAS VIOLATING ORDERS EVERY TIME I FIRED MY GUN.
SO EVERYTHING BONZO SAID ABOUT YOU WAS A LIE. YOU'RE NOT ONLY SHORT AND INCOMPETENT, YOU'RE INSUBORDINATE, TOO.
BUT I TURNED DEFEAT INTO A STALEMATE, ALL BY MYSELF.
WE'LL SEE HOW YOU DO ALL BY YOURSELF NEXT TIME.

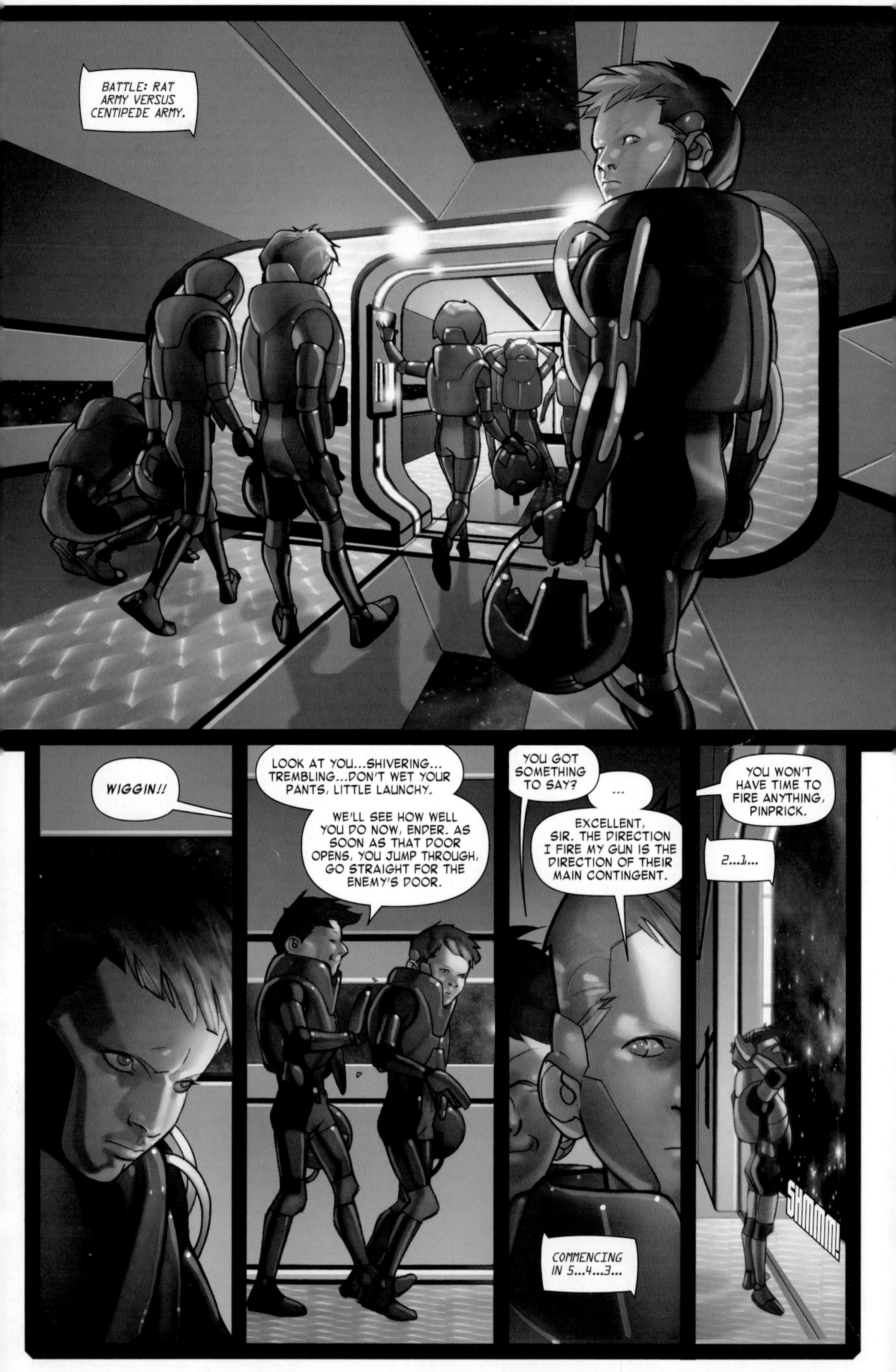
BATTLE: RAT ARMY VERSUS CENTIPEDE ARMY.
WIGGIN!!
LOOK AT YOU...SHIVERING... TREMBLING...DON'T WET YOUR PANTS, LITTLE LAUNCHY.
WE'LL SEE HOW WELL YOU DO NOW, ENDER. AS SOON AS THAT DOOR OPENS, YOU JUMP THROUGH, GO STRAIGHT FOR THE ENEMY'S DOOR.
YOU GOT SOMETHING TO SAY?
...
EXCELLENT, SIR. THE DIRECTION I FIRE MY GUN IS THE DIRECTION OF THEIR MAIN CONTINGENT.
COMMENCING IN 5...4...3...
YOU WON'T HAVE TIME TO FIRE ANYTHING, PINPRICK.
2...1...
SHMMM!

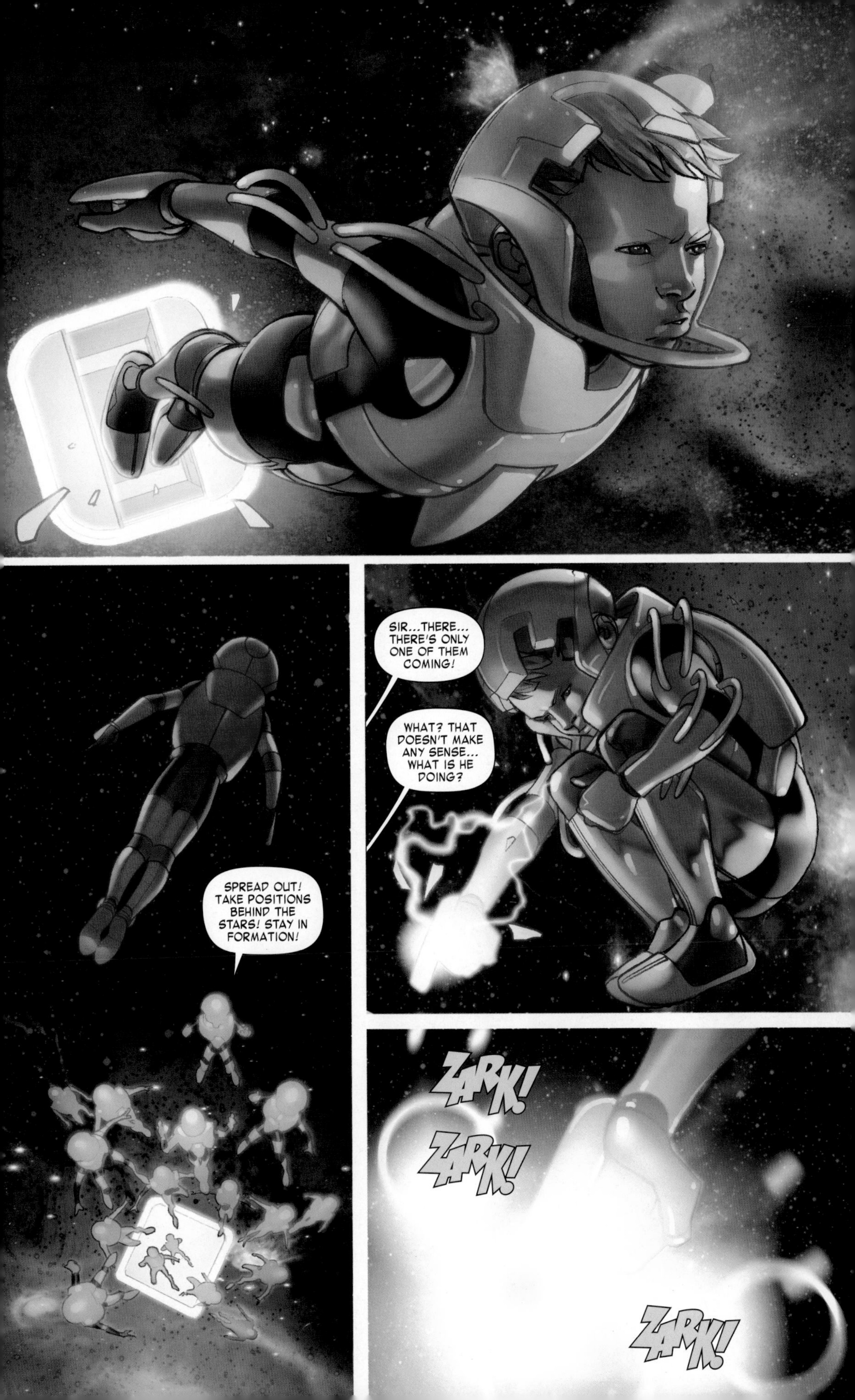
SIR...THERE... THERE'S ONLY ONE OF THEM COMING!
WHAT? THAT DOESN'T MAKE ANY SENSE... WHAT IS HE DOING?
SPREAD OUT! TAKE POSITIONS BEHIND THE STARS! STAY IN FORMATION!
ZARK!
ZARK!
ZARK!

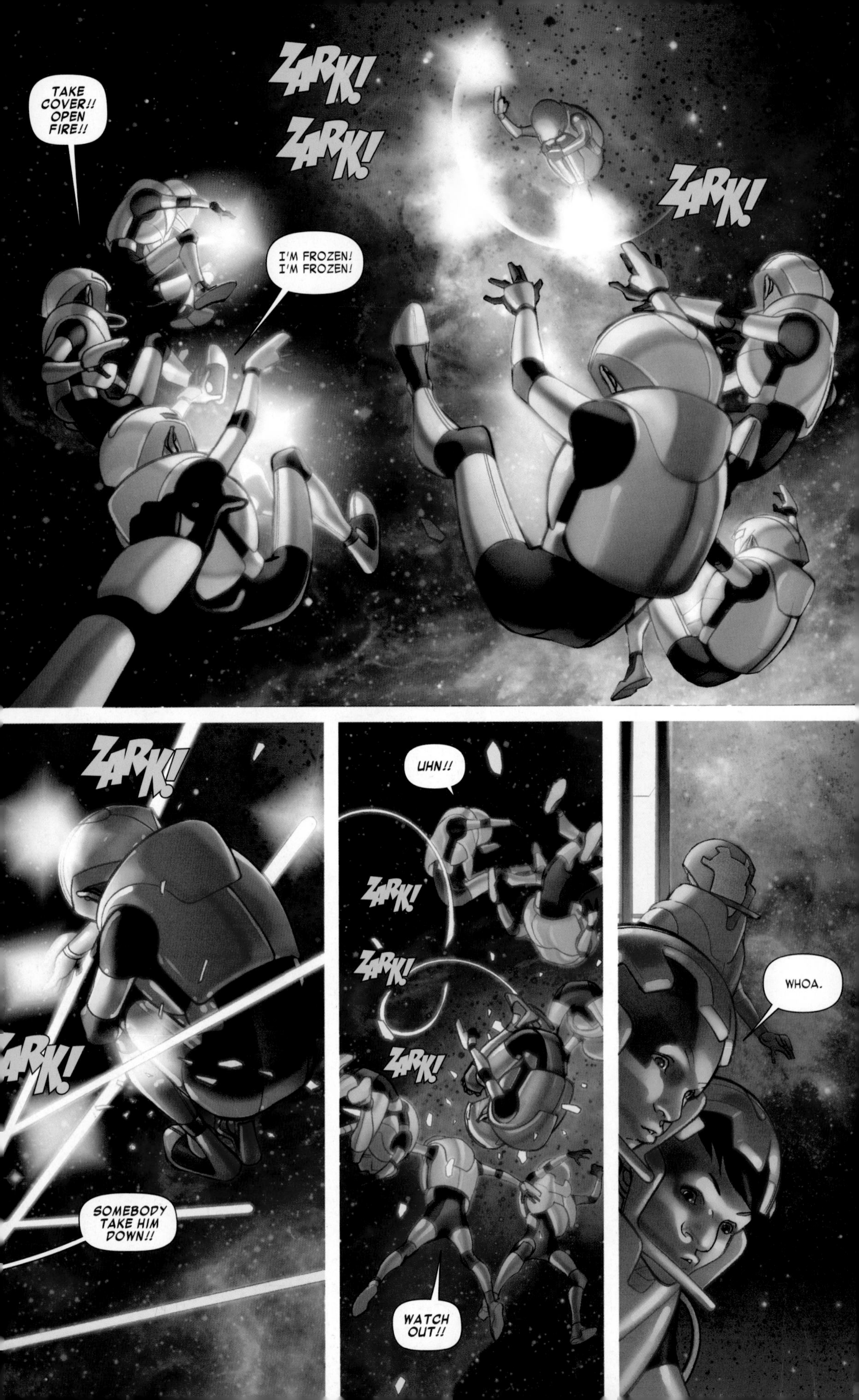
TAKE COVER!! OPEN FIRE!!
ZARK!
ZARK!
I'M FROZEN! I'M FROZEN!
ZARK!
ZARK!
SOMEBODY TAKE HIM DOWN!!
UHN!!
ZARK!
ZARK!
ZARK!
WATCH OUT!!
WHOA.

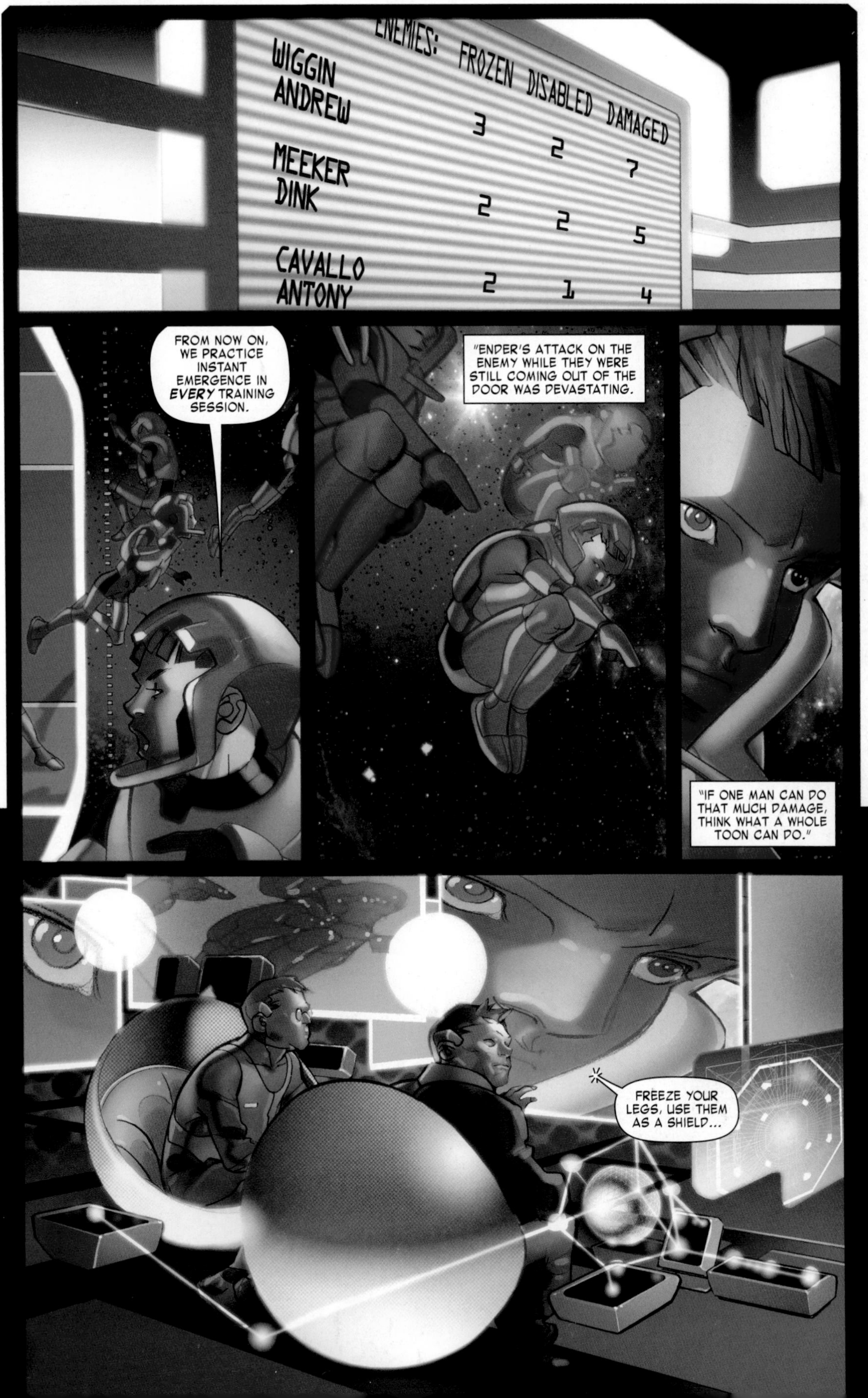
ENEMIES: FROZEN DISABLED DAMAGED
WIGGIN ANDREW 3 2 7
MEEKER DINK 2 2 5
CAVALLO ANTONY 2 1 4
FROM NOW ON, WE PRACTICE INSTANT EMERGENCE IN EVERY TRAINING SESSION.
"ENDER'S ATTACK ON THE ENEMY WHILE THEY WERE STILL COMING OUT OF THE DOOR WAS DEVASTATING.
"IF ONE MAN CAN DO THAT MUCH DAMAGE, THINK WHAT A WHOLE TOON CAN DO."
FREEZE YOUR LEGS, USE THEM AS A SHIELD...

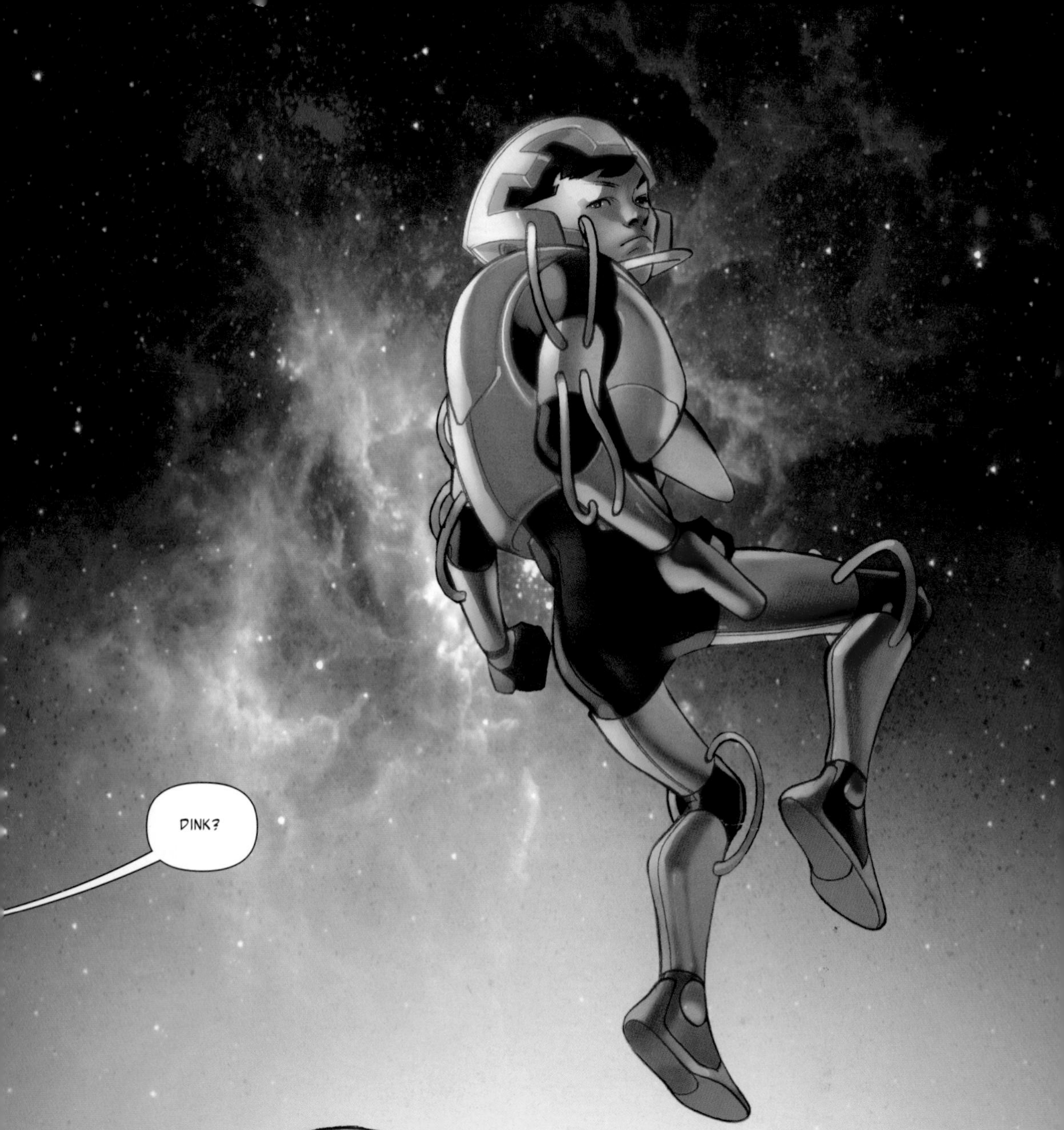
DINK?

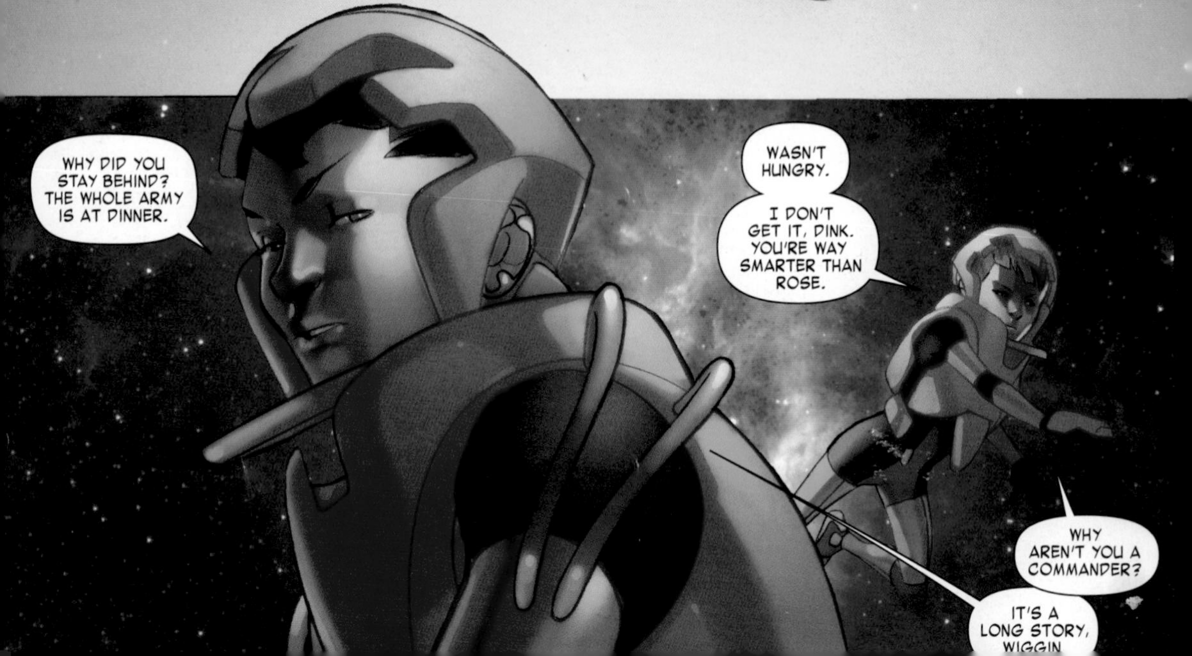
WHY DID YOU STAY BEHIND? THE WHOLE ARMY IS AT DINNER.
WASN'T HUNGRY.
I DON'T GET IT, DINK. YOU'RE WAY SMARTER THAN ROSE.
WHY AREN'T YOU A COMMANDER?
IT'S A LONG STORY,

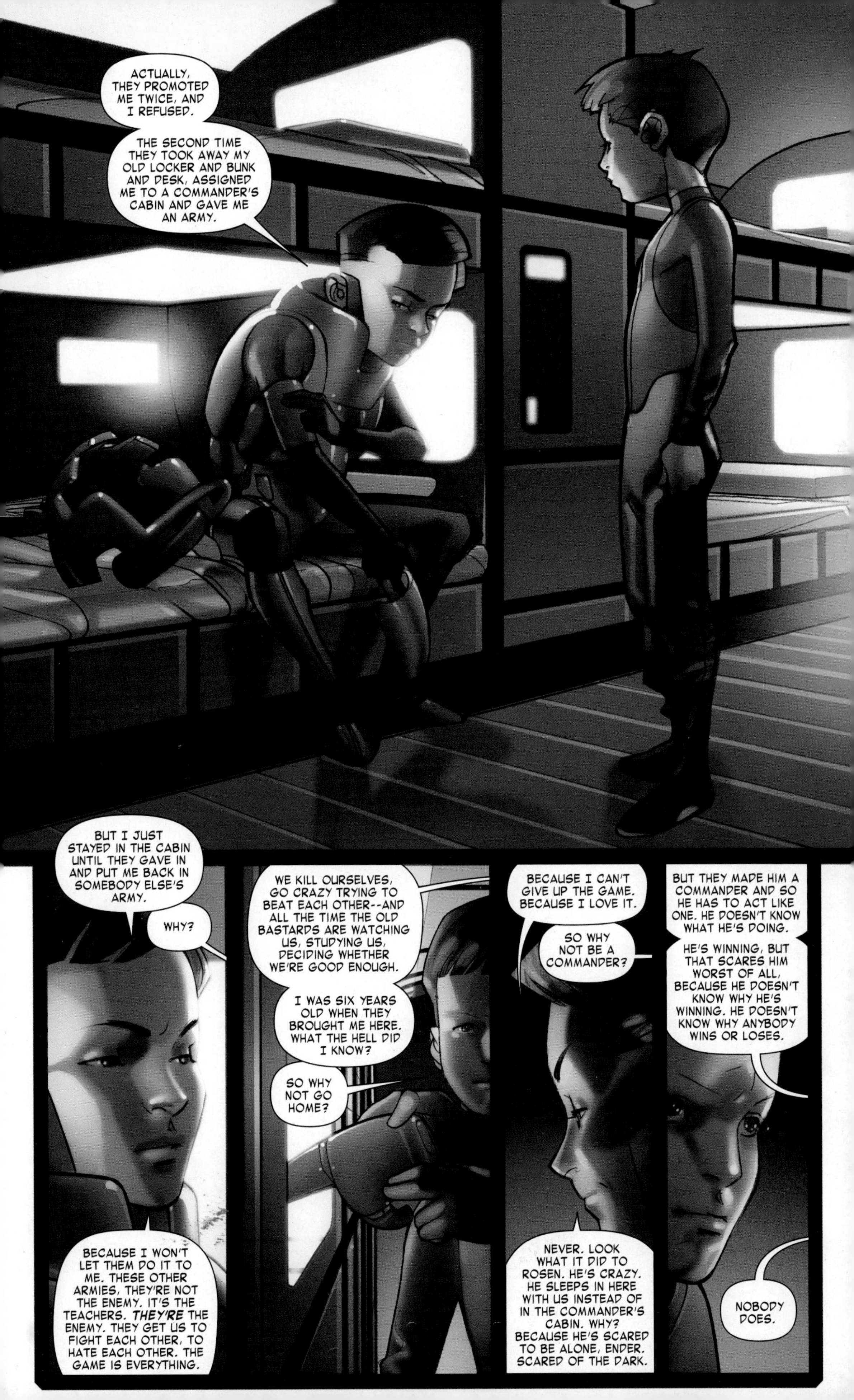
ACTUALLY, THEY PROMOTED ME TWICE, AND I REFUSED.
THE SECOND TIME THEY TOOK AWAY MY OLD LOCKER AND BUNK AND DESK, ASSIGNED ME TO A COMMANDER'S CABIN AND GAVE ME AN ARMY.
BUT I JUST STAYED IN THE CABIN UNTIL THEY GAVE IN AND PUT ME BACK IN SOMEBODY ELSE'S ARMY.
WHY?
BECAUSE I WON'T LET THEM DO IT TO ME. THESE OTHER ARMIES, THEY'RE NOT THE ENEMY. IT'S THE TEACHERS. *THEY'RE* THE ENEMY. THEY GET US TO FIGHT EACH OTHER, TO HATE EACH OTHER. THE GAME IS EVERYTHING.
WE KILL OURSELVES, GO CRAZY TRYING TO BEAT EACH OTHER--AND ALL THE TIME THE OLD BASTARDS ARE WATCHING US, STUDYING US, DECIDING WHETHER WE'RE GOOD ENOUGH.
I WAS SIX YEARS OLD WHEN THEY BROUGHT ME HERE. WHAT THE HELL DID I KNOW?
SO WHY NOT GO HOME?
BECAUSE I CAN'T GIVE UP THE GAME. BECAUSE I LOVE IT.
SO WHY NOT BE A COMMANDER?
NEVER. LOOK WHAT IT DID TO ROSEN. HE'S CRAZY. HE SLEEPS IN HERE WITH US INSTEAD OF IN THE COMMANDER'S CABIN. WHY? BECAUSE HE'S SCARED TO BE ALONE, ENDER. SCARED OF THE DARK.
BUT THEY MADE HIM A COMMANDER AND SO HE HAS TO ACT LIKE ONE. HE DOESN'T KNOW WHAT HE'S DOING.
HE'S WINNING, BUT THAT SCARES HIM WORST OF ALL, BECAUSE HE DOESN'T KNOW WHY HE'S WINNING. HE DOESN'T KNOW WHY ANYBODY WINS OR LOSES.
NOBODY DOES.

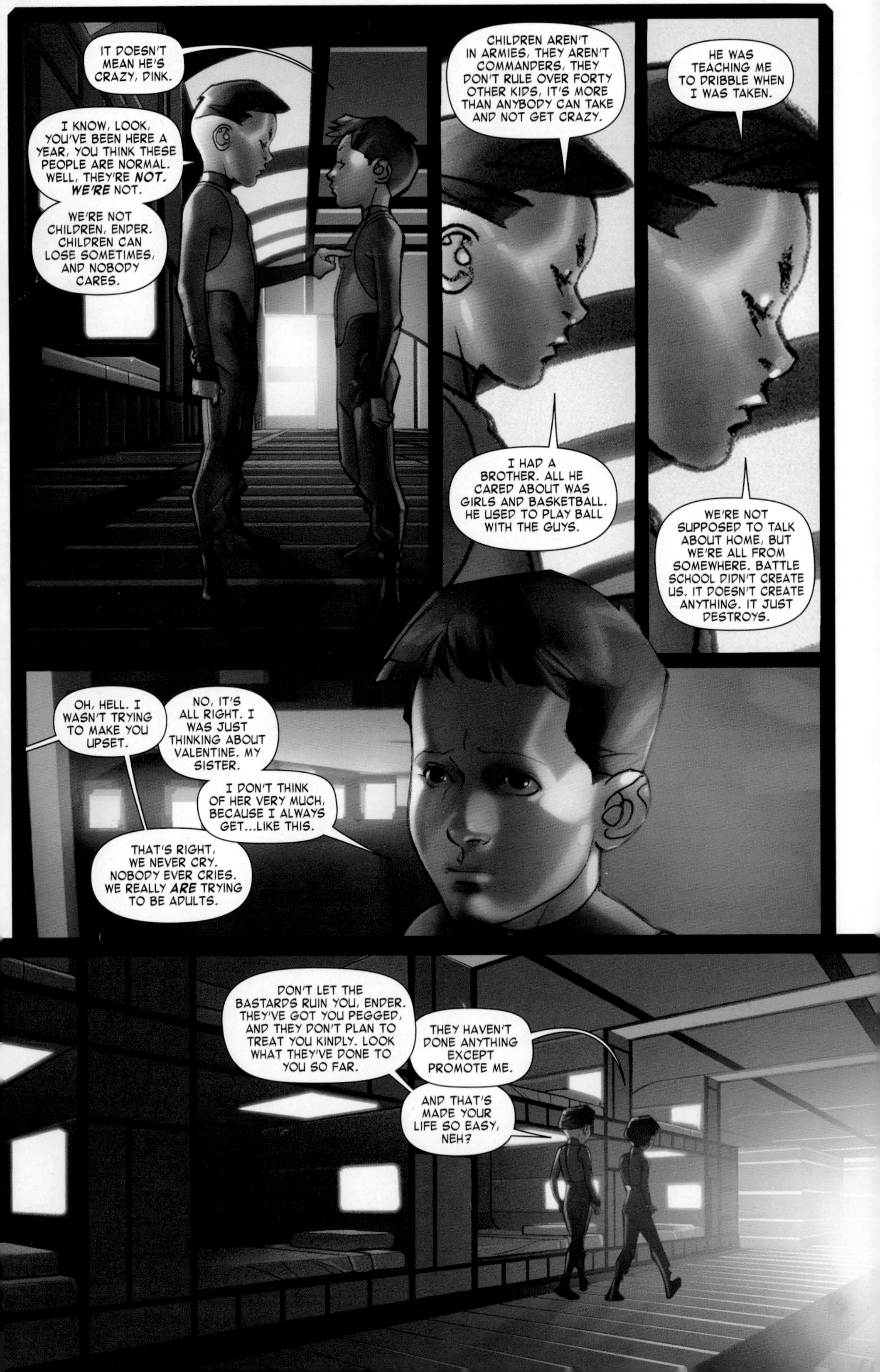
IT DOESN'T MEAN HE'S CRAZY, DINK.
I KNOW, LOOK, YOU'VE BEEN HERE A YEAR, YOU THINK THESE PEOPLE ARE NORMAL. WELL, THEY'RE *NOT.* *WE'RE* NOT.
WE'RE NOT CHILDREN, ENDER. CHILDREN CAN LOSE SOMETIMES, AND NOBODY CARES.
CHILDREN AREN'T IN ARMIES, THEY AREN'T COMMANDERS, THEY DON'T RULE OVER FORTY OTHER KIDS, IT'S MORE THAN ANYBODY CAN TAKE AND NOT GET CRAZY.
I HAD A BROTHER. ALL HE CARED ABOUT WAS GIRLS AND BASKETBALL. HE USED TO PLAY BALL WITH THE GUYS.
HE WAS TEACHING ME TO DRIBBLE WHEN I WAS TAKEN.
WE'RE NOT SUPPOSED TO TALK ABOUT HOME, BUT WE'RE ALL FROM SOMEWHERE. BATTLE SCHOOL DIDN'T CREATE US. IT DOESN'T CREATE ANYTHING. IT JUST DESTROYS.
OH, HELL. I WASN'T TRYING TO MAKE YOU UPSET.
NO, IT'S ALL RIGHT. I WAS JUST THINKING ABOUT VALENTINE. MY SISTER.
I DON'T THINK OF HER VERY MUCH, BECAUSE I ALWAYS GET...LIKE THIS.
THAT'S RIGHT, WE NEVER CRY. NOBODY EVER CRIES. WE REALLY *ARE* TRYING TO BE ADULTS.
DON'T LET THE BASTARDS RUIN YOU, ENDER. THEY'VE GOT YOU PEGGED, AND THEY DON'T PLAN TO TREAT YOU KINDLY. LOOK WHAT THEY'VE DONE TO YOU SO FAR.
THEY HAVEN'T DONE ANYTHING EXCEPT PROMOTE ME.
AND THAT'S MADE YOUR LIFE SO EASY, NEH?

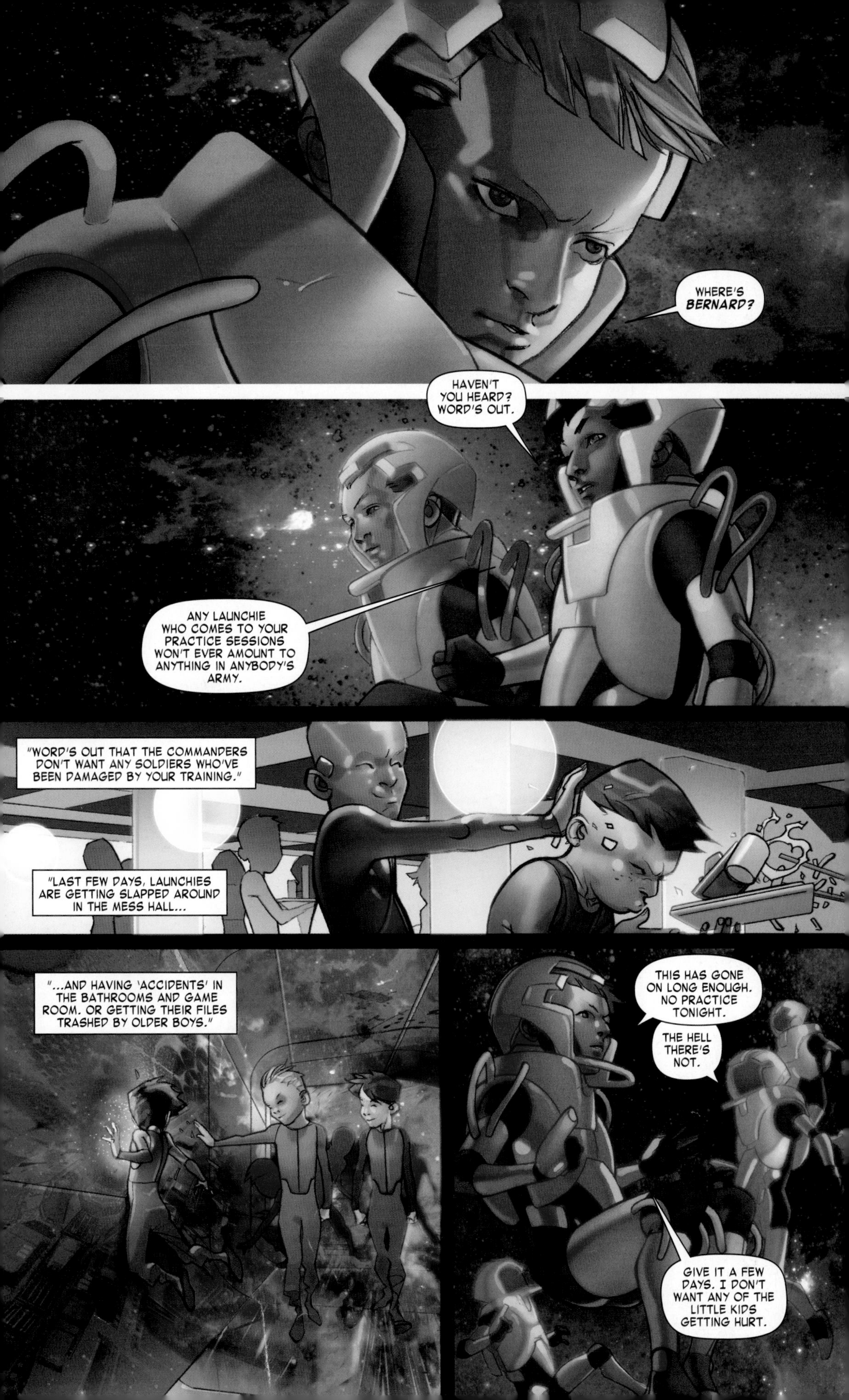
WHERE'S BERNARD?
HAVEN'T YOU HEARD? WORD'S OUT.
ANY LAUNCHIE WHO COMES TO YOUR PRACTICE SESSIONS WON'T EVER AMOUNT TO ANYTHING IN ANYBODY'S ARMY.
"WORD'S OUT THAT THE COMMANDERS DON'T WANT ANY SOLDIERS WHO'VE BEEN DAMAGED BY YOUR TRAINING."
"LAST FEW DAYS, LAUNCHIES ARE GETTING SLAPPED AROUND IN THE MESS HALL...
"...AND HAVING 'ACCIDENTS' IN THE BATHROOMS AND GAME ROOM. OR GETTING THEIR FILES TRASHED BY OLDER BOYS."
THIS HAS GONE ON LONG ENOUGH. NO PRACTICE TONIGHT.
THE HELL THERE'S NOT.
GIVE IT A FEW DAYS. I DON'T WANT ANY OF THE LITTLE KIDS GETTING HURT.

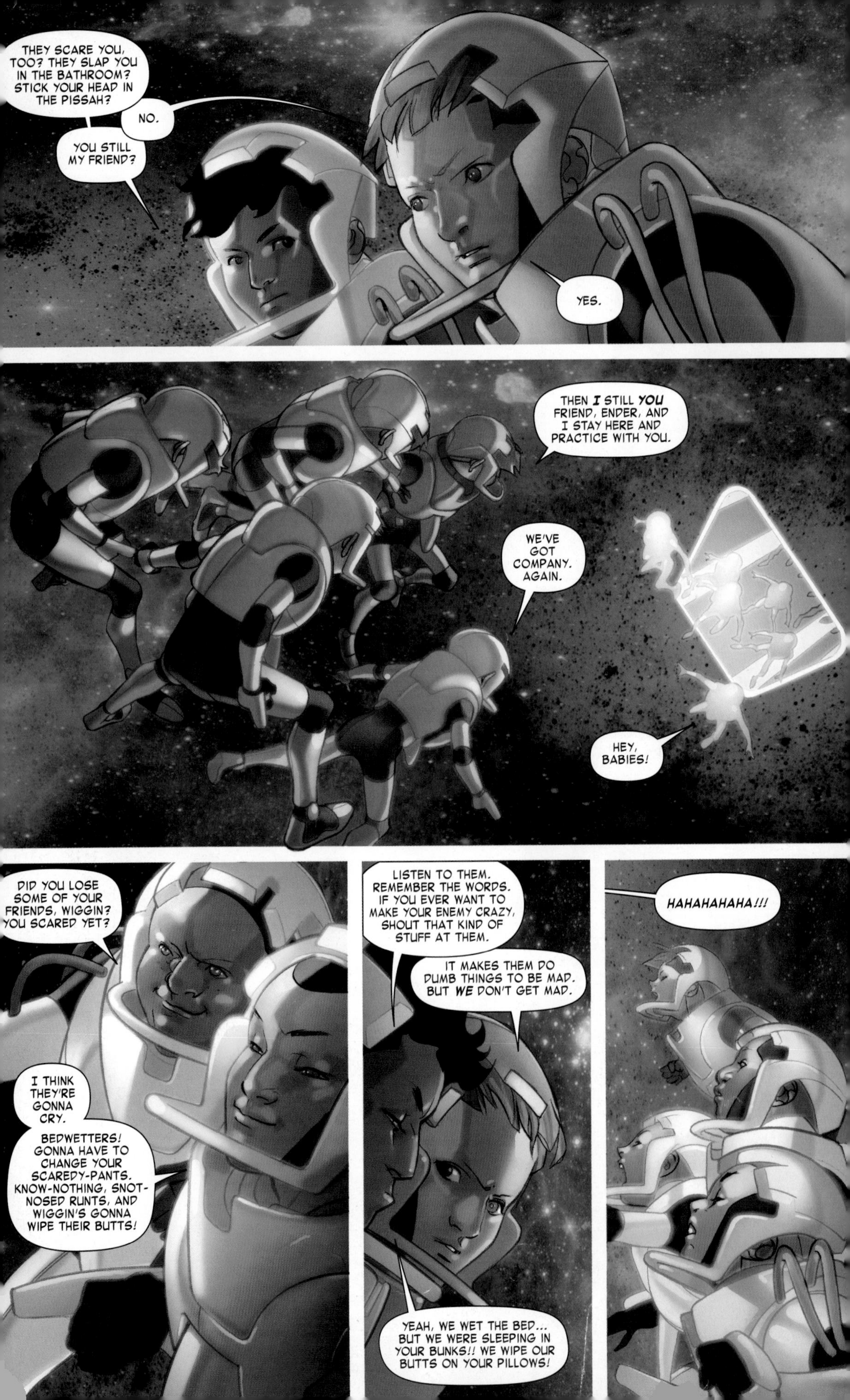
THEY SCARE YOU, TOO? THEY SLAP YOU IN THE BATHROOM? STICK YOUR HEAD IN THE PISSAH?
NO.
YOU STILL MY FRIEND?
YES.
THEN *I* STILL *YOU* FRIEND, ENDER, AND I STAY HERE AND PRACTICE WITH YOU.
WE'VE GOT COMPANY. AGAIN.
HEY, BABIES!
DID YOU LOSE SOME OF YOUR FRIENDS, WIGGIN? YOU SCARED YET?
I THINK THEY'RE GONNA CRY.
BEDWETTERS! GONNA HAVE TO CHANGE YOUR SCAREDY-PANTS. KNOW-NOTHING, SNOT-NOSED RUNTS, AND WIGGIN'S GONNA WIPE THEIR BUTTS!
LISTEN TO THEM. REMEMBER THE WORDS. IF YOU EVER WANT TO MAKE YOUR ENEMY CRAZY, SHOUT THAT KIND OF STUFF AT THEM.
IT MAKES THEM DO DUMB THINGS TO BE MAD. BUT *WE* DON'T GET MAD.
YEAH, WE WET THE BED... BUT WE WERE SLEEPING IN YOUR BUNKS!! WE WIPE OUR BUTTS ON YOUR PILLOWS!
HAHAHAHAHA!!!

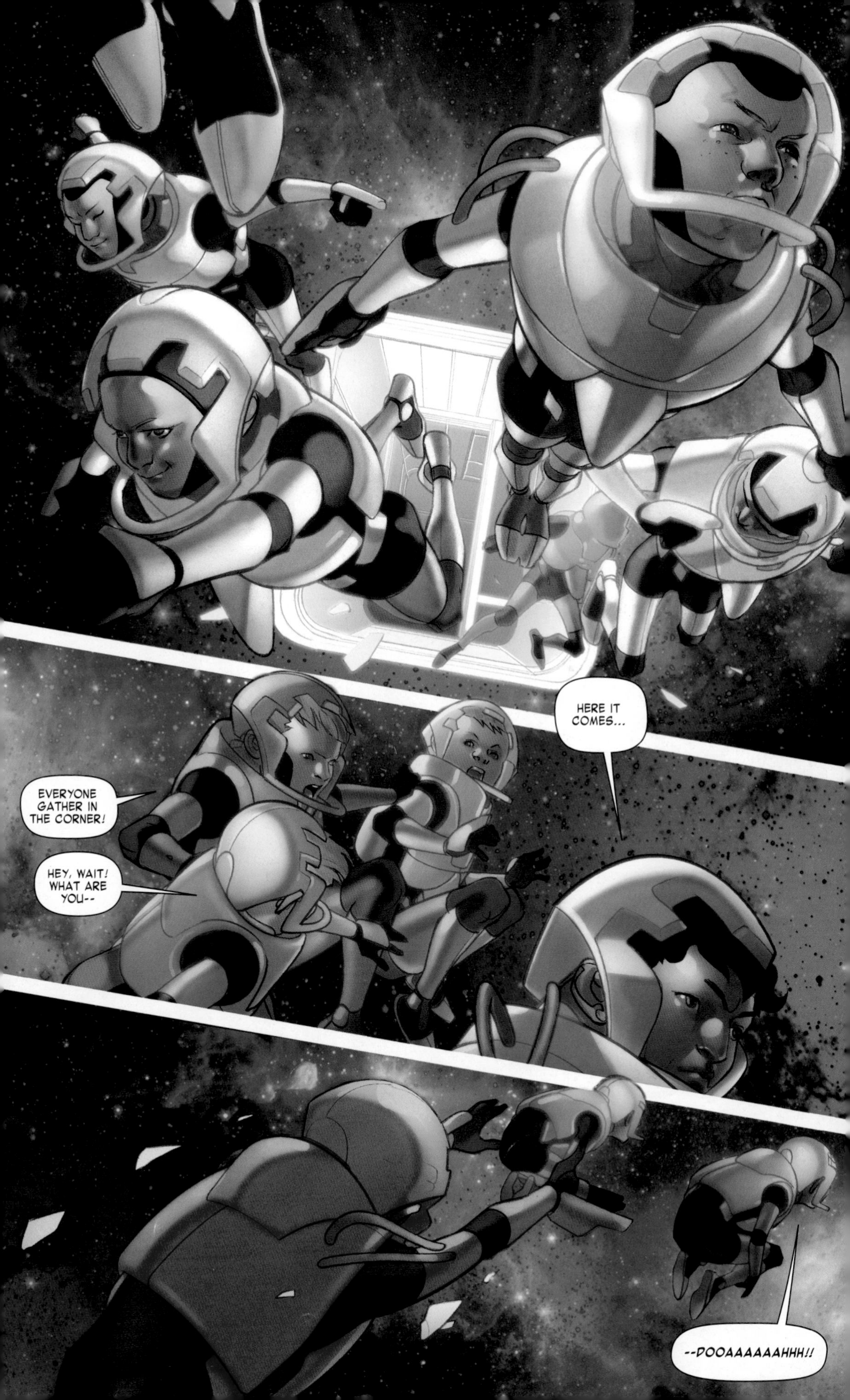
EVERYONE GATHER IN THE CORNER!
HEY, WAIT! WHAT ARE YOU--
HERE IT COMES...
--DOOAAAAAAHHH!!

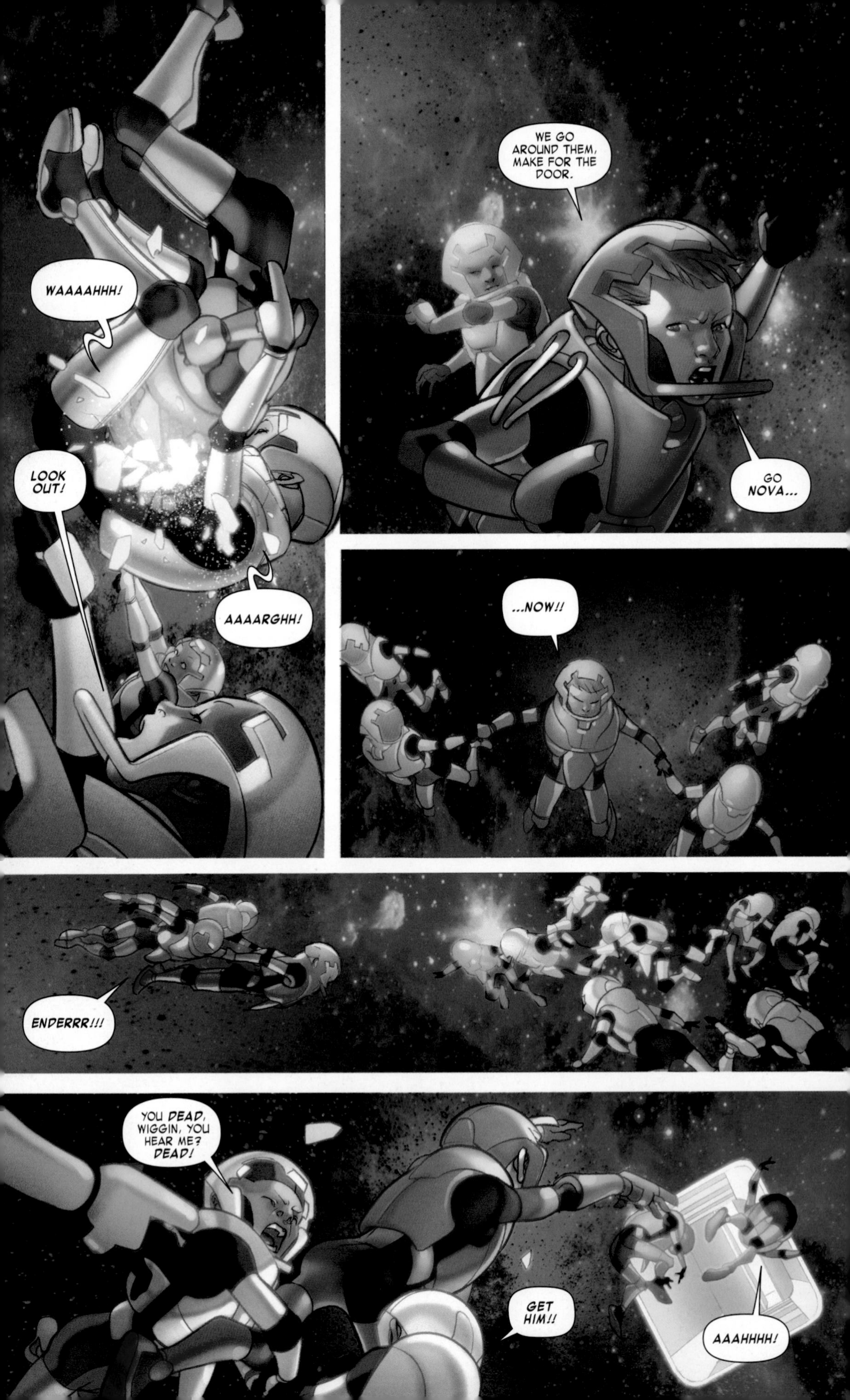
WAAAAHHH!
LOOK OUT!
AAAARGHH!
WE GO AROUND THEM, MAKE FOR THE DOOR.
GO NOVA...
...NOW!!
ENDERRR!!!
YOU DEAD, WIGGIN, YOU HEAR ME? DEAD!
GET HIM!!
AAAHHHH!

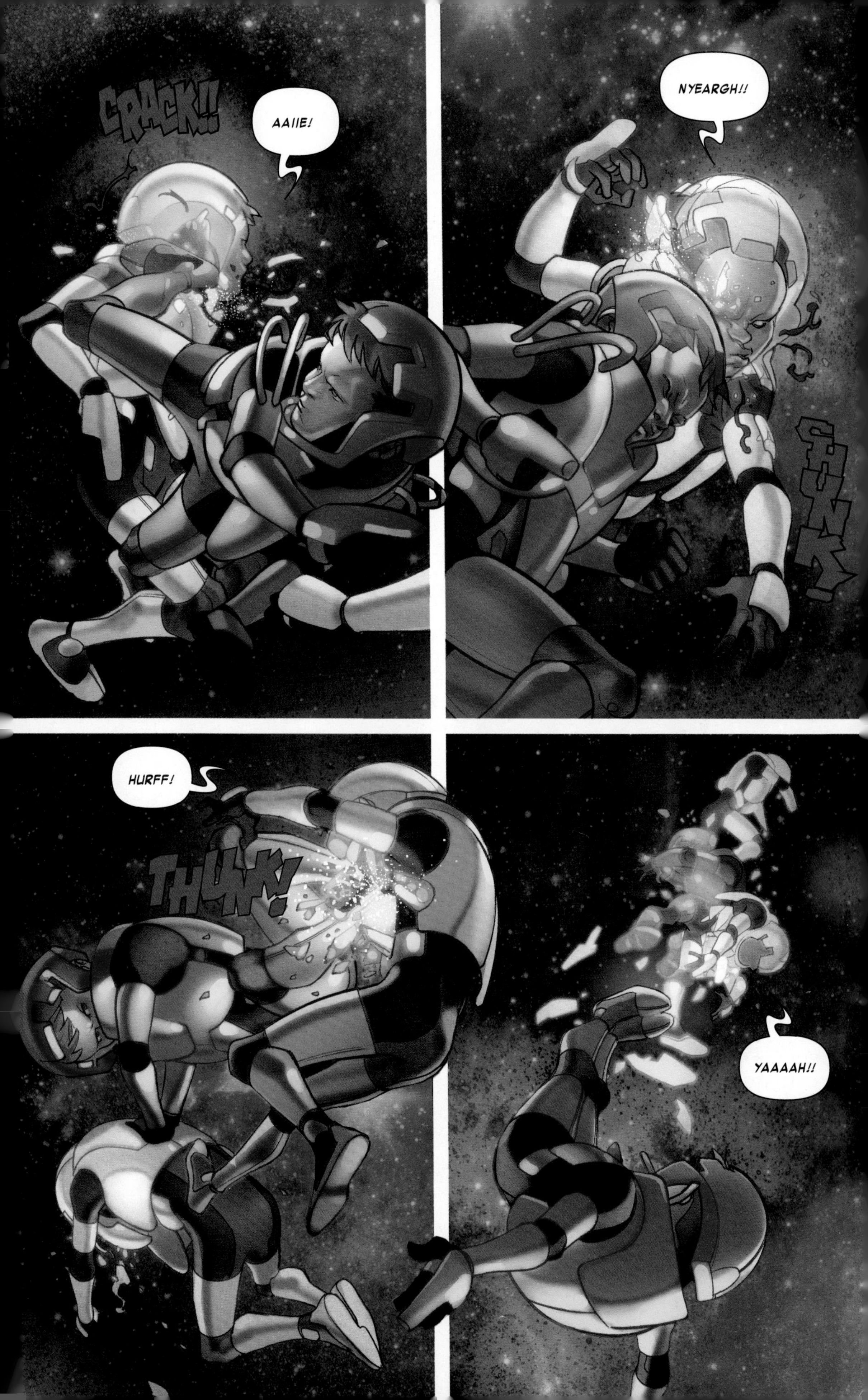
CRACK!!
AAIIE!
NYEARGH!!
CHUNK!
HURFF!
THUNK!
YAAAAH!!

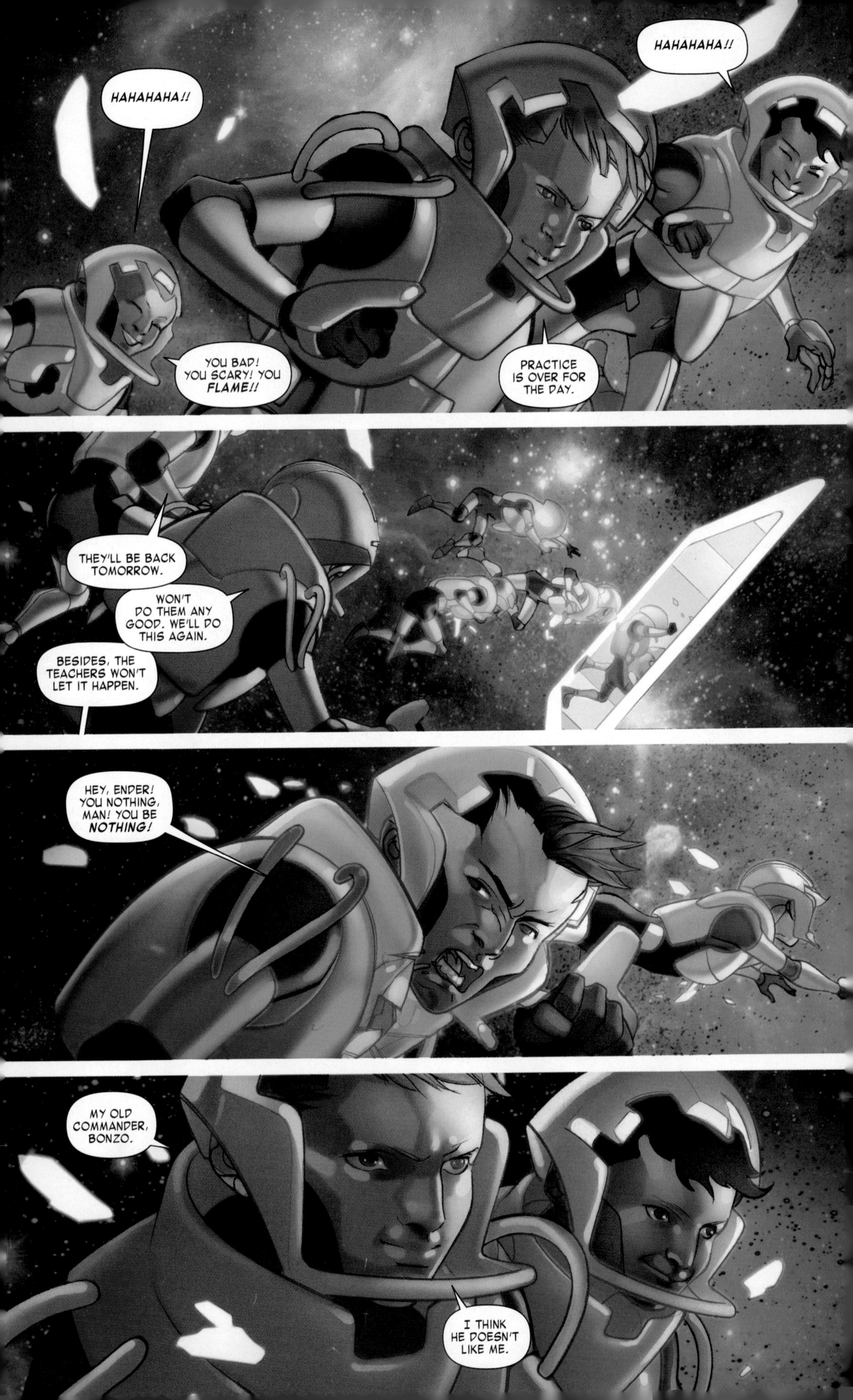
HAHAHAHA!!
HAHAHAHA!!
YOU BAD! YOU SCARY! YOU FLAME!!
PRACTICE IS OVER FOR THE DAY.
THEY'LL BE BACK TOMORROW.
WON'T DO THEM ANY GOOD. WE'LL DO THIS AGAIN.
BESIDES, THE TEACHERS WON'T LET IT HAPPEN.
HEY, ENDER! YOU NOTHING, MAN! YOU BE NOTHING!
MY OLD COMMANDER, BONZO.
I THINK HE DOESN'T LIKE ME.

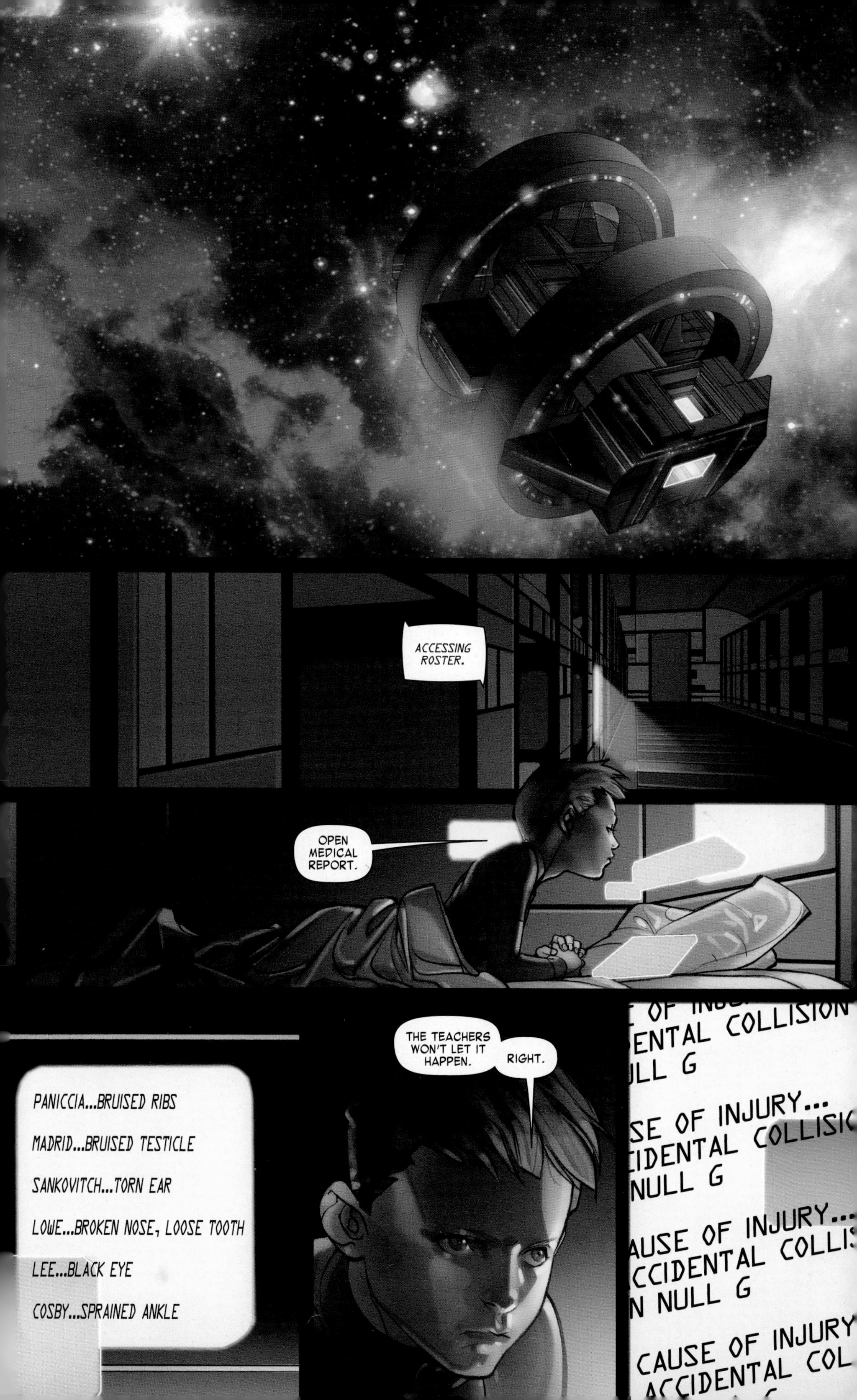
ACCESSING ROSTER.
OPEN MEDICAL REPORT.
PANICCIA...BRUISED RIBS
MADRID...BRUISED TESTICLE
SANKOVITCH...TORN EAR
LOWE...BROKEN NOSE, LOOSE TOOTH
LEE...BLACK EYE
COSBY...SPRAINED ANKLE
THE TEACHERS WON'T LET IT HAPPEN.
RIGHT.
ENTAL COLLISION
ULL G
SE OF INJURY...
CIDENTAL COLLISI
NULL G
CAUSE OF INJURY...
CCIDENTAL COLLI
N NULL G
CAUSE OF INJURY
ACCIDENTAL COL

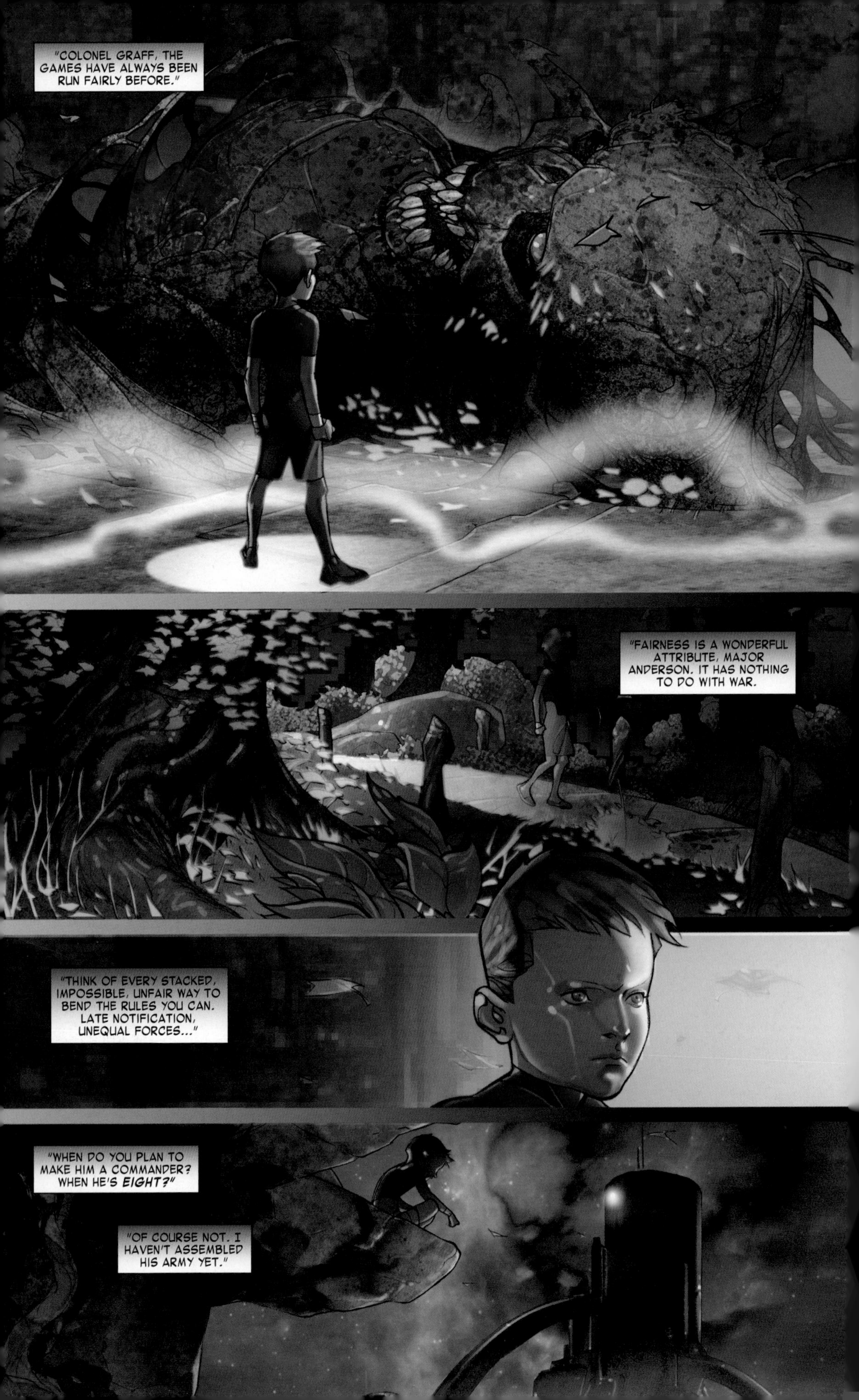
"COLONEL GRAFF, THE GAMES HAVE ALWAYS BEEN RUN FAIRLY BEFORE."
"FAIRNESS IS A WONDERFUL ATTRIBUTE, MAJOR ANDERSON. IT HAS NOTHING TO DO WITH WAR.
"THINK OF EVERY STACKED, IMPOSSIBLE, UNFAIR WAY TO BEND THE RULES YOU CAN. LATE NOTIFICATION, UNEQUAL FORCES..."
"WHEN DO YOU PLAN TO MAKE HIM A COMMANDER? WHEN HE'S *EIGHT?*"
"OF COURSE NOT. I HAVEN'T ASSEMBLED HIS ARMY YET."

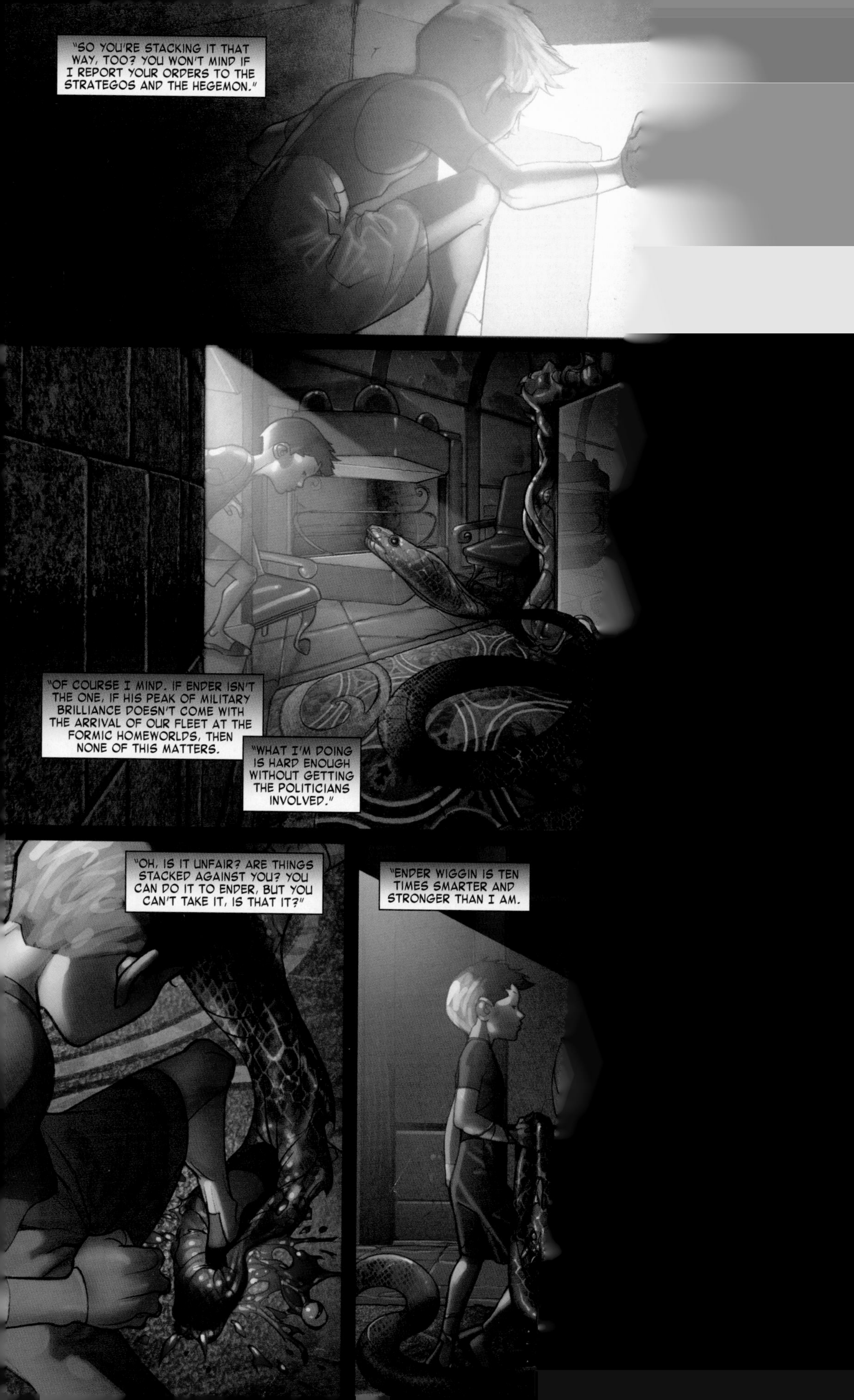
"SO YOU'RE STACKING IT THAT WAY, TOO? YOU WON'T MIND IF I REPORT YOUR ORDERS TO THE STRATEGOS AND THE HEGEMON."
"OF COURSE I MIND. IF ENDER ISN'T THE ONE, IF HIS PEAK OF MILITARY BRILLIANCE DOESN'T COME WITH THE ARRIVAL OF OUR FLEET AT THE FORMIC HOMEWORLDS, THEN NONE OF THIS MATTERS.
"WHAT I'M DOING IS HARD ENOUGH WITHOUT GETTING THE POLITICIANS INVOLVED."
"OH, IS IT UNFAIR? ARE THINGS STACKED AGAINST YOU? YOU CAN DO IT TO ENDER, BUT YOU CAN'T TAKE IT, IS THAT IT?"
"ENDER WIGGIN IS TEN TIMES SMARTER AND STRONGER THAN I AM.

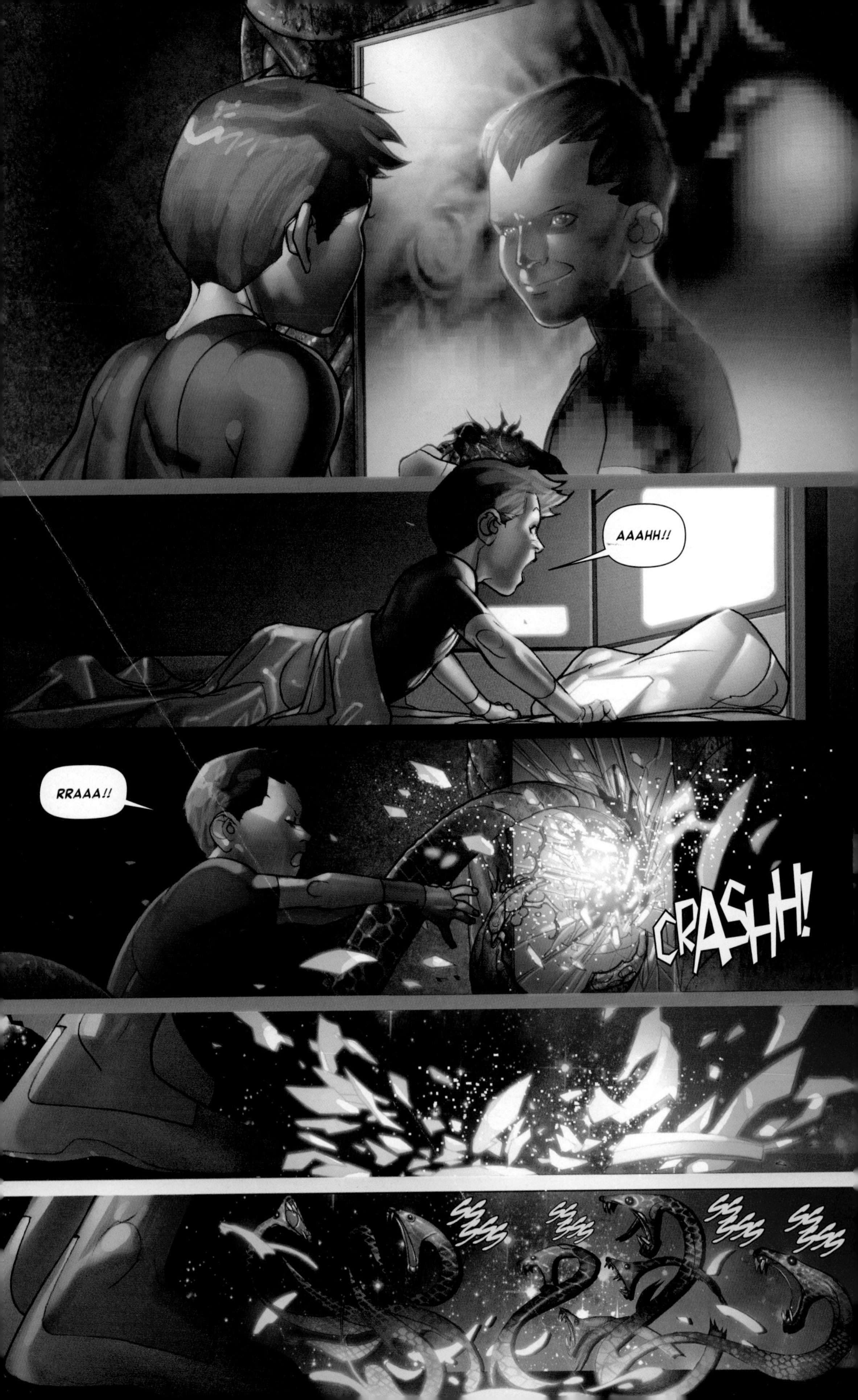
AAAHH!!
RRAAA!!
CRASHH!
SSSS

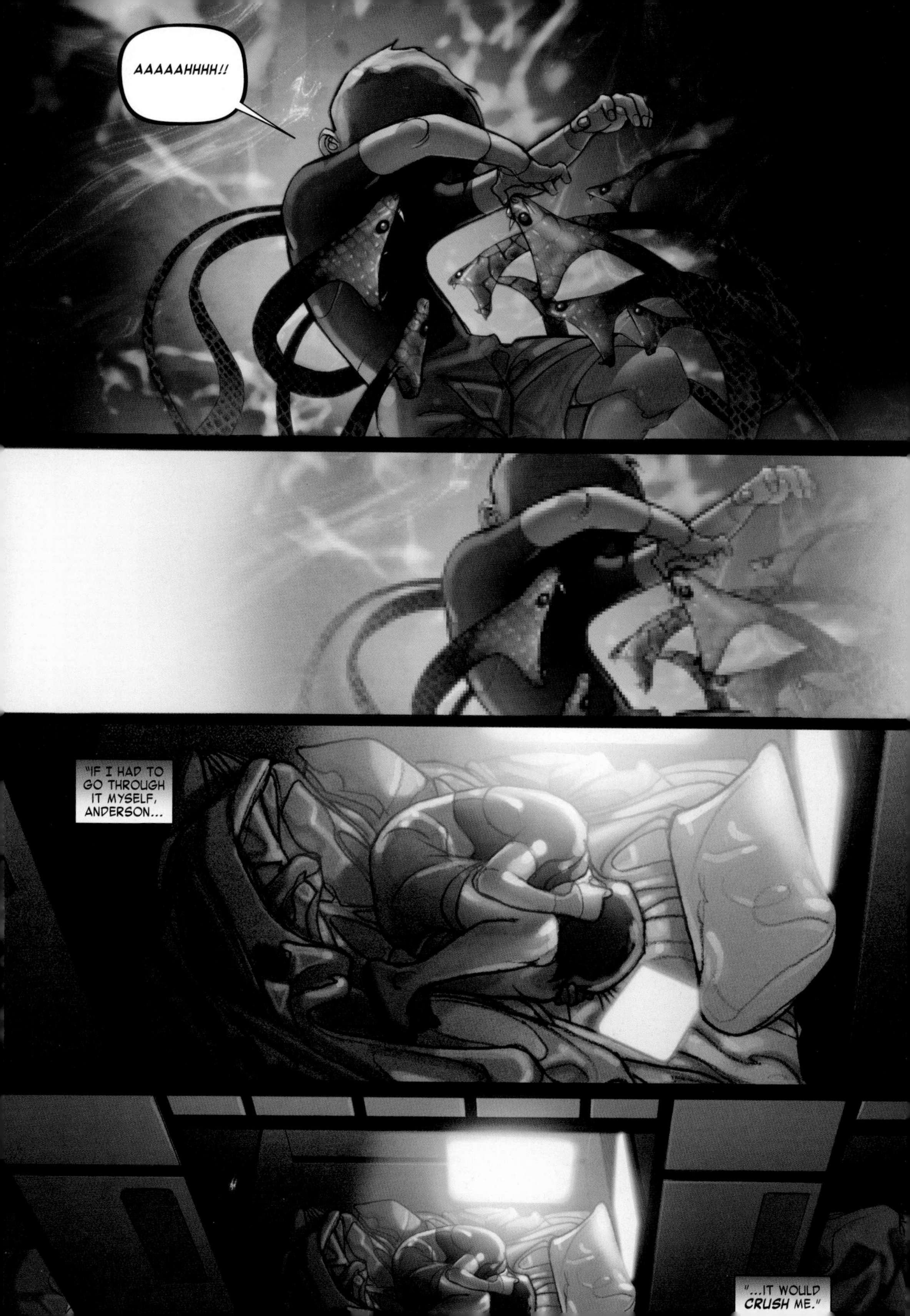
AAAAAHHHH!!
"IF I HAD TO GO THROUGH IT MYSELF, ANDERSON...
"...IT WOULD CRUSH ME."

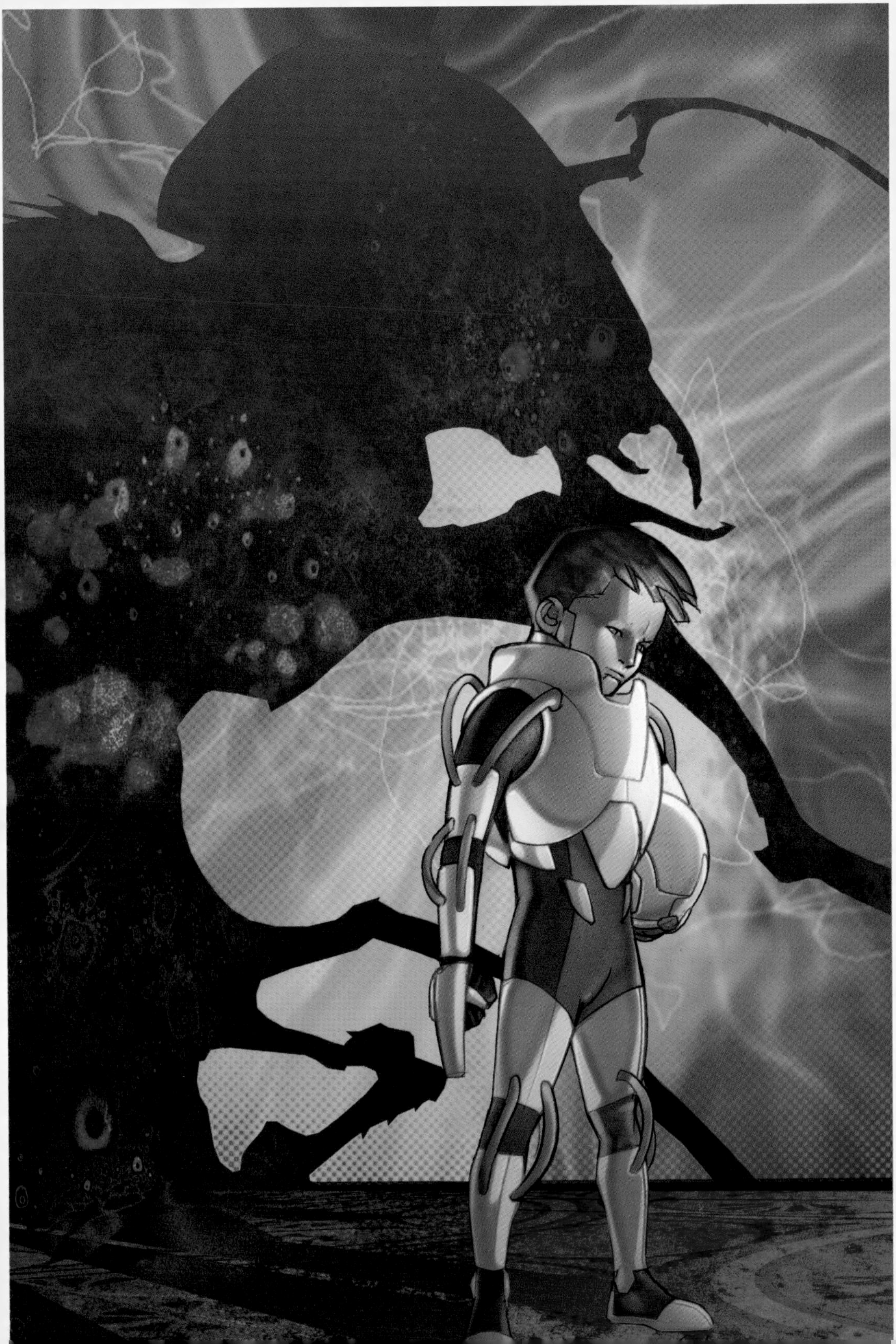

BATTLE SCHOOL VIDEO LOG 9509502

EMERGENCY MEETING/RE: MIND GAME (REF: WIGGIN, ANDREW
SESSION 5902) PARTICIPANTS: GRAFF, IMBU

GRAFF: How in hell did the computer do that?

IMBU: I don't know.

G: How could it pick up a picture of Ender's brother and put in into the
graphics in this Fairyland routine?

I: Fairyland was programmed in, but we don't have any experience
with the End of the World.

G: I don't like having the computer screw around with Ender's mind
that way. Peter Wiggin is the most potent person in his life, except
maybe his sister Valentine.

I: The mind game was designed to help shape the students, to help
them find worlds they can be comfortable in.

G: You don't get it, do you Major Imbu? I don't WANT Ender being
comfortable with the end of the world.

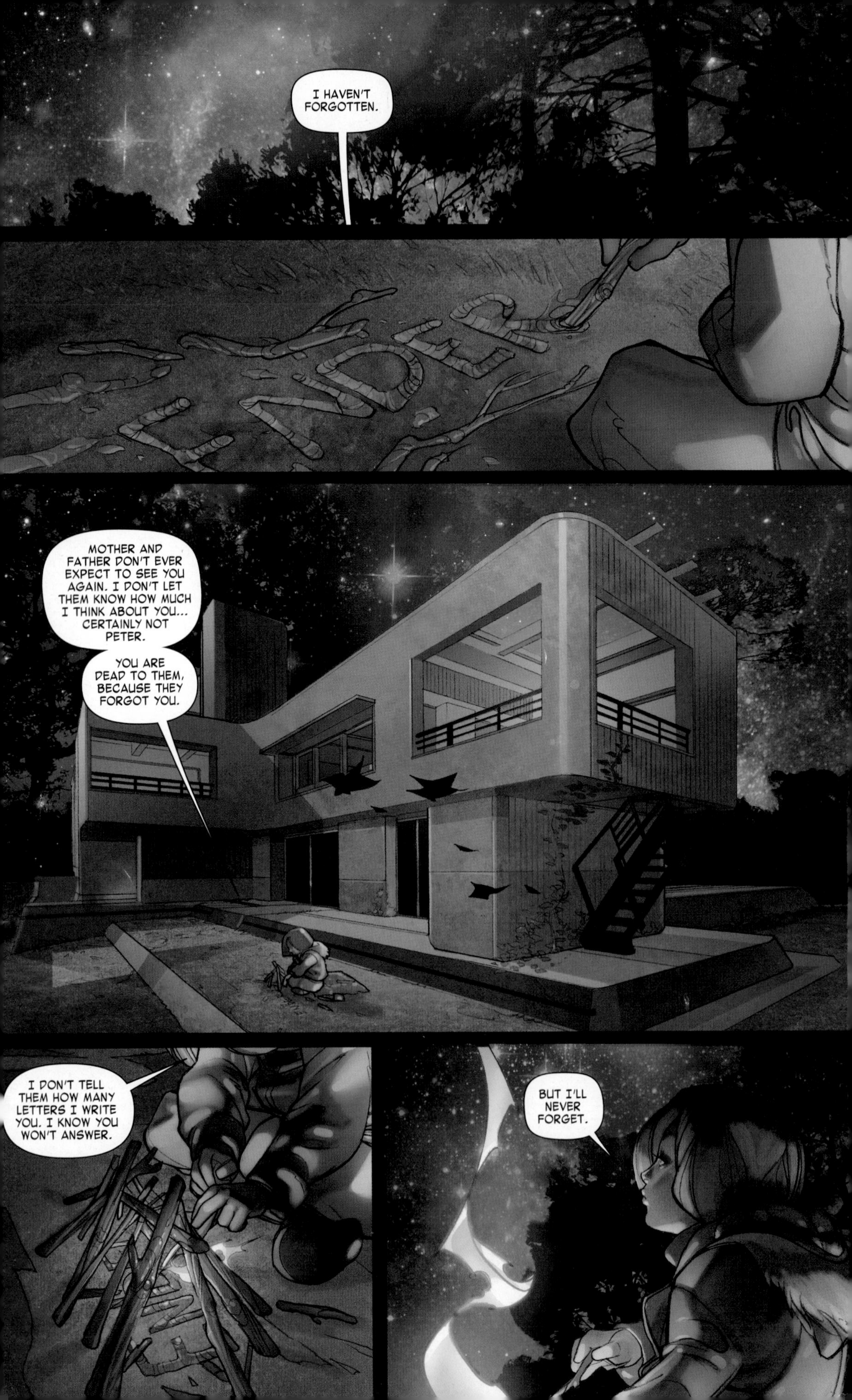
I HAVEN'T FORGOTTEN.
MOTHER AND FATHER DON'T EVER EXPECT TO SEE YOU AGAIN. I DON'T LET THEM KNOW HOW MUCH I THINK ABOUT YOU... CERTAINLY NOT PETER.
YOU ARE DEAD TO THEM, BECAUSE THEY FORGOT YOU.
I DON'T TELL THEM HOW MANY LETTERS I WRITE YOU. I KNOW YOU WON'T ANSWER.
BUT I'LL NEVER FORGET.

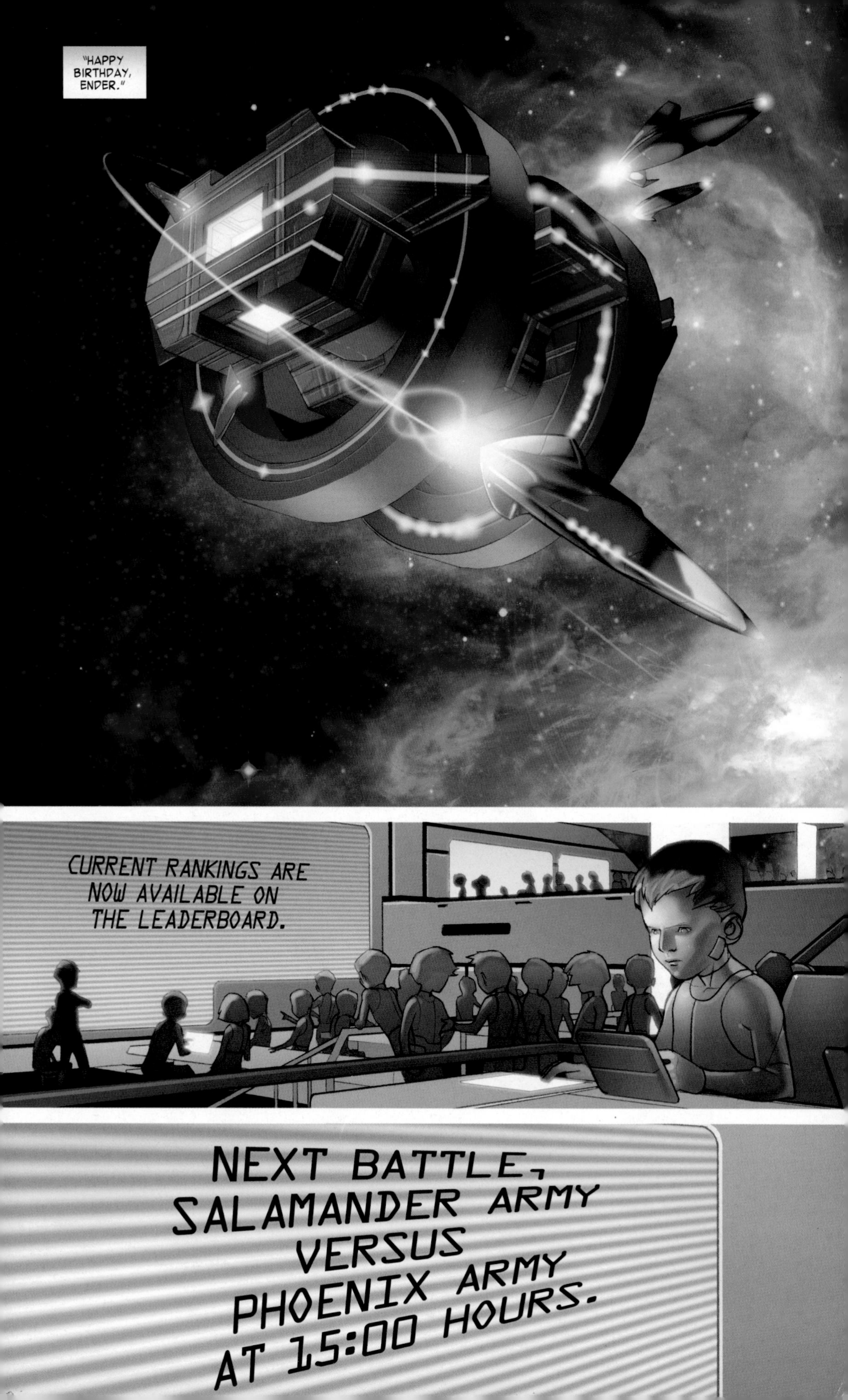
"HAPPY BIRTHDAY, ENDER."
CURRENT RANKINGS ARE NOW AVAILABLE ON THE LEADERBOARD.
NEXT BATTLE, SALAMANDER ARMY VERSUS PHOENIX ARMY AT 15:00 HOURS.

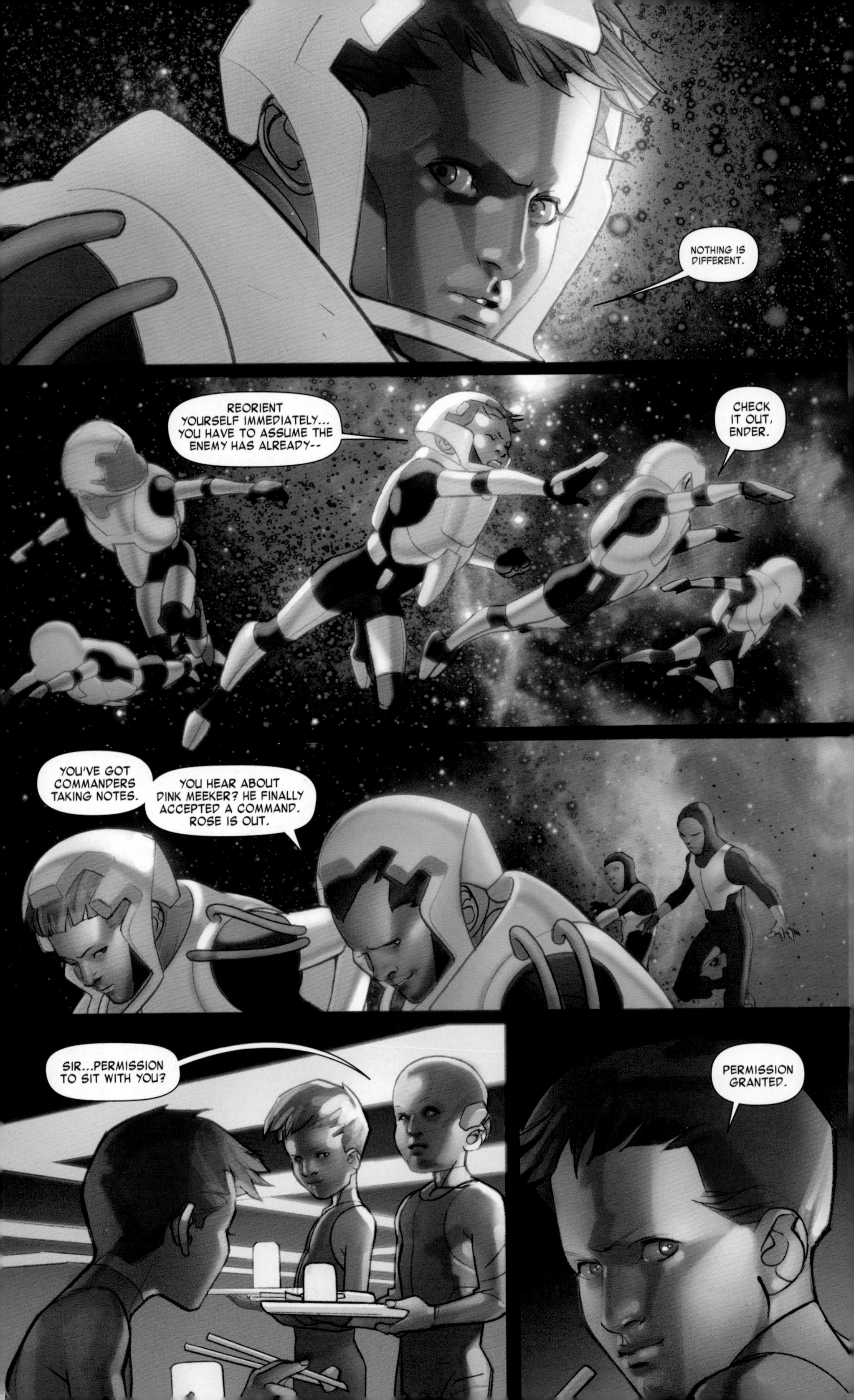
NOTHING IS DIFFERENT.
REORIENT YOURSELF IMMEDIATELY... YOU HAVE TO ASSUME THE ENEMY HAS ALREADY--
CHECK IT OUT, ENDER.
YOU'VE GOT COMMANDERS TAKING NOTES.
YOU HEAR ABOUT DINK MEEKER? HE FINALLY ACCEPTED A COMMAND. ROSE IS OUT.
SIR...PERMISSION TO SIT WITH YOU?
PERMISSION GRANTED.

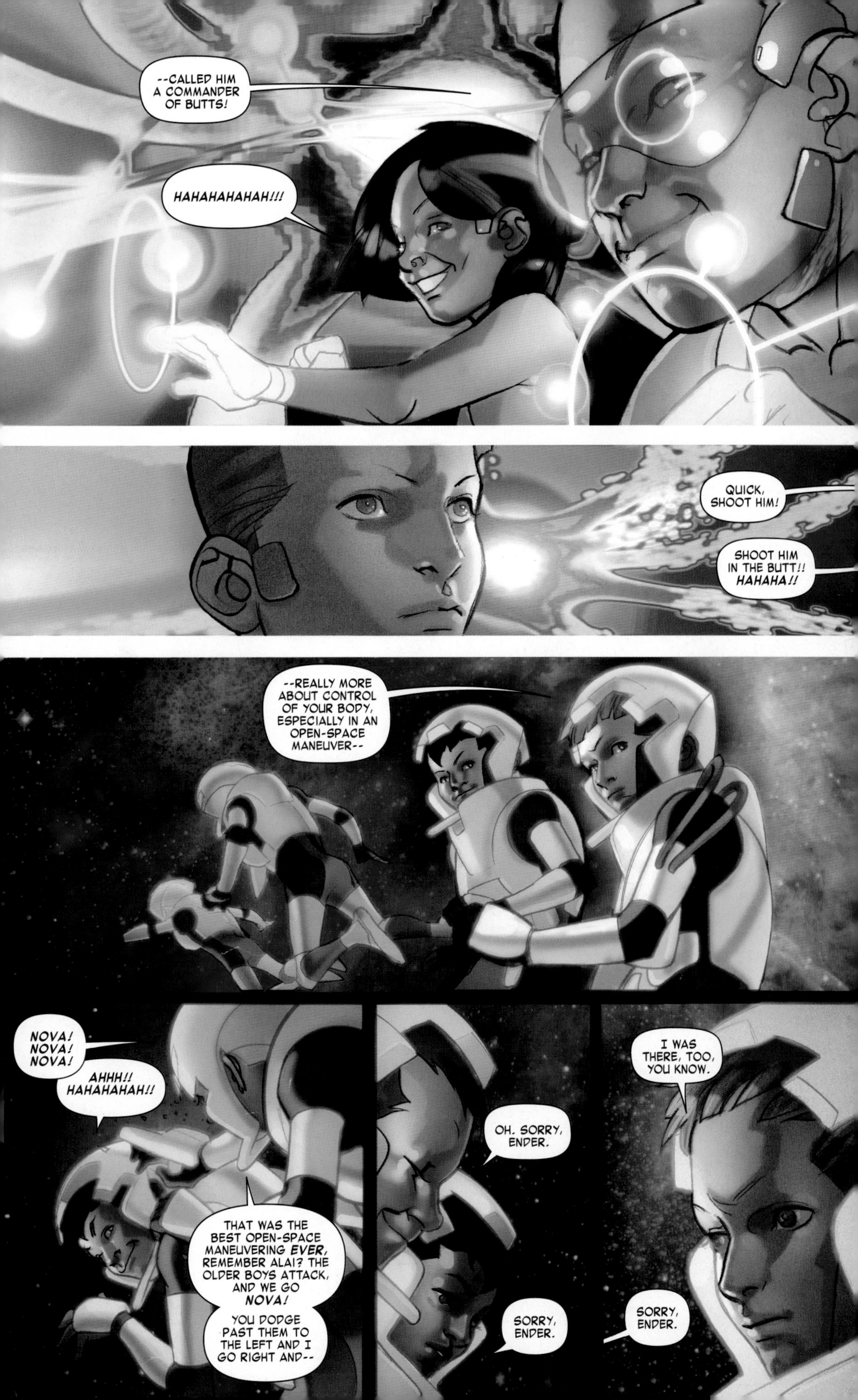
--CALLED HIM A COMMANDER OF BUTTS!
HAHAHAHAHAH!!!
QUICK, SHOOT HIM!
SHOOT HIM IN THE BUTT!! HAHAHA!!
--REALLY MORE ABOUT CONTROL OF YOUR BODY, ESPECIALLY IN AN OPEN-SPACE MANEUVER--
NOVA! NOVA! NOVA!
AHHH!! HAHAHAHAH!!
THAT WAS THE BEST OPEN-SPACE MANEUVERING EVER, REMEMBER ALAI? THE OLDER BOYS ATTACK, AND WE GO NOVA!
YOU DODGE PAST THEM TO THE LEFT AND I GO RIGHT AND--
OH. SORRY, ENDER.
SORRY, ENDER.
I WAS THERE, TOO, YOU KNOW.
SORRY, ENDER.

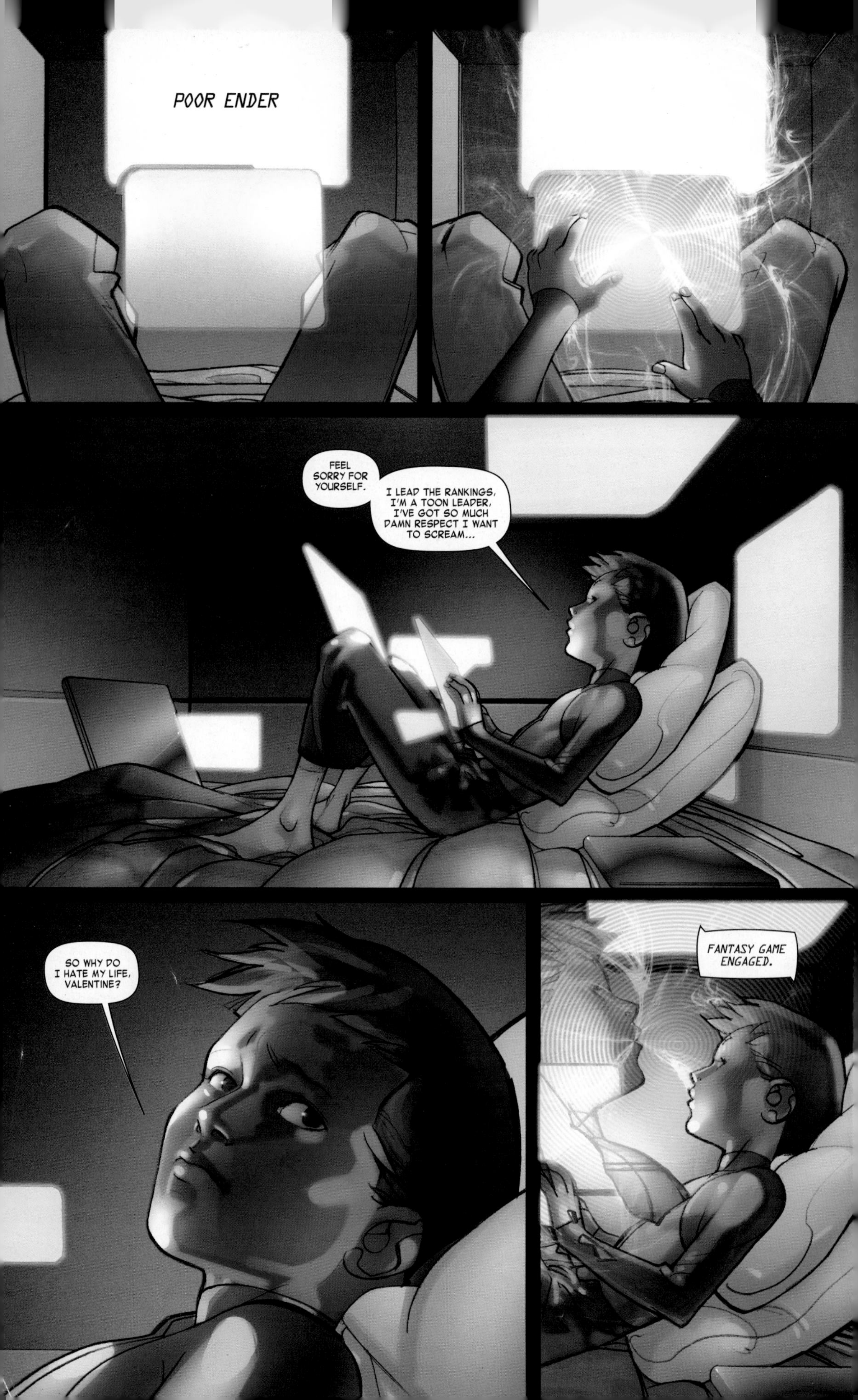
POOR ENDER
FEEL SORRY FOR YOURSELF.
I LEAD THE RANKINGS, I'M A TOON LEADER, I'VE GOT SO MUCH DAMN RESPECT I WANT TO SCREAM...
SO WHY DO I HATE MY LIFE, VALENTINE?
FANTASY GAME ENGAGED.

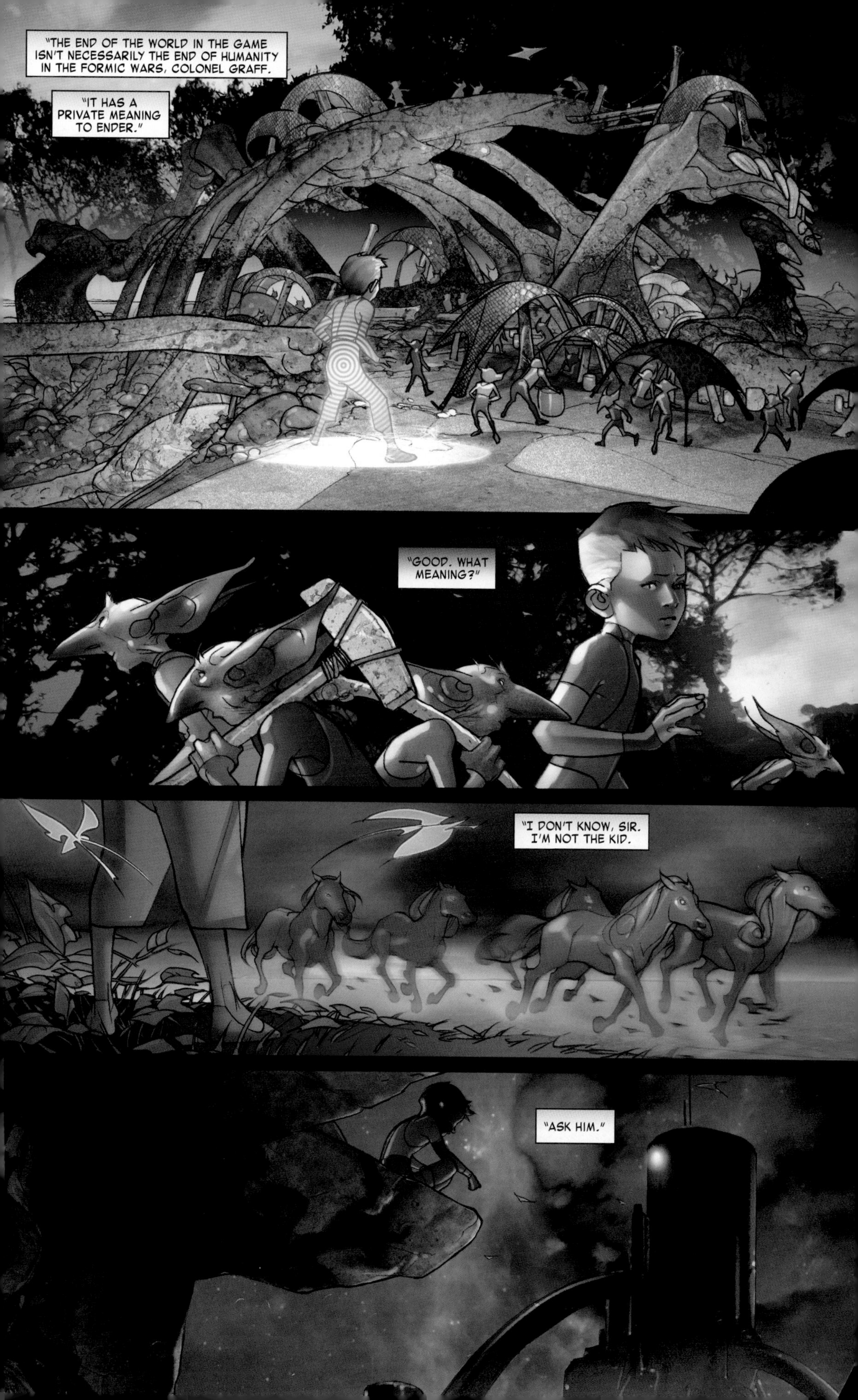
"THE END OF THE WORLD IN THE GAME ISN'T NECESSARILY THE END OF HUMANITY IN THE FORMIC WARS, COLONEL GRAFF.
"IT HAS A PRIVATE MEANING TO ENDER."
"GOOD. WHAT MEANING?"
"I DON'T KNOW, SIR. I'M NOT THE KID.
"ASK HIM."

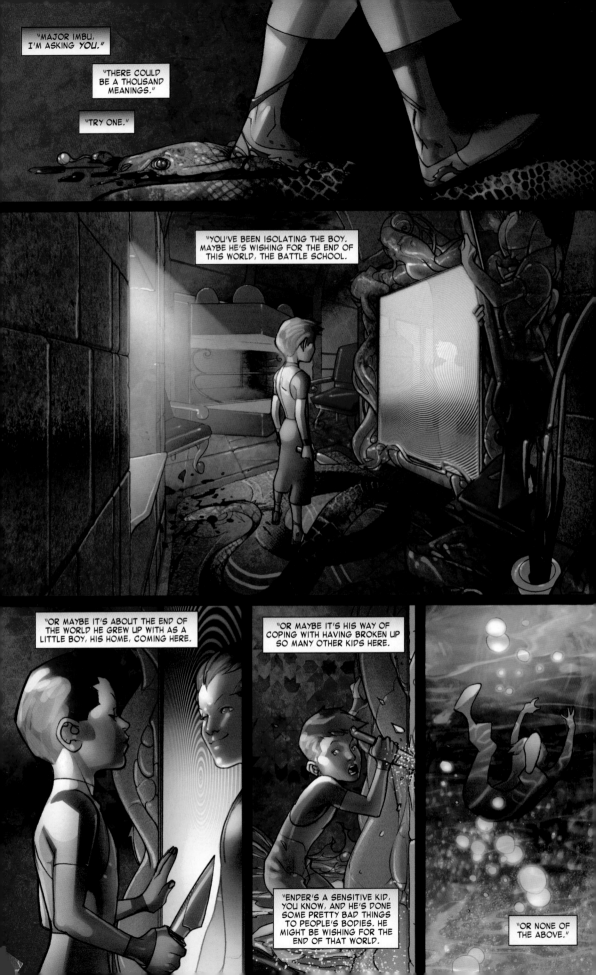

"MAJOR IMBU, I'M ASKING *YOU.*"

"THERE COULD BE A THOUSAND MEANINGS."

"TRY ONE."

"YOU'VE BEEN ISOLATING THE BOY. MAYBE HE'S WISHING FOR THE END OF THIS WORLD, THE BATTLE SCHOOL."

"OR MAYBE IT'S ABOUT THE END OF THE WORLD HE GREW UP WITH AS A LITTLE BOY, HIS HOME, COMING HERE."

"OR MAYBE IT'S HIS WAY OF COPING WITH HAVING BROKEN UP SO MANY OTHER KIDS HERE."

"ENDER'S A SENSITIVE KID, YOU KNOW, AND HE'S DONE SOME PRETTY BAD THINGS TO PEOPLE'S BODIES. HE MIGHT BE WISHING FOR THE END OF THAT WORLD.

"OR NONE OF THE ABOVE."

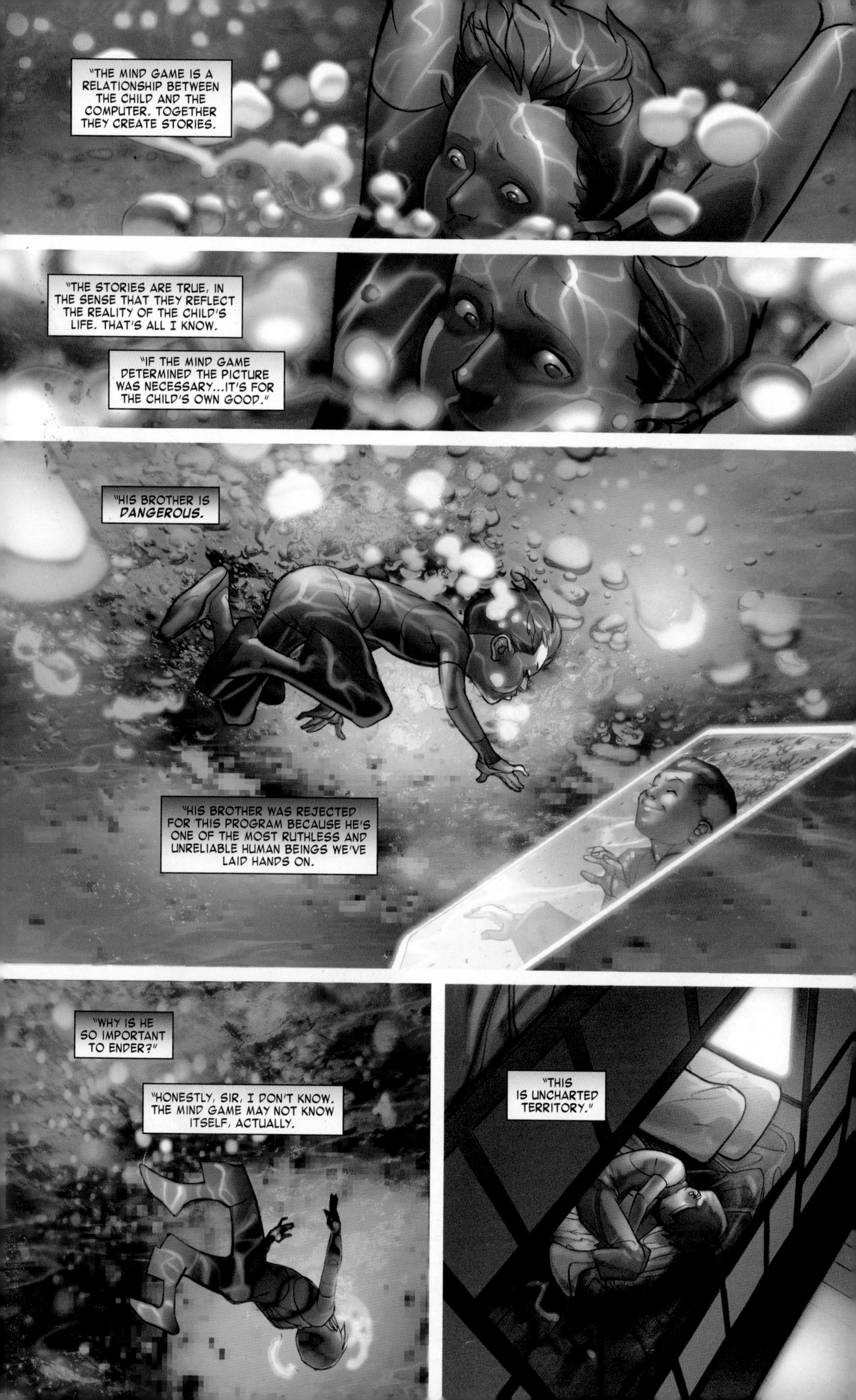
"THE MIND GAME IS A RELATIONSHIP BETWEEN THE CHILD AND THE COMPUTER. TOGETHER THEY CREATE STORIES.
"THE STORIES ARE TRUE, IN THE SENSE THAT THEY REFLECT THE REALITY OF THE CHILD'S LIFE. THAT'S ALL I KNOW.
"IF THE MIND GAME DETERMINED THE PICTURE WAS NECESSARY...IT'S FOR THE CHILD'S OWN GOOD."
"HIS BROTHER IS DANGEROUS.
"HIS BROTHER WAS REJECTED FOR THIS PROGRAM BECAUSE HE'S ONE OF THE MOST RUTHLESS AND UNRELIABLE HUMAN BEINGS WE'VE LAID HANDS ON.
"WHY IS HE SO IMPORTANT TO ENDER?"
"HONESTLY, SIR, I DON'T KNOW. THE MIND GAME MAY NOT KNOW ITSELF, ACTUALLY.
"THIS IS UNCHARTED TERRITORY."

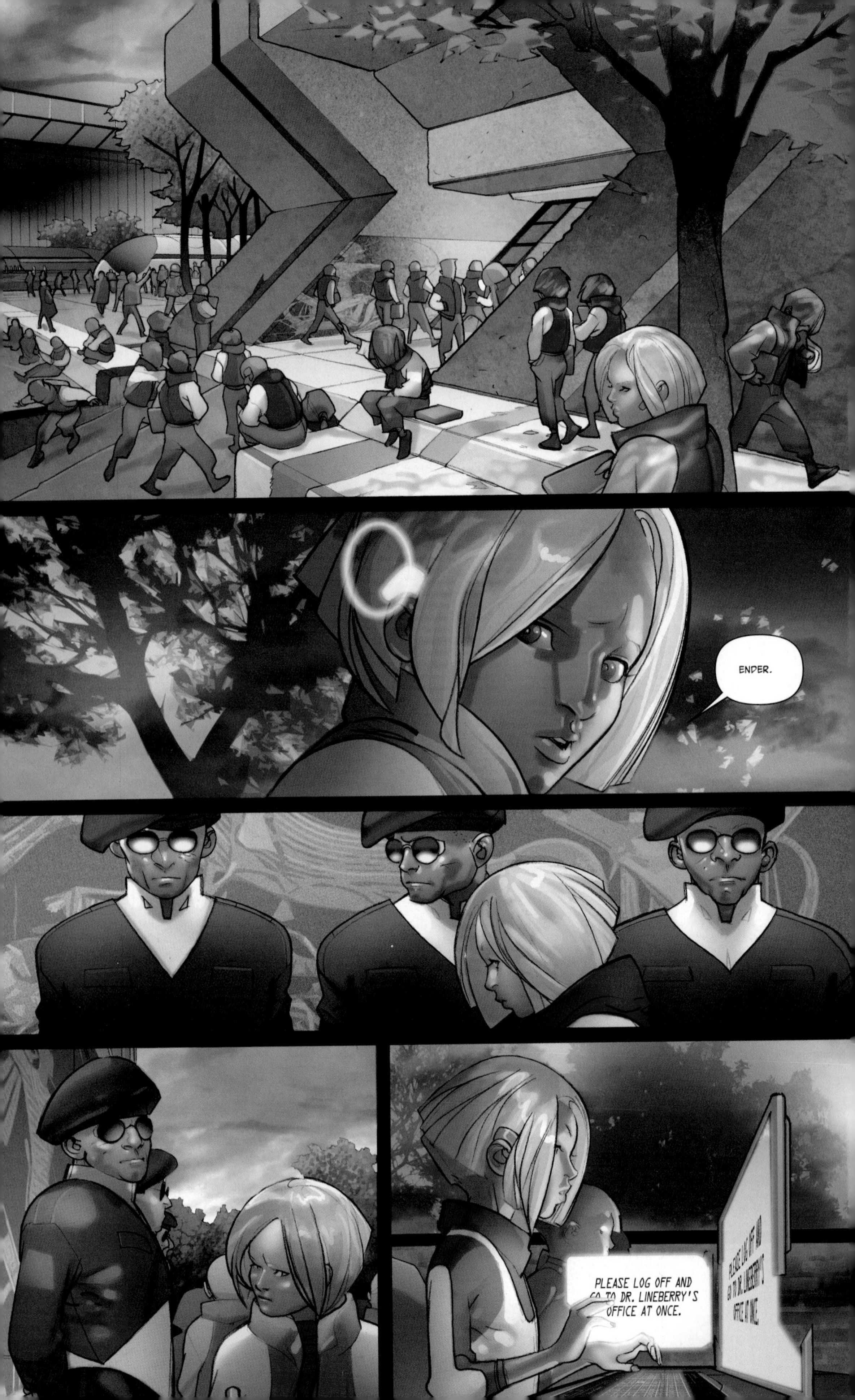
ENDER.
PLEASE LOG OFF AND GO TO DR. LINEBERRY'S OFFICE AT ONCE.

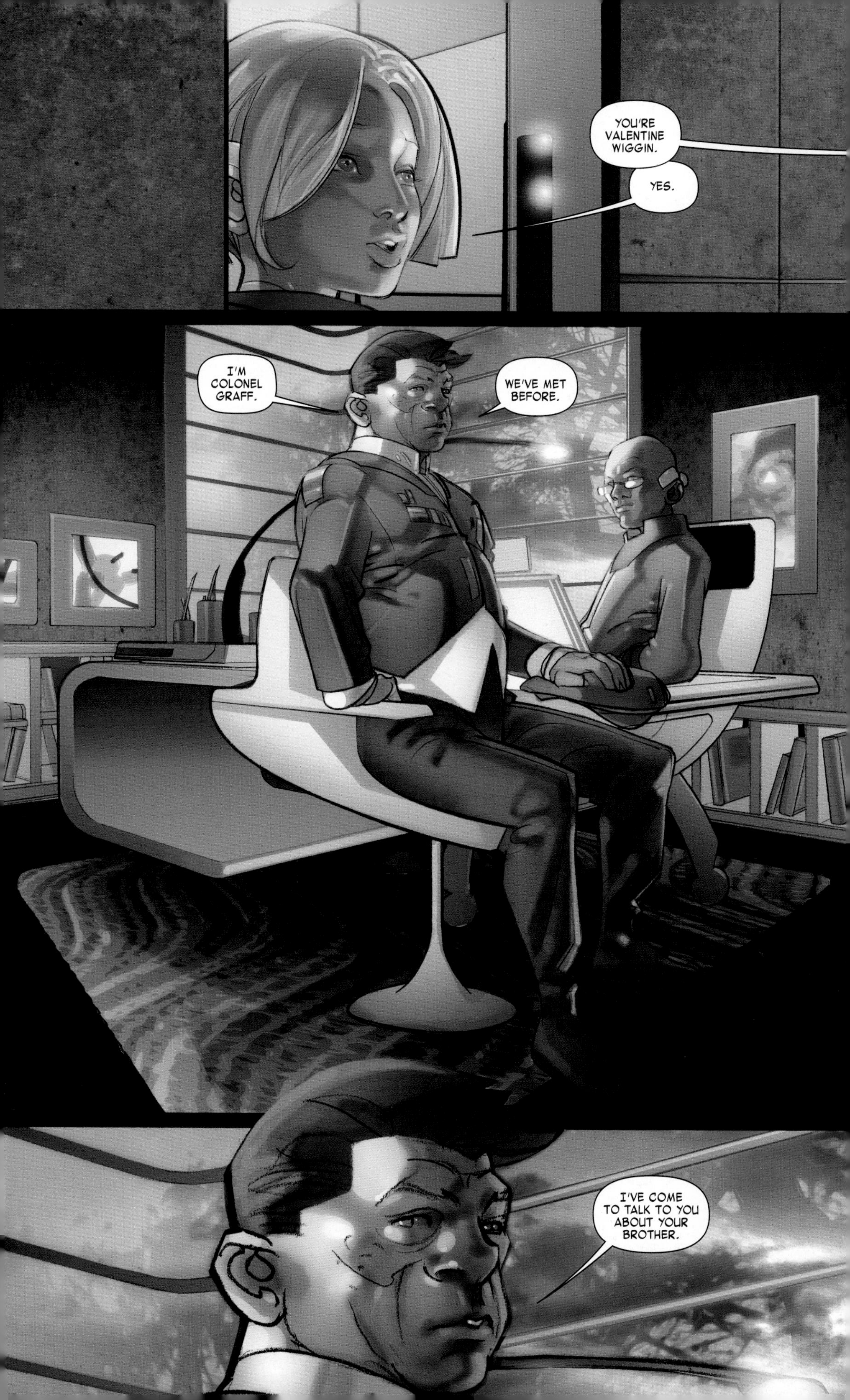
YOU'RE VALENTINE WIGGIN.
YES.
I'M COLONEL GRAFF.
WE'VE MET BEFORE.
I'VE COME TO TALK TO YOU ABOUT YOUR BROTHER.

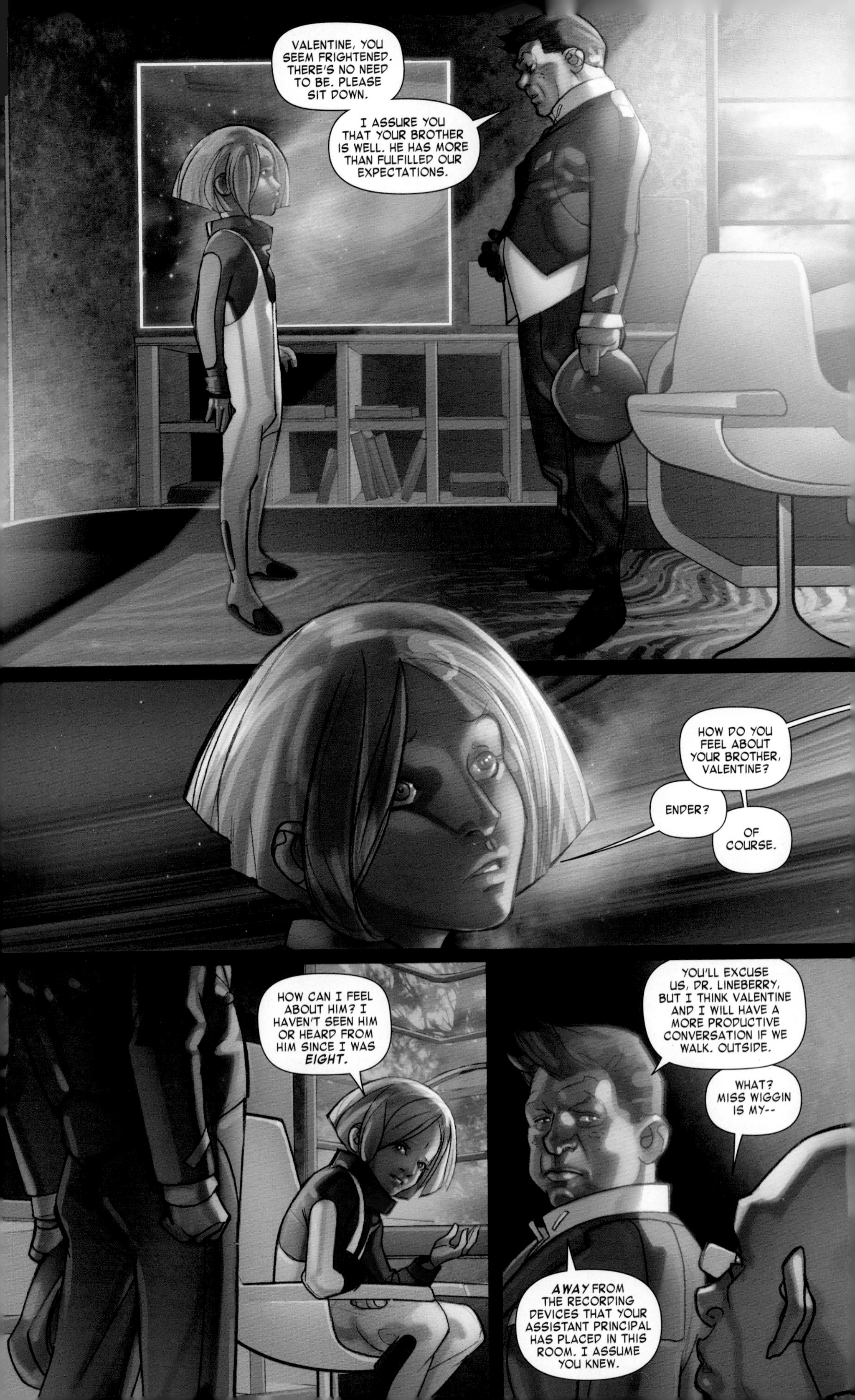
VALENTINE, YOU SEEM FRIGHTENED. THERE'S NO NEED TO BE. PLEASE SIT DOWN.
I ASSURE YOU THAT YOUR BROTHER IS WELL. HE HAS MORE THAN FULFILLED OUR EXPECTATIONS.
HOW DO YOU FEEL ABOUT YOUR BROTHER, VALENTINE?
ENDER?
OF COURSE.
HOW CAN I FEEL ABOUT HIM? I HAVEN'T SEEN HIM OR HEARD FROM HIM SINCE I WAS *EIGHT*.
YOU'LL EXCUSE US, DR. LINEBERRY, BUT I THINK VALENTINE AND I WILL HAVE A MORE PRODUCTIVE CONVERSATION IF WE WALK. OUTSIDE.
WHAT? MISS WIGGIN IS MY--
AWAY FROM THE RECORDING DEVICES THAT YOUR ASSISTANT PRINCIPAL HAS PLACED IN THIS ROOM. I ASSUME YOU KNEW.

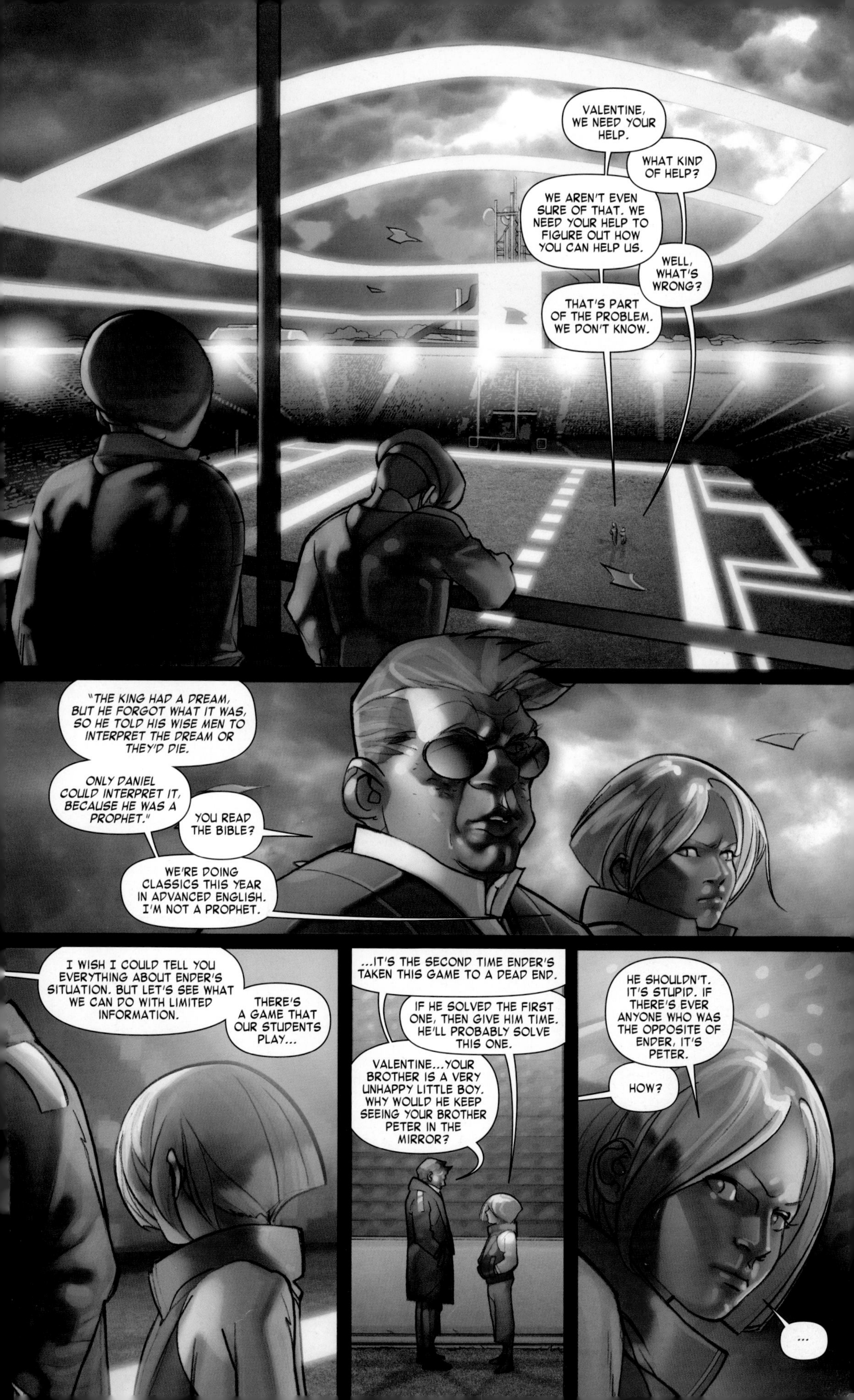
VALENTINE, WE NEED YOUR HELP.
WHAT KIND OF HELP?
WE AREN'T EVEN SURE OF THAT. WE NEED YOUR HELP TO FIGURE OUT HOW YOU CAN HELP US.
WELL, WHAT'S WRONG?
THAT'S PART OF THE PROBLEM. WE DON'T KNOW.
"THE KING HAD A DREAM, BUT HE FORGOT WHAT IT WAS, SO HE TOLD HIS WISE MEN TO INTERPRET THE DREAM OR THEY'D DIE.
ONLY DANIEL COULD INTERPRET IT, BECAUSE HE WAS A PROPHET."
YOU READ THE BIBLE?
WE'RE DOING CLASSICS THIS YEAR IN ADVANCED ENGLISH. I'M NOT A PROPHET.
I WISH I COULD TELL YOU EVERYTHING ABOUT ENDER'S SITUATION. BUT LET'S SEE WHAT WE CAN DO WITH LIMITED INFORMATION.
THERE'S A GAME THAT OUR STUDENTS PLAY...
...IT'S THE SECOND TIME ENDER'S TAKEN THIS GAME TO A DEAD END.
IF HE SOLVED THE FIRST ONE, THEN GIVE HIM TIME. HE'LL PROBABLY SOLVE THIS ONE.
VALENTINE...YOUR BROTHER IS A VERY UNHAPPY LITTLE BOY. WHY WOULD HE KEEP SEEING YOUR BROTHER PETER IN THE MIRROR?
HE SHOULDN'T. IT'S STUPID. IF THERE'S EVER ANYONE WHO WAS THE OPPOSITE OF ENDER, IT'S PETER.
HOW?
...

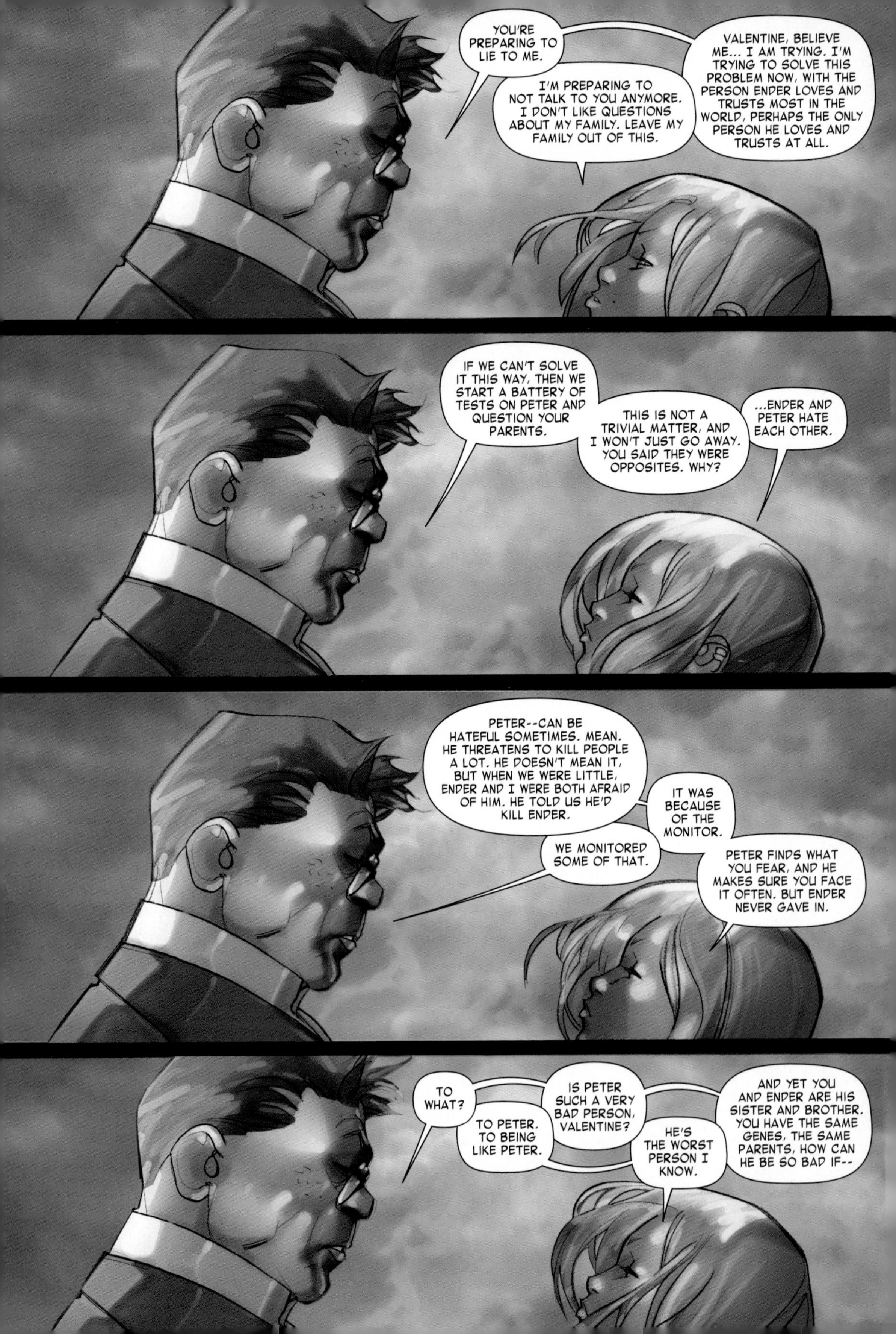

YOU'RE PREPARING TO LIE TO ME.
I'M PREPARING TO NOT TALK TO YOU ANYMORE. I DON'T LIKE QUESTIONS ABOUT MY FAMILY. LEAVE MY FAMILY OUT OF THIS.
VALENTINE, BELIEVE ME... I AM TRYING. I'M TRYING TO SOLVE THIS PROBLEM NOW, WITH THE PERSON ENDER LOVES AND TRUSTS MOST IN THE WORLD, PERHAPS THE ONLY PERSON HE LOVES AND TRUSTS AT ALL.
IF WE CAN'T SOLVE IT THIS WAY, THEN WE START A BATTERY OF TESTS ON PETER AND QUESTION YOUR PARENTS.
THIS IS NOT A TRIVIAL MATTER, AND I WON'T JUST GO AWAY. YOU SAID THEY WERE OPPOSITES. WHY?
...ENDER AND PETER HATE EACH OTHER.
PETER--CAN BE HATEFUL SOMETIMES. MEAN. HE THREATENS TO KILL PEOPLE A LOT. HE DOESN'T MEAN IT, BUT WHEN WE WERE LITTLE, ENDER AND I WERE BOTH AFRAID OF HIM. HE TOLD US HE'D KILL ENDER.
WE MONITORED SOME OF THAT.
IT WAS BECAUSE OF THE MONITOR.
PETER FINDS WHAT YOU FEAR, AND HE MAKES SURE YOU FACE IT OFTEN. BUT ENDER NEVER GAVE IN.
TO WHAT?
TO PETER. TO BEING LIKE PETER.
IS PETER SUCH A VERY BAD PERSON, VALENTINE?
HE'S THE WORST PERSON I KNOW.
AND YET YOU AND ENDER ARE HIS SISTER AND BROTHER. YOU HAVE THE SAME GENES, THE SAME PARENTS, HOW CAN HE BE SO BAD IF--

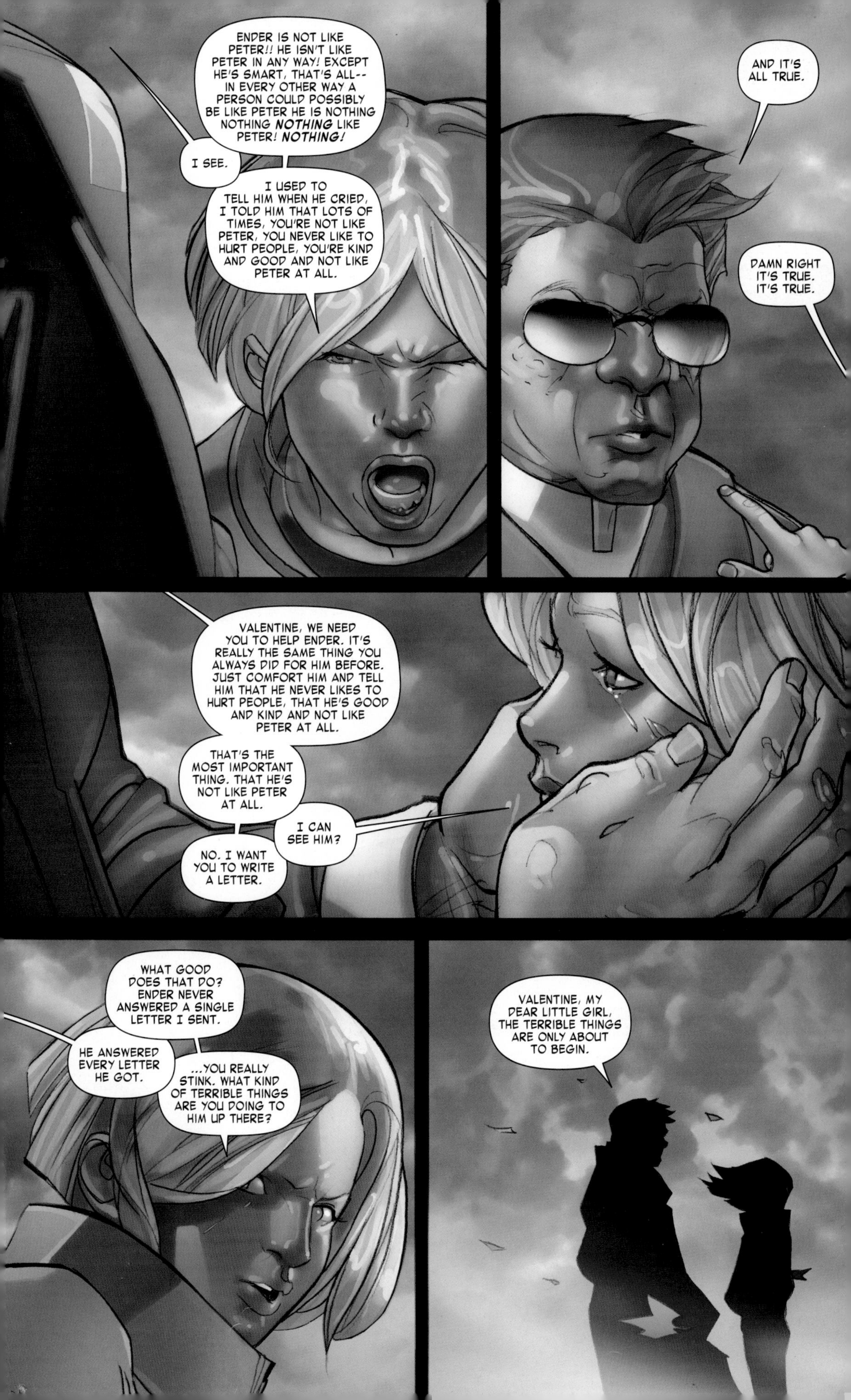
ENDER IS NOT LIKE PETER!! HE ISN'T LIKE PETER IN ANY WAY! EXCEPT HE'S SMART, THAT'S ALL-- IN EVERY OTHER WAY A PERSON COULD POSSIBLY BE LIKE PETER HE IS NOTHING NOTHING ***NOTHING*** LIKE PETER! ***NOTHING!***
I SEE.
I USED TO TELL HIM WHEN HE CRIED, I TOLD HIM THAT LOTS OF TIMES, YOU'RE NOT LIKE PETER, YOU NEVER LIKE TO HURT PEOPLE, YOU'RE KIND AND GOOD AND NOT LIKE PETER AT ALL.
AND IT'S ALL TRUE.
DAMN RIGHT IT'S TRUE. IT'S TRUE.
VALENTINE, WE NEED YOU TO HELP ENDER. IT'S REALLY THE SAME THING YOU ALWAYS DID FOR HIM BEFORE. JUST COMFORT HIM AND TELL HIM THAT HE NEVER LIKES TO HURT PEOPLE, THAT HE'S GOOD AND KIND AND NOT LIKE PETER AT ALL.
THAT'S THE MOST IMPORTANT THING. THAT HE'S NOT LIKE PETER AT ALL.
I CAN SEE HIM?
NO. I WANT YOU TO WRITE A LETTER.
WHAT GOOD DOES THAT DO? ENDER NEVER ANSWERED A SINGLE LETTER I SENT.
HE ANSWERED EVERY LETTER HE GOT.
...YOU REALLY STINK. WHAT KIND OF TERRIBLE THINGS ARE YOU DOING TO HIM UP THERE?
VALENTINE, MY DEAR LITTLE GIRL, THE TERRIBLE THINGS ARE ONLY ABOUT TO BEGIN.

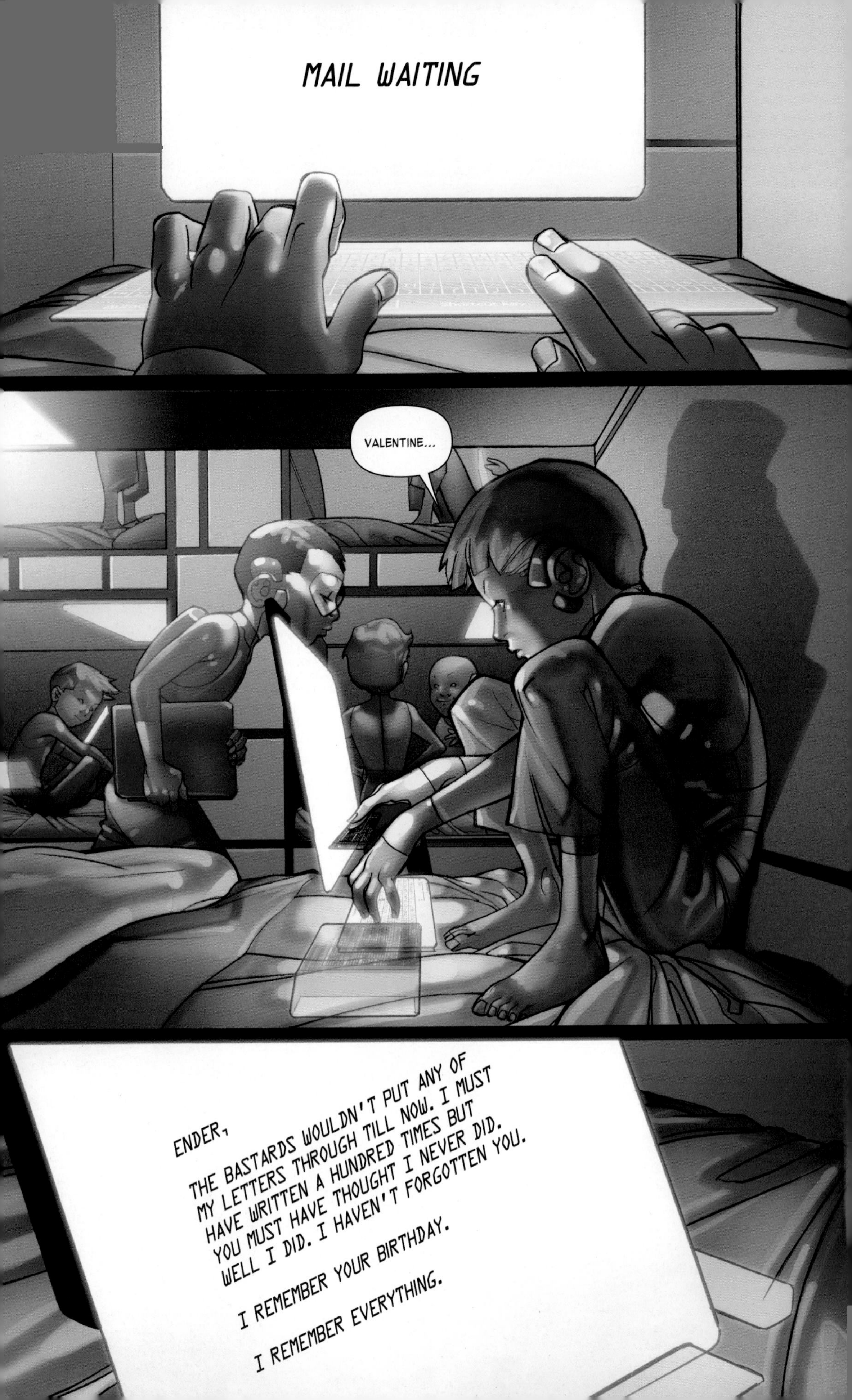
MAIL WAITING
VALENTINE...
ENDER,
THE BASTARDS WOULDN'T PUT ANY OF MY LETTERS THROUGH TILL NOW. I MUST HAVE WRITTEN A HUNDRED TIMES BUT YOU MUST HAVE THOUGHT I NEVER DID. WELL I DID. I HAVEN'T FORGOTTEN YOU.
I REMEMBER YOUR BIRTHDAY.
I REMEMBER EVERYTHING.

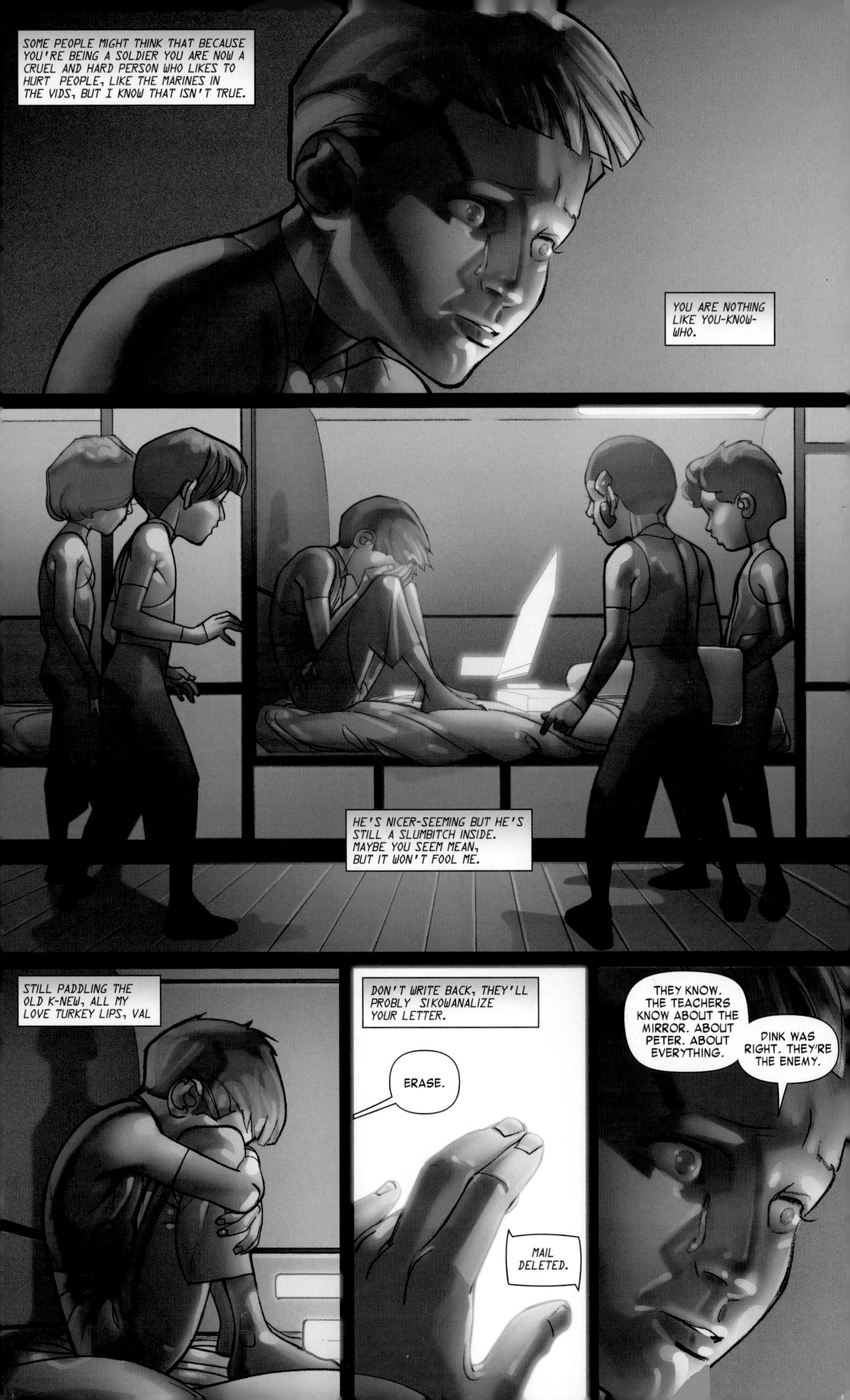
SOME PEOPLE MIGHT THINK THAT BECAUSE YOU'RE BEING A SOLDIER YOU ARE NOW A CRUEL AND HARD PERSON WHO LIKES TO HURT PEOPLE, LIKE THE MARINES IN THE VIDS, BUT I KNOW THAT ISN'T TRUE.
YOU ARE NOTHING LIKE YOU-KNOW-WHO.
HE'S NICER-SEEMING BUT HE'S STILL A SLUMBITCH INSIDE. MAYBE YOU SEEM MEAN, BUT IT WON'T FOOL ME.
STILL PADDLING THE OLD K-NEW, ALL MY LOVE TURKEY LIPS, VAL
DON'T WRITE BACK, THEY'LL PROBLY SIKOWANALIZE YOUR LETTER.
ERASE.
MAIL DELETED.
THEY KNOW. THE TEACHERS KNOW ABOUT THE MIRROR. ABOUT PETER. ABOUT EVERYTHING.
DINK WAS RIGHT. THEY'RE THE ENEMY.

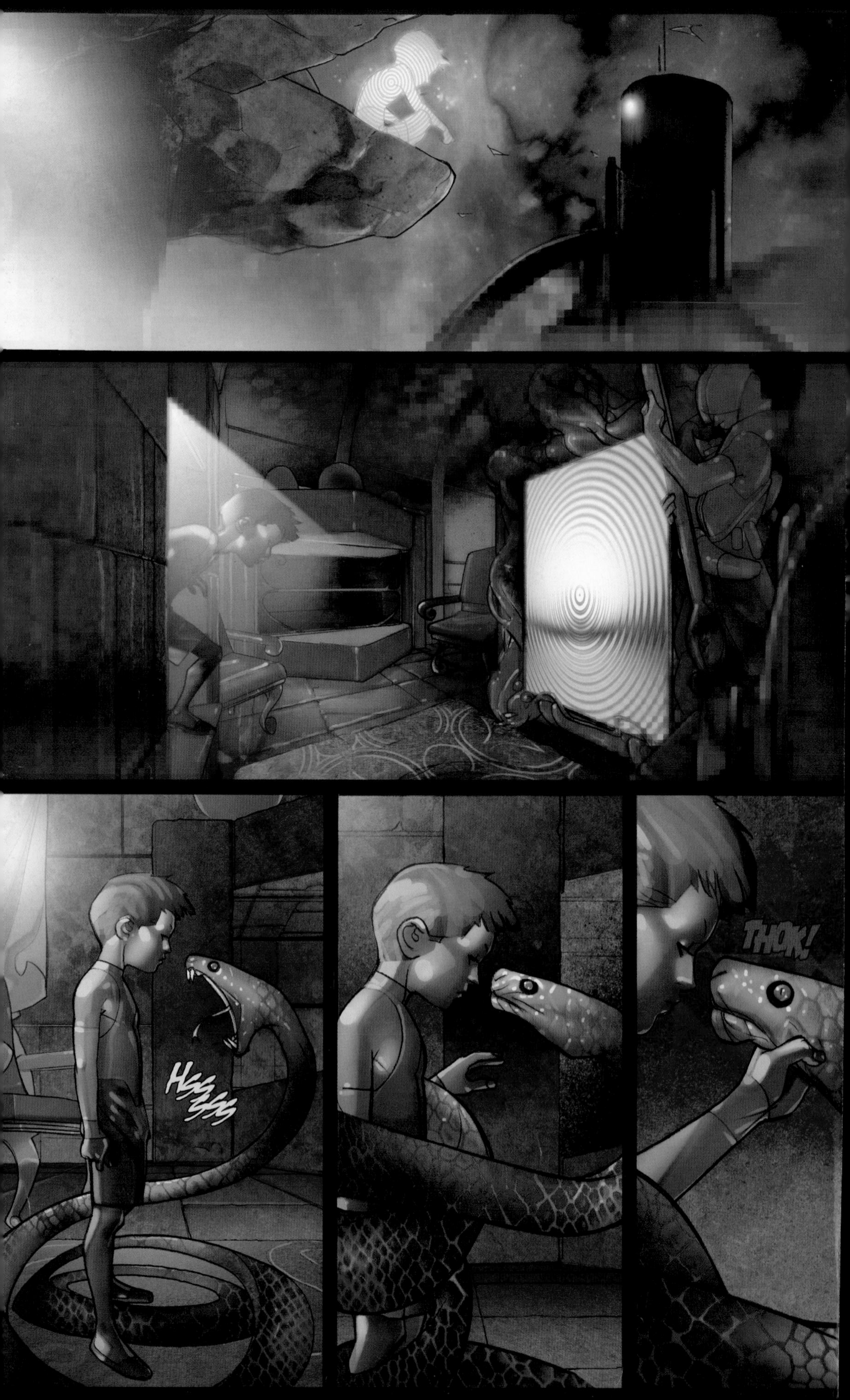
HSSSSS
THOK!

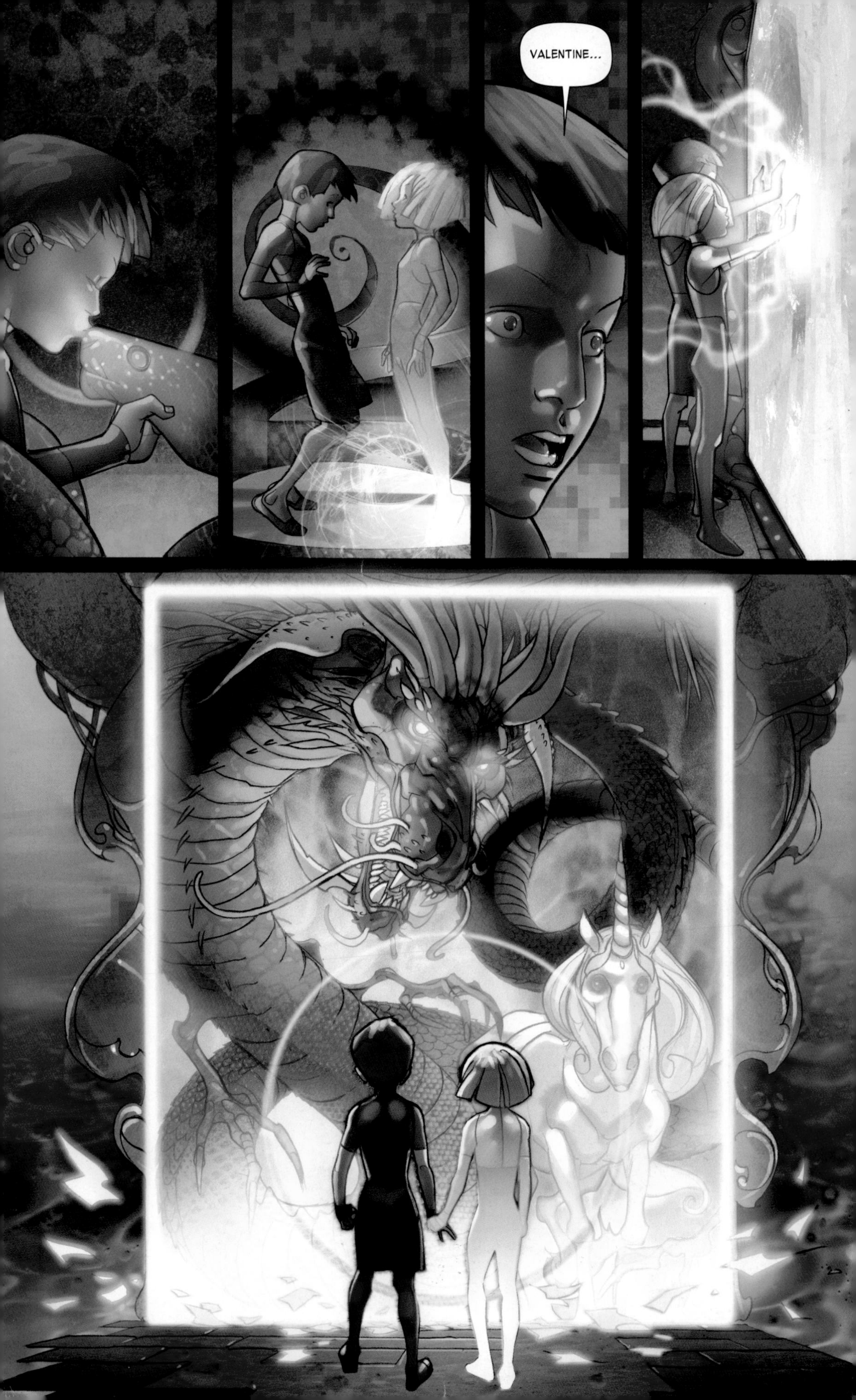
VALENTINE...

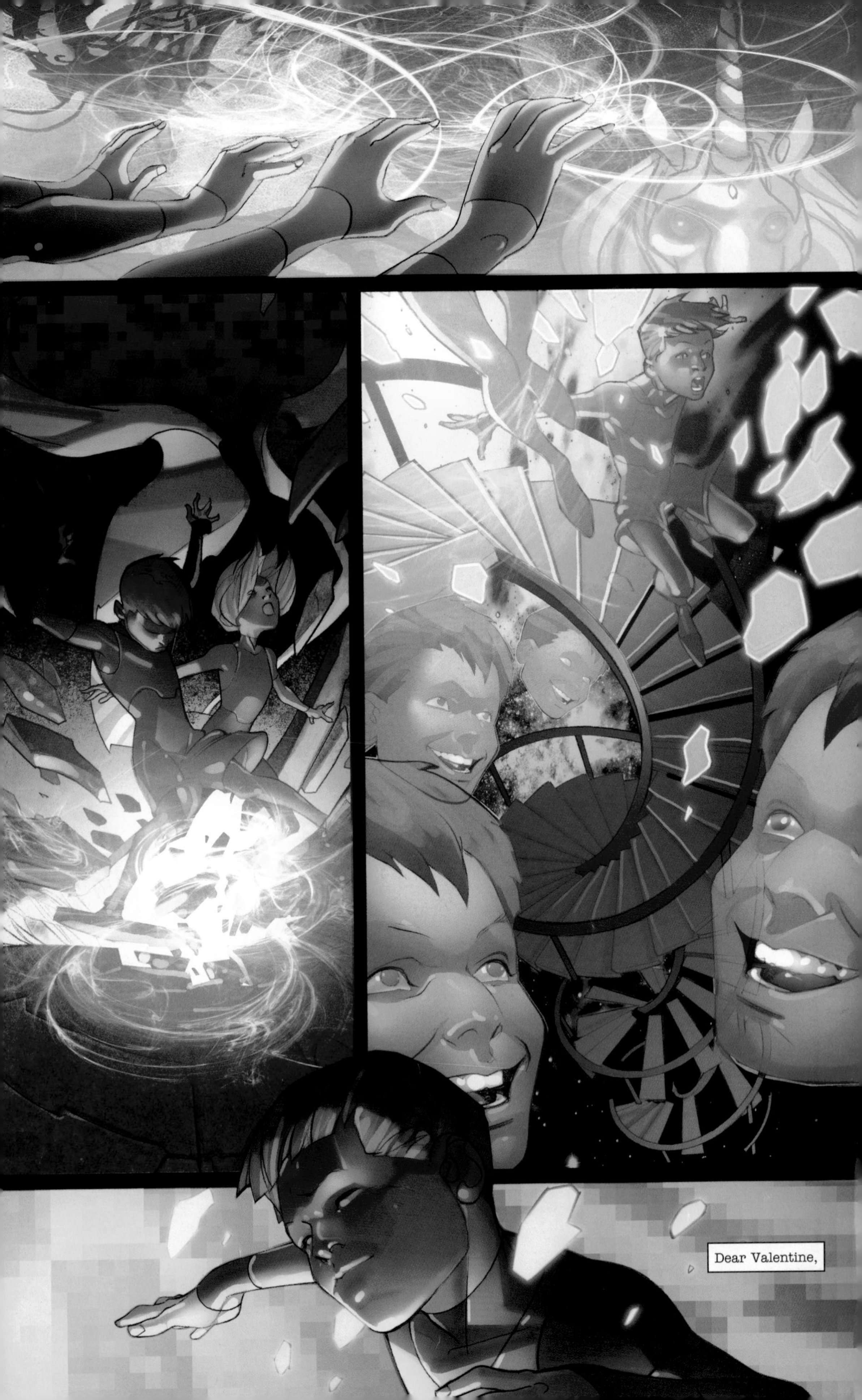
Dear Valentine,

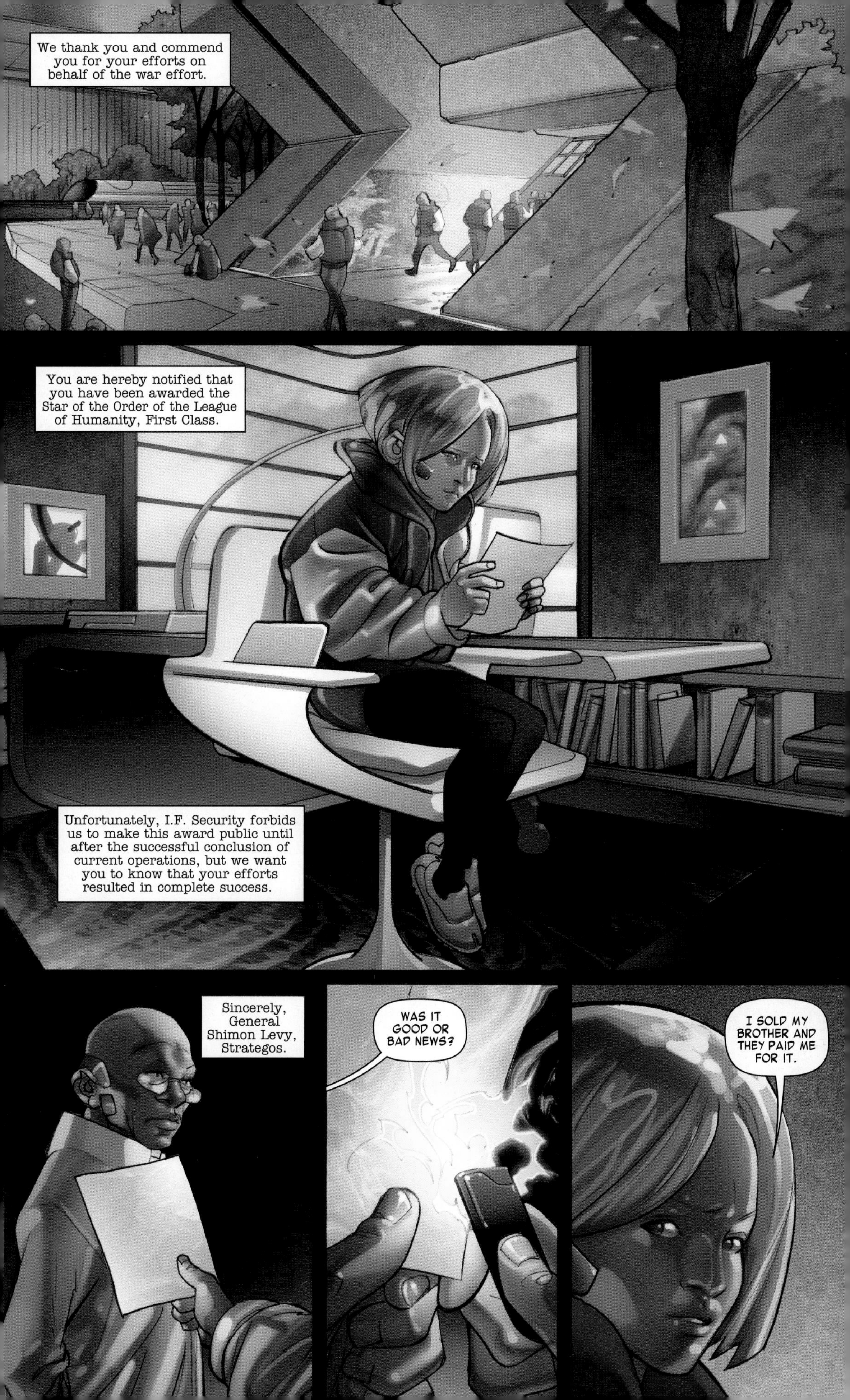
We thank you and commend you for your efforts on behalf of the war effort.
You are hereby notified that you have been awarded the Star of the Order of the League of Humanity, First Class.
Unfortunately, I.F. Security forbids us to make this award public until after the successful conclusion of current operations, but we want you to know that your efforts resulted in complete success.
Sincerely, General Shimon Levy, Strategos.
WAS IT GOOD OR BAD NEWS?
I SOLD MY BROTHER AND THEY PAID ME FOR IT.

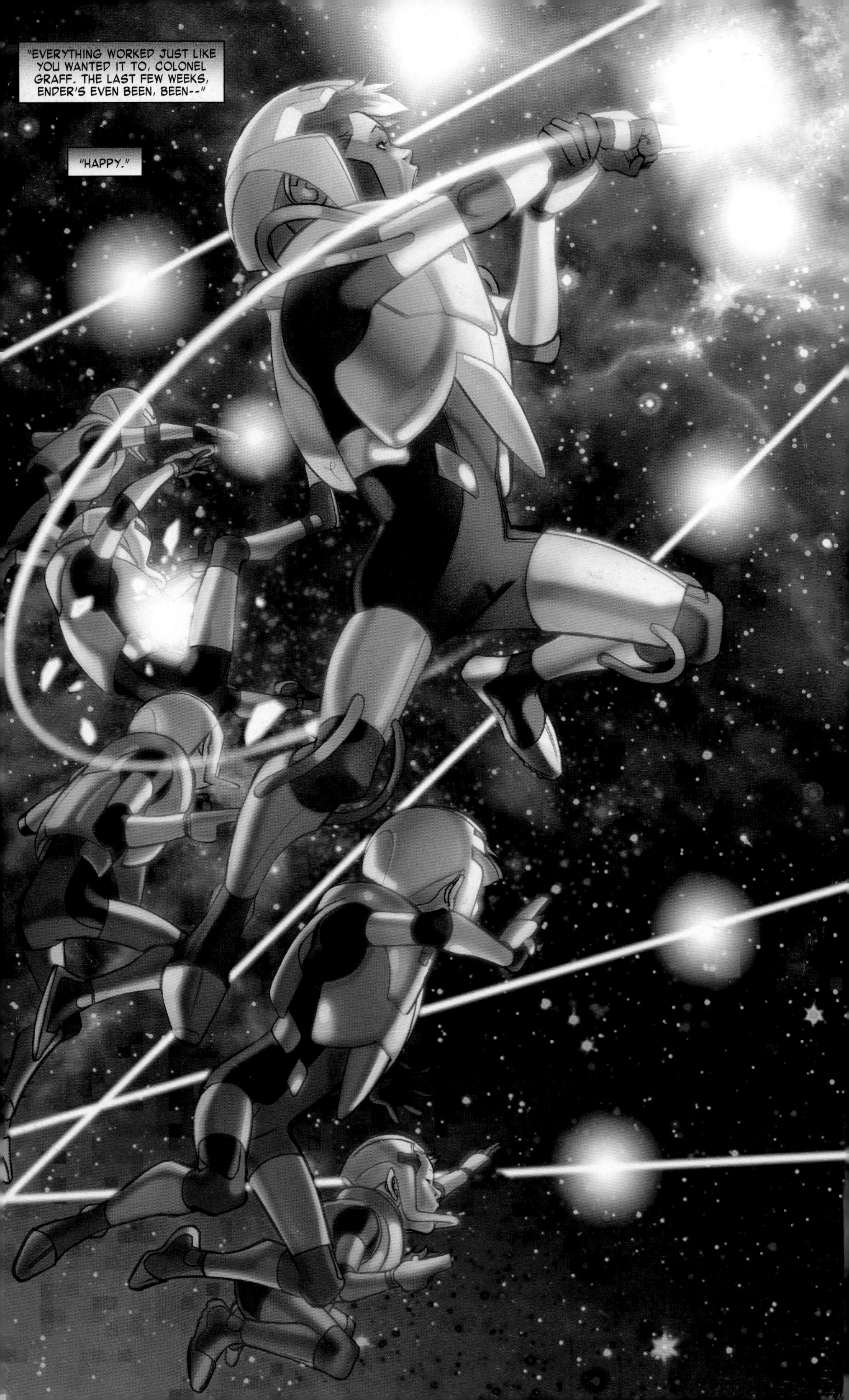
"EVERYTHING WORKED JUST LIKE YOU WANTED IT TO, COLONEL GRAFF. THE LAST FEW WEEKS, ENDER'S EVEN BEEN, BEEN--"
"HAPPY."

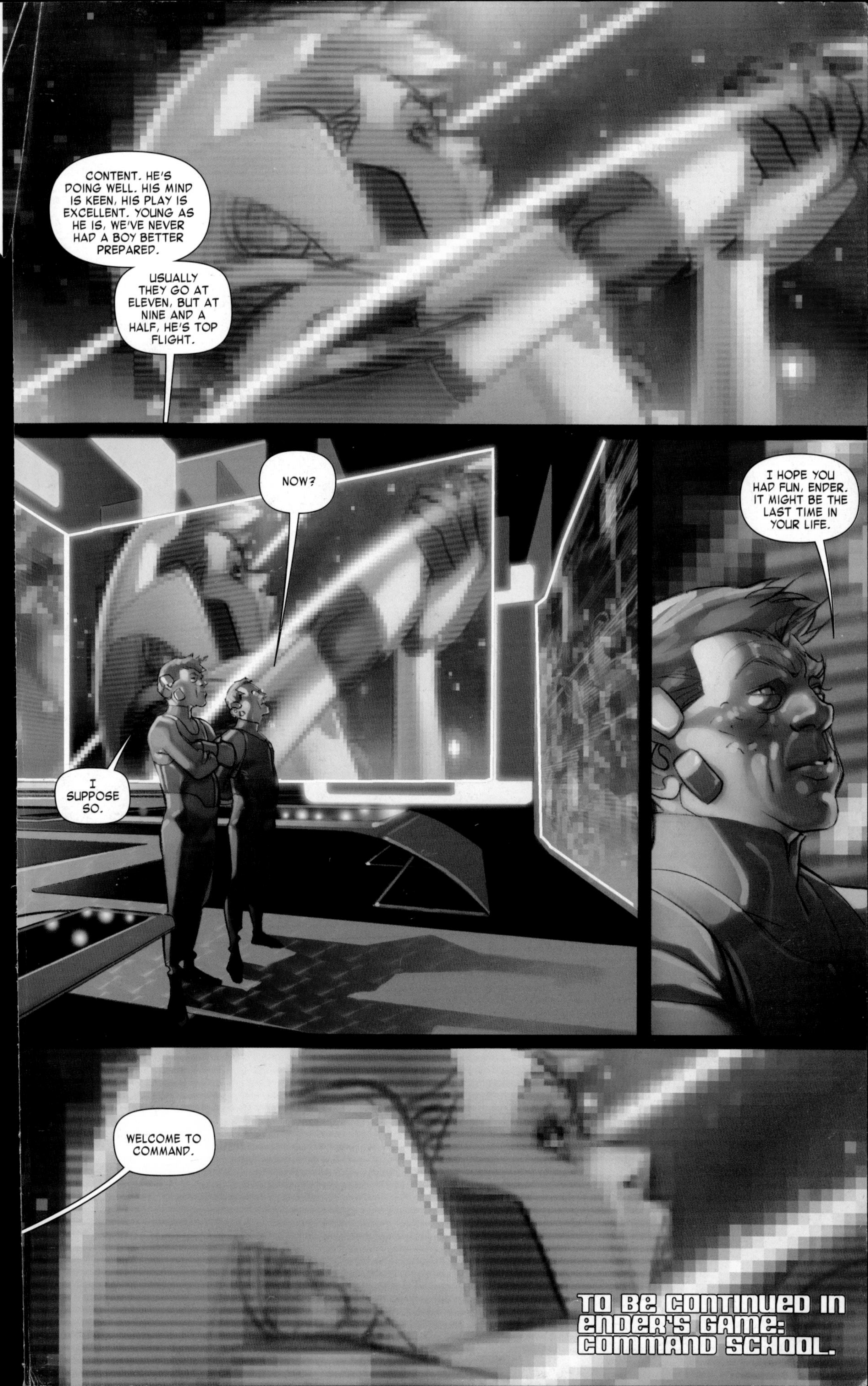
CONTENT. HE'S DOING WELL. HIS MIND IS KEEN, HIS PLAY IS EXCELLENT. YOUNG AS HE IS, WE'VE NEVER HAD A BOY BETTER PREPARED.
USUALLY THEY GO AT ELEVEN, BUT AT NINE AND A HALF, HE'S TOP FLIGHT.
NOW?
I SUPPOSE SO.
I HOPE YOU HAD FUN, ENDER. IT MIGHT BE THE LAST TIME IN YOUR LIFE.
WELCOME TO COMMAND.
TO BE CONTINUED IN ENDER'S GAME: COMMAND SCHOOL.

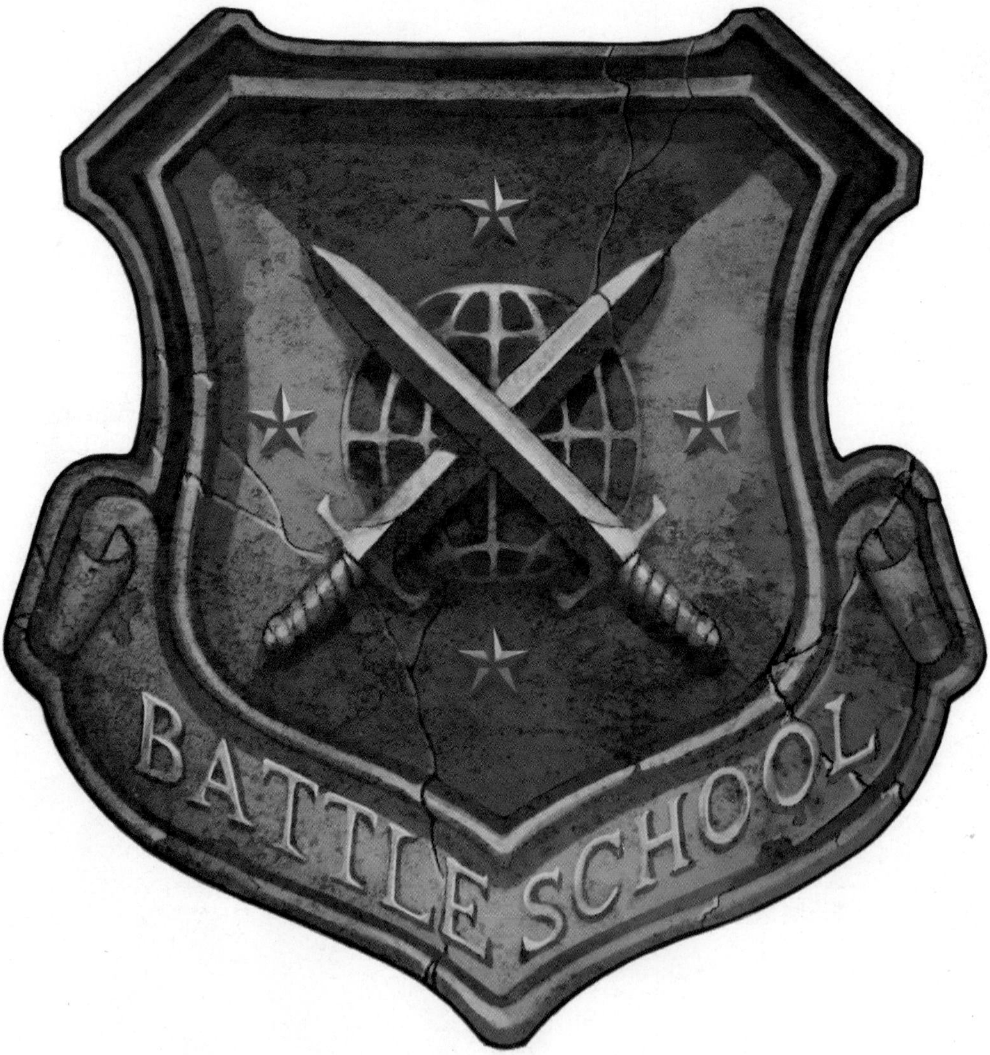
BATTLE SCHOOL

#1 SYMBOL VARIANT